The Evolution of Global Internet Governance

Roxana Radu • Jean-Marie Chenou • Rolf H. Weber
Editors

The Evolution of Global Internet Governance

Principles and Policies in the Making

Springer

Editors
Roxana Radu
Graduate Institute of International and Development Studies
Geneva, Switzerland

Jean-Marie Chenou
IEPI-CRII
Université de Lausanne
Lausanne, Switzerland

Rolf H. Weber
University of Zurich Faculty of Law
Zurich, Switzerland

ISBN 978-3-642-45298-7 ISBN 978-3-642-45299-4 (eBook)
DOI 10.1007/978-3-642-45299-4
Springer Heidelberg New York Dordrecht London

Library of Congress Control Number: 2014935884

Co-Publication with Schulthess Juristische Medien AG

ISBN 978-3-7255-6908-3. www.schulthess.com

Published by Springer-Verlag GmbH Berlin Heidelberg 2014

Printed on acid-free paper

Springer is part of Springer Science+Business Media (www.springer.com)

Contents

Editors

Roxana Radu, PhD candidate at the Graduate Institute of International and Development Studies (Geneva) and research fellow, Center for Media and Communication Studies, Central European University (Budapest).

Jean-Marie Chenou, Teaching assistant and PhD candidate, IEPI-CRII, Université de Lausanne

Rolf H. Weber, Professor Dr. iur. University of Zurich, Visiting Professor at Hong Kong University and Attorney-at-Law in Zurich

Bibliography

Abbate, Janet. 1999. *Inventing the Internet.* Cambridge, MA and London: MIT Press.

Abbott, K.W. and Snidal, D., 2000. Hard and Soft Law in International Governance, *International Organizations,* 54(3), pp. 421–456.

ACLU *et al.,* 2012. *Declaration of Internet Freedom* [online], 4 July. Available from: http://www.internetdeclaration.org/ [Accessed 20 August 2013].

Adas, M., 2006. *Dominance by Design: Technological Imperatives and America's Civilizing Mission.* Cambridge: Belknap Press.

Aguiar, L. and Martens, B., 2013. Digital music consumption on the internet: evidence from clickstream data. *Digital Economy Working Paper* 2013/04. Seville: European Commission Joint Research Centre Technical Reports, Institute for Prospective Technical Studies.

Alexander, F., 2011. Towards an Open and Innovative Internet. *MIND Paper Series,* No. 2, September. Berlin: Internet & Gesellschaft Colaboratory.

Aljazeera, 2012. Internet freedom tops Dubai summit agenda, *Aljazeera* [online], 3 December. Available from: http://www.aljazeera.com/news/middleeast/2012/12/20121236252823671.html [Accessed 20 August 2013].

Alker, H.R., Jr., 1973. Ón political capabilities in a schedule sense: measuring power, integration, and development. *In:* H.R. Alker, Jr., K.W. Deutsch, and A.H. Stoetzel (eds.) *Mathematical approaches to politics.* San Francisco: Jossey-Bass, pp. 307–73.

Anderson, K., 2005. Squaring the Circle? Reconciling Sovereignty and Global Governance through Global Government Network. Review of *A New World Order,* by Anne-Marie. Slaughter. *Harvard Law Review,* 118, pp. 1255–1312.

Arab States, 2012. *Arab States Common Proposals.* Document 64(Add.23)-E. November 2012. [online] Available from: <http://www.internetgovernance.org/wordpress/wp-content/uploads/T09-WTSA-12-C-0064.pdf> [Accessed 23 July 2013].

Assaf, D., 2007. Government Intervention in Information Infrastructure Protection. *In:* E. Goetz & S. Shenoi (eds), *Critical Infrastructure Protection,* Boston: Springer, pp. 29–39.

Assaf, D., 2008. Models of critical information infrastructure protection. *International Journal of Critical Infrastructure Protection.* 1(0), pp. 6–14.

Assaf, D., 2009. Conceptualising the use of public-private partnerships as a regulatory arrangement in critical information infrastructure protection. *In:* A. Peters et al. (eds), *Non-State Actors as Standard Setters,* Cambridge: Cambridge University Press, pp. 61–83.

Association for Progressive Communications, 2006. *Internet Rights Charter* [online] Available from http://www.apc.org/node/5677 [Accessed 17 July 2013].

AT Kearney, 2010. *A Viable Future Model for the Internet* [online] Available from: http://www.atkearney.com/index.php/Publications/a-viable-future-model-for-the-internet.html [Accessed 16 July 2013].

Aviram, A., 2004. Network Responses to Network Threats: The Evolution Into Private Cyber-Security Associations, *SSRN eLibrary.*

Banks, K., 2005. Summitry & Strategies. *Index on Censorship* [online] Available from: http://www.tandfonline.com/doi/abs/10.1080/03064220500258992 [Accessed 25 August 2013].

Barabas, E. and Bankston, K., 2013. It's Not Just About the US: How the NSA Threatens Human Rights Internationally. *Center for Democracy and Technology* [online], 12 June 2013. Available from: https://www.cdt.org/blogs/1206it's-not-just-about-us-how-nsa-threatens-human-rights-internationally [Accessed 15 June 2013].

Barlow, J. P., 1996. *Declaration of Independence of Cyberspace* [online], 8 February. Available from: https://projects.eff.org/~barlow/Declaration-Final.html [Accessed 20 August 2013].

Barme, G. R. and Ye, S., 1997. The Great Firewall of China: At ISPs, Internet cafes, even state censorship committees, we meet the wired of China, *Wired,* no. 5, June 1997, pp. 138–149.

Barnes, B. and Law, J., 1976. Whatever should be done with indexical expressions? *Theory and Society,* 3(2), pp. 223–37.

Barnett, M. and Duvall, R., 2005. Power in international politics. *International Organization,* 59(1), pp. 39–75.

Barry, E., 2009. Protests in Moldova Explode, With Help of Twitter, *The New York Times* [online], 7 April. Available from: http://www.nytimes.com/2009/04/08/world/europe/08moldova.html?pagewanted=all [Accessed 28 August 2013].

Bauer, J., and van Eeten, M., 2009. Cybersecurity: Stakeholder incentives, externalities, and policy options, *Telecommunications Policy,* 33(10–11), pp. 706–19.

Bauwens, V. 2012. Evolving towards a Partner State in an Ethical Economy. *In:* A. Botero, A. Gryf Paterson & J. Saad-Sulonen (eds), *Towards Peer Production In Public Services: Cases From Finland,* Helsinki: Aalto University, pp. 34–49.

BBC News, 2007. Call for blogging code of conduct, *BBC News* [online], 28 March. Available from: http://news.bbc.co.uk/2/hi/technology/6502643.stm [Accessed 23 August 2013].

BCG (Boston Consulting Group), 2012. *The Internet Economy in the G-20* [online] Available from: https://www.bcgperspectives.com/content/articles/media_entertainment_strategic_planning_4_2_trillion_opportunity_internet_economy_g20/#chapter1 [Accessed 19 June 2013].

Benkler. Y., 2000. Internet Regulation: a Case Study in the Problem of Unilateralism. *European Journal of International Law,* 11(1), pp. 171–185.

Benkler, Y., 2006. *The Wealth of Networks: How Social Production Transforms Markets and Freedom.* New Haven: Yale University Press.

Benkler, Y., 2013. Practical Anarchism: Peer Mutualism, Market Power, and the Fallible State. *Politics & Society,* 41(2), pp. 213–51.

Benkler, Y. and Nissenbaum, H., 2006. Commons-based Peer Production and Virtue. *Journal of Political Philosophy,* 14(4), pp. 394–419.

Bennett, D., 2011. The FBI seizes the three biggest US poker websites, Business Insider [online], 15 April 2011. Available from: http://www.businessinsider.com/online-poker-websites-fraud-2011-4 [Accessed 29 August 2013].

Bernstein, S. and Cashore, B., 2007. Can non-state global governance be legitimate? An analytical framework. *Regulation & Governance,* 1(4), pp. 347–371.

Black, E.J., 2011. Recognition of Internet freedom as a trade issue growing, *The Huffington Post* [online], 23 September. Available from: http://www.huffingtonpost.com/edward-j-black/internet-censorship_b_975658.html [Accessed 30 August 2013].

Black, J., 2008. Constructing and contesting legitimacy and accountability in polycentric regulatory regimes. *Regulation & Governance,* 2(2), pp. 137–164.

Blackman, C. 2013. The future of multilateralism in the governance of communications. *Info.* 15 (1), editorial.

Bosco, D., 2013. Brazil Wants UN to Help Safeguard Internet, *Foreign Policy* [online], 8 July 2013. Available from: http://bosco.foreignpolicy.com/posts/2013/07/08/brazil_wants_un_to_help_safeguard_internet [Accessed 14 July 2013].

Braithwaite, J. and Drahos, P., 2000. *Global Business Regulation.* Cambridge: Cambridge University Press.

Brock, G.W., 1994. *Telecommunication Policy for the Information Age: From Monopoly to Competition.* Cambridge: Harvard University Press.

Brookings, 2013.The NSA Versus the Global Internet: How Online Surveillance Could Impact Internet Governance. *Brookings workshop,* 20 June 2013. Summary available from: http://www.brookings.edu/events/2013/06/20-nsa-surveillance-internet-governance [Accessed 25 June 2013].

Brousseau, É., 2005. Multilevel Governance of the Digital Space: Does a "second rank" Institutional Framework exist? *In:* É. Brousseau et N. Curien (eds.) *Internet and Digital Economics Principles, Methods and Applications.* Cambridge: Cambridge University Press, pp. 617–649.

Bucak, S.; 2012. NANOG Rhetoric and WCIT-12 Reality. *The Global Journal* [online], 2 December 2012. Available from: http://theglobaljournal.net/article/view/930/ [Accessed 16 July 2013].

Buzan, B., Wæver, O. and de Wilde, J., 1998. *Security: A New Framework for Analysis.* Boulder: Lynne Rienner Publishers.

Caney, S., 2006. *Justice Beyond Borders: A Global Political Theory.* Oxford: Oxford University Press.

Carney, M., 1998. The Competitiveness of Networked Production: The Role of Trust and Asset Specificity, *Journal of Management Studies,* 35(4), pp. 457–79.

Cerf, V. G., 2012. Forward for EURid, *UNESCO World Report on Internationalized Domain Names Development, EU Insights* [online] Available from: http://www.eurid.eu/files/publ/insights_2012_idnreport.pdf [Accessed 26 June 2013].

Cerf, V. G., 2012a. Keep the Internet Open, *New York Times* [online], 24 May 2012. Available from: http://www.nytimes.com/2012/05/25/opinion/keep-the-internet-open.html?_r=0 [Accessed 27 June 2013].

Cerf, V. G., 2012b. Father of the Internet: Why we must fight for its freedom, *CNN* [online], 30 November. Available from: http://edition.cnn.com/2012/11/29/business/opinion-cerf-google-internet-freedom [Accessed 29 July 2013].

CERN (China Education and Research Network), 2001. Evolution of Internet in China, *CERN.* [online] Available from: http://www.edu.cn/introduction_1378/20060323/t20060323_4285.shtml [Accessed 27 June 2013].

Cerny, P. G., 2010. *Rethinking World Politics. A Theory of Transnational Neopluralism.* New York, NY: Oxford University Press.

de Certeau, M., 1984. *The practice of everyday life.* Translated by S. Rendall. Berkeley: University of California Press.

Chiariglione, L., 2000. Communication standards: Götterdämmerung? *In* A. Puri and T. Chen (eds.) *Multimedia systems, standards, and networks,* New York: Marcel Dekker, pp. 1–22.

Chick, W.B., 2010. Customary Internet-Ional Law: Creating a body of Customary Law for Cyberspace. *Computer Law & Security Review,* 26, pp. 2–22.

China, Russia, Tajikistan and Uzbekistan, 2011. *International Code of Conduct for Information Security* [online], 12 September 2011. Available from: http://www.fmprc.gov.cn/eng/wjdt/wshd/t858978.htm [Accessed 13 July 2013].

Chowdary, T. H., 1998. Telecom Liberalization and Competition in Developing Countries. *Telecommunications Policy,* 22(4–5), pp. 259–265.

Christou, G. and Simpson, S., 2007. Gaining a Stake in Global Internet Governance: The EU, ICANN and Strategic Norm Manipulation. *European Journal of Communication,* 22(2), pp. 147–164.

Clinton, H., 2010. *Remarks on Internet Freedom* [online], 21 January 2010. Available from: http://www.state.gov/secretary/rm/2010/01/135519.htm [Accessed 28 August 2013].

Clinton, H., 2011. I*nternet Rights and Wrongs: Choices & Challenges in a Networked World* [online], 15 February. Available from: http://www.state.gov/secretary/rm/2011/02/156619.htm [Accessed 28 August 2013].

CNNIC (China Internet Information Network) & CIS (Internet Society of China), 2002. *Suggestions on ICANN Reform* [online] Available from: http://www.cnnic.cn/gjjl/gjy-jydt/200312/t20031213_27765.htm [Accessed 28 June 2013].

CNNIC (China Internet Information Network), 2008. 中国互联网络发展状况统计报告 Zhongguo Hulianwang Fazhan Tongji Baogao, Statistical Report on Internet Development in China, *CNNIC* [online], July 2008. Available from: http://www.cnnic.net.cn/hlwfzyj/hlwxzbg/200906/P020120709345337342613.doc [Accessed 27 June 2013].

CNNIC (China Internet Information Network), 2011. Memorabilia of the Development of the Internet in China, *CNNIC* [online] Available from: http://www.isc.org.cn/english/Review/listinfo-15323.html [Accessed 27 June 2013].

CNNIC (China Internet Information Network), 2013. 中国互联网络发展状况统计报告 Zhongguo Hulianwang Fazhan Tongji Baogao, Statistical Report on Internet Development in China, CNNIC [online], January 2013. Available from: http://www.cnnic.cn/hlwfzyj/hlwxzbg/hlwtjbg/201301/P020130122600399530412.pdf [Accessed 27 June 2013].

Cogburn, D.L., 2003. Governing Global Information and Communication Policy: Emergent Regime Formation and the Impact on Africa, *Telecommunications Policy,* 27(1–2), pp. 135–153.

Cogburn, D.L., 2005. *Global Internet Governance: Who's Winning, Who's Losing, and Who Cares?* Paper presented at the Annual Meeting of the American Political Science Association, Washington, D.C.

Cogburn, D. L., Mueller, M., McKnight, L; Klein, H. and Mathiason, J., 2005. The US Role in Global Internet Governance. *IEEE Communications Magazine,* 43(12), pp. 12–14.

Cohen, N., 2009. Twitter on the Barricades: Six Lessons Learned, *The New York Times* [online], 20 June. Available from: http://www.nytimes.com/2009/06/21/weekinreview/21cohenweb.html [Accessed 28 August 2013].

Committee, International Ad Hoc. 1997. "Final Report of the International Ad Hoc Committee: Recommendations for Administration and Management of gTLDs".

Constitutional Council (France), 2009. *Act furthering the diffusion and protection of creation on the Internet.* Decision n° 2009-580, 10 June 2009.

Cooper, A., Tschofenig, H., Aboba, B., Peterson, J., Morris, J., Hansen, M., Smith, R., 2013. *Privacy Considerations for Internet Protocols.* RFC 6973, Internet Engineering Task Force, July 2013.

Council of Europe, 2013. Draft Compendium of existing rights for internet users, *OECD* [online], 7 March 2013. Available from: http://www.coe.int/t/dghl/standardsetting/media/msi-dui/MSI-DUI(2013)03_en_pdf.pdf [Accessed 23 July 2013].

Cowhey, P. F., 1990. The International Telecommunications Regime: The Political Roots of Regimes for High Technology. *International Organization,* 44(2), pp. 169–199.

Crawford, Susan, 2013. *Captive Audience: The Telecom Industry and Monopoly in the New Guilded Age.* New Haven: Yale University Press.

Crépin-Leblond, O.M.J, 2011. Bottom Up vs. Top Down. *MIND Paper Series,* No. 2, September 2011. Berlin: Internet& Gesellschaft Colaboratory.

CSFI (Cyber-Security Forum Initiative), 2013. *About CSFI* [online] Available from: http://www.csfi.us/?page=about [Accessed 1 September 2013].

CS-IEG (Civil Society Informal Experts Group), 2013. Statement by Civil Society Informal Experts Group members at WTPF 2013 [online] Available from: https://docs.google.com/document/d/1FZr-9sN_OOWDfs6fwHfYZi49RcK5V9Y04lNeRekeybg/edit?pli=1 [Accessed 1 September 2013].

CSTD (Commission on Science and Technology for Development), 2013. *Questionnaire of the Working Group on Enhanced Cooperation* [online] Available from: http://unctad.org/meetings/en/SessionalDocuments/2013_WGEC_Questionnaire.pdf [Accessed 20 August 2013].

CSTD (Commission on Science and Technology for Development), 2013a. *Composition of the Working Group on Enhanced Cooperation* [online] Available from: http://unctad.org/Sections/un_cstd/docs/cstd2013d02_Composition.pdf [Accessed 20 August 2013].

CSTDWG (Working Group on improvements to the Internet Governance Forum), 2011. Working Group on improvements to the Internet Governance Forum, *Commission on Science and Technology for Development (CSTD)* [online] Available from: http://www.unctad.info/en/CstdWG, [Accessed 29 August 2013].

Cuba, 2013. *Proposal presented at the Fifth Meeting of National Coordinators of the Community of Latin American and Caribbean States* (CELAC), 9–10 May 2013.

Curran, J., 2013. Comment to "Can't Sell your IPv4 Numbers: Try Leasing Them", *Internet Governance Project* [online], 29 April 2013. Available from: http://www.Internetgovernance.org/2013/04/28/cant-sell-your-ipv4-numbers-try-leasing-them/ [Accessed 10 June 2013].

Cutler, C.A., Haufler V. and Porter T. (eds.), 1999. *Private Authority in International Affairs,* Albany: SUNY Press.

Dafermos, G., 2012. Authority In Peer Production: The Emergence Of Governance In The FreeBSD Project, *Journal of Peer Production* (1).

Dahl, R.A., 1957. The concept of power. *Behavioral Science,* 2(3), pp. 201–15.

David, P.A., 1985. Clio and the economics of QWERTY. *American Economic Review,* 75(2), pp. 332–37.

Deibert, R., 2011, Tracking the emerging arms race in cyberspace. *Bulletin of the Atomic Scientists,* 67(1), pp. 1–8.

Deibert, R. and Rohozinski, R., 2008. Good for Liberty, Bad for Security? Global Civil Society and the Securitization of the Internet. In: R. Deibert et al (eds.) *Access Denied: The Practice and Policy of Global Internet Filtering,* Cambridge: MIT Press, pp. 123–149.

DeNardis, L., 2009. *Protocol Politics: The Globalization of Internet Governance.* Cambridge: MIT Press.

Deutsch, K.W., 1963. *The nerves of government: models of political communication and control.* New York: Free Press of Glencoe.

Devaney, T., 2011. FCC official: Internet freedom threatened, *Washington Times* [online], 19 December. Available from: http://www.washingtontimes.com/news/2011/dec/19/fcc-official-delivers-warning-on-threat-to-interne/?page=all [Accessed 20 August 2013].

DHS (Department of Homeland Security), 2010. Computer Network Security & Privacy Protection, *Department of Homeland Security* [online], 19 February 2010. Available from: http://www.dhs.gov/xlibrary/assets/privacy/privacy_cybersecurity_white_paper.pdf [Accessed 20 August 2013].

DHS (Department of Homeland Security), 2010a. Privacy Impact Assessment for the Initiative Three Exercises, *Department of Homeland Security* [online], 18 March 2010. Available from: http://www.dhs.gov/xlibrary/assets/privacy/privacy_pia_nppd_initiative3 exercise.pdf [Accessed 20 August 2013].

DHS (Department of Homeland Security), 2012. Privacy Compliance Review of the EINSTEIN Program, *Department of Homeland Security* [online], 3 January 2013. Available from: http://www.dhs.gov/xlibrary/assets/privacy/privacy_privcomrev_nppd_ein.pdf [Accessed 20 August 2013].

DHS (Department of Homeland Security), 2013. Privacy Impact Assessment for the Enhanced Cybersecurity Services (ECS), *Department of Homeland Security* [online], 16 January 2013. Available from: http://www.dhs.gov/sites/default/files/publications/privacy/privacy_pia_nppd_ecs_jan2013.pdf [Accessed 20 August 2013].

Doria, A., 2013. *Intro to ICANN Structure* [online] Available from: https://docs.google.com/presentation/d/1rn4hmXVAkQw46O7zawgj9aMpWOKbNrODYj7j2xYGw2I/edit?usp=sharing [Accessed 29 august 2013].

Drake, W.J., 2000. The Rise and Decline of the International Telecommunications Regime. *In:* C. T. Marsden, *Regulating the Global Information Society.* London: Routledge, pp. 124–177.

Drake, W.J., 2004. Reframing Internet Governance Discourse: Fifteen Baseline Propositions. *In:* D. MacLean (ed.). *Internet Governance: A Grand Collaboration.* New York: United Nations Information and Communication Technology Taskforce, pp. 122–161.

Drake,W.J. (ed.), 2005. *Reforming Internet Governance: Perspectives from the UN Working Group on Internet Governance,* New York: United Nations Information and Communication Technologies Task Force.

Drake, W. J., 2008. Introduction: The Distributed Architecture of Network Global Governance. *In:* W. J. Drake and E. J. Wilson III (eds.), *Governing Global Electronic Networks.* Cambridge and London: MIT Press, pp. 1–79.

Drake, W.J., 2011. Multistakeholderism: Internal Limitations and External Limits. *MIND Paper Series,* No. 2, September 2011. Berlin: Internet& Gesellschaft Colaboratory.

Drake, W. J. and Nicolaïdis, K. 1992. Ideas, Interests, and Institutionalization: Trade in Services and the Uruguay Round. *International Organization,* 46(1), pp. 37–100.

Drake, W. J. and Wilson III, E.J. (2008). *Governing Global Electronic Networks. International Perspectives on Policy and Power.* Cambridge: MIT Press.

Drezner, D., 2004. Global Governance of the Internet: Bringing the State Back In. *Political Science Quarterly,* 119(3), pp. 477–498.

Drezner, D., 2007. *All Politics is Global: Explaining International Regulatory Regimes.* Princeton and Oxford: Princeton University Press.

Dufborg, A, 2005. The Preparatory Process and WSIS II. In Hellström; J., *The World Summit on the Information Society—A summit of Solutions?* Collegium for Development Studies, Publication no. 28, Uppsala: Uppsala Universitet, pp. 17–22.

Dugdale, A., 2012. The End Of Internet Freedom? U.N. Opens Ten-Day Talks On Web Regulation, *Fast Company* [online], 3 December 2012. Available from: http://www.fast company.com/3003568/end-internet-freedom-un-opens-ten-day-talks-web-regulation [Accessed 20 August 2013].

Dunn-Cavelty, M. 2008. *Cyber-Security and Threat Politics: US Efforts to Secure the Information Age.* London: Routledge.

Dunn-Cavelty, M., and Suter, M., 2009. Public–Private Partnerships are no silver bullet: An expanded governance model for Critical Infrastructure Protection. *International Journal of Critical Infrastructure Protection,* 2(4), pp. 179–87.

Dutton, W.H. and Peltu, M., 2005. The Emerging Internet Governance Mosaic: Connecting the Pieces, *OII Forum Discussion Paper,* No. 5, Oxford: Oxford Internet Institute, University of Oxford.

Eagleton-Pierce, M., 2013. *Symbolic power in the World Trade Organization.* Oxford: Oxford University Press.

Ebenstein, A., Ebenstein, W. and Fogelman, E., 2000. Today's ISMS, 11th Editon. Upper Saddle River: Prentice Hall. First published in 1954.

Eilstrup-Sangiovanni, M., 2007. *Varieties of Cooperation: Government Networks in International Security.* [online] Available from: http://cadmus.iue.it/dspace/handle/1814/7503 [Accessed 29 August 2013].

Ermert, M. and Hughes, C R, 2003. What's in a name? China and the domain name system. In: C R Hughes and G. Wacke (eds.) *China and the Internet: Politics of the Digital Leap Forward.* London: Routledge, pp. 127–138.

Esterhuysen, A., 2011, A long Way to Go. *MIND Paper Series,* No. 2, September 2011. Berlin: Internet & Gesellschaft Colaboratory.

EURid (European Registry of Internet Domain Names) and UNESCO (United Nations Educational Scientific and Cultural Organization), 2012. *EURid—UNESCO World Report on Internationalized Domain Names Development, EU Insights* [online] Available from: http://www.eurid.eu/files/publ/insights_2012_idnreport.pdf [Accessed 26 June 2013].

European Commission, 2013. EU-US Transatlantic Trade and Investment Partnership. Technical Barriers to Trade. *Initial EU Position Paper* [online] Available from: http://trade.ec.europa.eu/doclib/docs/2013/july/tradoc_151627.pdf [Accessed 29 August 2013].

European Commission, 2013a. Impact Assessment—Accompanying the document "Proposal for a Directive of the European Parliament and of the Council Concerning measures to ensure a high level of network and information security across the Union [online] Available from: http://www.statewatch.org/news/2013/feb/eu-com-network-info-security-swd-31-13.pdf [Accessed 1 May 2013].

European Commission, 2013b. Proposal for a directive of the European Parliament and of the Council concerning measures to ensure a high common level of network and information security across the Union. COM(2013) 48 final [online] Available from: http://www.eeas.europa.eu/policies/eu-cyber-security/cybsec_directive_en.pdf [1 May 2013].

European Network and Information Security Agency, 2011. *Cooperative Models for Effective Public Private Partnerships—Desktop Research Report* [online] Available from: http://www.enisa.europa.eu/act/res/other-areas/national-public-private-partnerships-ppps/desktop-reserach-on-public-private-partnership [Accessed 21 July 2013].

European Newspaper Publishing Association, 2013. European Publishers Urge European Commission to Challenge Google Further, Press Release, *ENPA* [online], 25 June 2013. Available from: http://www.enpa.be/en/news/press-release-european-publishers-urge-european-commission-to-challenge-google-further_98.aspx [Accessed 26 June 2013].

Fassbender, B., 1998. The United Nations Charter as Constitution of the International Community, *Columbia Journal of Transnational Law,* 36(3), pp. 529–620.

Fernández González, J.A., 2011. Economic sustainability of international telecommunication networks. *Info,* 13(11), p. 6.

Flyverbom, M. 2011. *The Power of Networks: Organizing the Global Politics of the Internet.* Edward Elgar Pub. http://books.google.com/books?id=yHpxUYsaiYYC.

Fransen, L., 2012. Multi-stakeholder governance and voluntary programme interactions: Legitimation policies in the institutional design of Corporate Social Responsibility. *Socio-Economic Review,* 10, pp. 163–192.

Froomkin, M.A., 1997. The Internet as a source of regulatory arbitrage. *In:* B. Kahin et C. Nesson (eds.) *Borders in Cyberspace: Information Policy and the Global Information Infrastructure.* Cambridge: MIT Press, pp. 129–163.

Froomkin, M.A., 2000. Wrong Turn in Cyberspace: Using ICANN to Route Around the APA and the Constitution. *Duke Law Journal,* 50(1), pp. 17–184.

Froomkin, A. M. (2002). ICANN 2.0: Meet the New Boss. *Loyola of Los Angeles Law Review, 36,* 1087.

Fuchs, D.A., 2007. *Business Power in Global Governance,* Boulder: Lynne Rienner.

GAO (U.S. Government Accountability Office), 2011. Information Security: Weaknesses Continue Amid New Federal Efforts to Implement Requirements, *GAO* [online] Report No. 12-137, 3 October 2011. Available from: http://www.gao.gov/products/GAO-12-137 [Accessed 20 August 2013].

Garfinkel, H., 1967. *Studies in ethnomethodology.* Englewood Cliffs: Prentice-Hall.

Geist, M., 2012. UN Internet meeting about who pays, not who rules: Geist, *The Star* [online], 25 November 2012. Available from: http://www.thestar.com/business/2012/11/25/un_internet_meeting_about_who_pays_not_who_rules_geist.html [Accessed 16 July 2013].

Ghonim, Y., 2011. The Egyptian People Are the Leaders and Heroes of This Revolution. Interview by Anderson Cooper, *CNN* [online], 11 February 2011. Available from: http://transcripts.cnn.com/TRANSCRIPTS/1102/11/bn.02.html [Accessed 28 August 2013].

Goldsmith, J., 2000. Unilateral Regulation of the Internet: a Modest Defence. *European Journal of International Law,* 11(1), pp. 135–148.

Goldsmith, J., 2010. Can we stop the global cyber arms race? *The Washington Post* [online], 1 February 2010. Available from: http://articles.washingtonpost.com/2010-02-01/opinions/36895669_1_botnets-cyber-attacks-computer-attacks [Accessed 20 August 2013].

Goldsmith J.and Wu, T., 2006. *Who controls the Internet? Illusions of a borderless world,* New York: Oxford University Press.

Google, 2012. *Take Action* [online] Available from: http://www.google.com/intl/en/take action/whats-at-stake/ [Accessed 29 July 2013].

Google, 2013. Financials, *Google.com* [online] Available from: https://www.google.com/finance?fstype=ii&q=NASDAQ:GOOG [Accessed 29 August 2013].

Global Network Initiative, 2013. *Who we are. What we do. Why it matters* [online] Available from: https://globalnetworkinitiative.org/sites/default/files/GNI_brochure.pdf [Accessed 29 August 2013].

Grant, R.W. and Keohane, R.O., 2005. Accountability and Abuses of Power in World Politics. *American Political Science Review,* 99(1), pp. 29–43.

Graz, J.-C. and Noelke, A. (eds.) 2008. *Transnational Private Governance and Its Limits.* New York: Routledge.

Grossman, L. K., 1996. *The electronic republic: reshaping democracy in the information age.* New York: Penguin Books.

Gurstein, M., 2012. (Whose) Hands off (What) Internet: Reflections on WCIT 2012, *Gurstein's Community Informatics* [online], 9 December 2012. Available from: http://gurstein.wordpress.com/2012/12/09/whose-hand-off-what-internet-some-reflections-on-wcit-2012/ [Accessed 16 July 2013].

Gurumurthy, K., and Gurumurthy, A., 2008. Internet Governance and Development Agenda. *Economic and Political Weekly,* 43(14), pp. 19–23.

Habermas, J., 1992. *Faktizität und Geltung, Beiträge zur Diskurstheorie des Rechts und des demokratischen Rechtstaats.* Frankfurt a.M.: Suhrkamp.

Hall, B. R. and Biersteker, T. (eds.) 2002. *The Emergence of Private Authority in Global Governance.* Cambridge: Cambridge University Press.

Hansen, L. and Nissenbaum, H. (2009) Digital Disaster, Cyber Security and the Copenhagen School. *International Studies Quarterly,* 53(4), pp. 1155–1175.

Héritier, A. and Lehmkuhl, D., 2011. New Modes of Governance and Democratic Accountability. *Government and Opposition,* 46, pp. 126–144.

Hill, R., 2013. WCIT: failure or success, impasse or way forward. *International Journal of Law and Information Technology,* 21(3), pp. 313–328.

Hill, R., 2014. The Internet, its governance, and the multi-stakeholder model. *Info,* 16(1), forthcoming.

Hills, J., 2007. *Telecommunications and Empire.* Champaign: University of Illinois Press.

Holitscher; M., 2005. Co-Regulation for Internet Governance? *In:*D. Stauffacher and W. Kleinwächter (eds.) *The World Summit on the Information Society. Moving from the Past into the Future,* New York: The United Nations Information and Communication Technologies Task Force, pp. 256–260.

Hopf, T., 2010. The logic of habit in international relations. *European Journal of International Relations,* 16(4), pp. 539–61.

Howson, A., 2009. Cultural Relativism, *EBSCO Research Starters* [online]. Available from: http://www.ebscohost.com/uploads/imported/thisTopic-dbTopic-1247.pdf [Accessed 23 July 2013].

Hruska, J., 2013. The NSA's Prism leak could fundamentally change or break the entire Internet, *Extreme Tech* [online], 10 June 2013. Available from: http://www.extremetech.com/computing/157761-the-nsas-prism-leak-could-fundamentally-change-or-break-the-entire-internet [Accessed 13 June 2013].

Huston, G., 2012. Calling Stumps at WCIT: Win, Lose or Draw?, *The ISP Column* [online], December 2012. Available from: http://www.potaroo.net/ispcol/2012-12/stumps.html [Accessed 4 June 2013].

Huston, G., 2013. Addressing 2012—Another One Bites the Dust, *The ISP Column* [online], January 2013. Available from: http://www.potaroo.net/ispcol/2013-01/2012.html [Accessed 22 June 2013].

Huston, G., 2013a. An End-to-End View of Telecommunications Policy Frameworks, *Information document for WTPF-13, ITU* [online] Available from: http://www.itu.int/md/S13-WTPF13IEG3-INF-0001/en [Accessed 20 August 2013].

IAHC (International Ad Hoc Committee), 1997. Generic Top-Level Domain Names. Memorandum of Understanding (gTLD-MoU) [online] Available from: http://web.archive.org/web/19971211190257/http://www.gtld-mou.org/gTLD-MoU.html [Accessed 10 June 2013].

ICANN (Internet Corporation for Assigned Names and Numbers), 2000. Comment on NSI Registry Multilingual Domain Name Testbed (25 August). Retrieved on 9 August 2013 from http://www.icann.org/en/news/announcements/announcement-25aug00-en.htm.

ICANN (Internet Corporation for Assigned Names and Numbers), 2001. *A Unique, Authoritative Root for the DNS* [online] Available from: http://www.icann.org/en/about/unique-authoritative-root [Accessed 25 June 2013].

ICANN (Internet Corporation for Assigned Names and Numbers), 2002a. *Bylaws for Internet Corporation for Assigned Names and Numbers. A california Nonprofit Public-Benefit Corporation.* Internet Corporation for Assigned Names and Numbers.

ICANN (Internet Corporation for Assigned Names and Numbers), 2002b. Advisory: Court Ruling in Auerbach v. ICANN Lawsuit [online] Available from: http://www.icann.org/en/news/announcements/advisory-29jul02-en.htm [Accessed 9 September 2013].

ICANN (Internet Corporation for Assigned Names and Numbers), 2012. *gTLD Applicant Guidebook, version 4 June* [online] Available from: http://newgtlds.icann.org/en/applicants/agb [28 August 2013].

ICANN (Internet Corporation for Assigned Names and Numbers), 2013. Comments on the new gTLD batching process from the Internet Society of China. Retrieved August 15, 2013, from http://www.icann.org/en/news/correspondence/isc-to-icann-10may12-en.

ICANN At-Large Community, 2013. *What is At-Large?* [online] Available from: from www.atlarge.icann.org [Accessed 9 September 2013].

IGF (Internet Governance Forum), 2010. *Managing Critical Internet Resources* [online], 15 September 2010. Available from: http://intgovforum.org/cms/component/content/article/102-transcripts2010/643-resources [Accessed 19 June 2013].

India, 2011. *Statement before the UN General Assembly* [online], 26 October 2011. Available from: http://www.un.int/india/2011/ind1945.pdf [Accessed 15 July 2013].

India, Brazil and South Africa, 2011. *Proposal for a United Nations Committee for Internet-Related Policies* [online], 26 October 2011. Available from: http://news.dot-nxt.com/2011/10/27/un-ga-india-cirp-proposal [Accessed 13 July 2013].

IETF (Internet Engineering Task Force), n.d. Internationalized Domain Name—Charter for Working Group. Retrieved on 17 April from http://datatracker.ietf.org/wg/idn/charter/.

Internet Rights and Principles Coalition, 2009 (constantly revised). *The Charter of Human Rights and Principles for the Internet* [online] Available from: http://internetrightsandprinciples.org/wpcharter/ [Accessed 17 July 2013].

Internet Society, 2013. *Statement on the Importance of Open Global Dialogue Regarding Online Privacy* [online], 12 June 2013. Available from: http://www.internetsociety.org/

news/internet-society-statement-importance-open-global-dialogue-regarding-online-privacy [Accessed 15 June 2013].

Internet Society, 2013a. Internet Society Launches a Questionnaire on Multistakeholder Participation in Internet governance [online], 2 August 2013. Available from http://www.internetsociety.org/news/internet-society-launches-questionnaire-multistakeholder-participation-internet-governance [Accessed 29 August 2013].

Internetworldstats, 2013. World Internet Users Statistics Usage and World Population Stats [online] Available from: www.internetworldstats.com [Accessed 29 August 2013].

Irion, K., 2012. *The Governance of Network and Information Security in the European Union: The European Public-Private Partnership for Resilience (EP3R).*

Irion, K. and Radu, R., 2014. Delegation to independent regulatory authorities in the media sector: a paradigm shift through the lens of regulatory theory. *In:* Schulz, W., Valcke, P. and Irion, K. (eds.), *The Independence of the Media and Its Regulatory Agencies,* Chicago: Chicago University Press, forthcoming.

ISOC (Internet Society), OECD (Organization for Economic Co-operation and Development) and UNESCO (United Nations Educational Scientific and Cultural Organization), 2011. *The relationship between local content, Internet development and access prices* [online], 6th Annual meeting of the Internet Governance Forum (IGF), Nairobi, Kenya, 27–30 September. Available from: http://www.unesco.org/new/fileadmin/MULTIMEDIA/HQ/CI/CI/pdf/local_content_study.pdf [Accessed 19 June 2013].

ITU (International Telecommunication Union) and TeleGeography Inc., 1999. Direction of Traffic: Trading Telecom Minutes, *ITU ICT Data and Statistics* [online], October 1999. Available from: http://www.itu.int/ITU-D/ict/publications/dot/1999/index.html [Accessed 16 July 2013].

ITU (International Telecommunication Union). 2006. *Review of the International Telecommunication Regulations,* ITU Admin. Council Res. 146 [online] Available from: http://www.itu.int/ITU-T/itr-eg/files/resolution146.pdf [Accessed 29 August 2013].

ITU (International Telecommunication Union). 2012. *Proposals received from the ITU Member States for the Work of the Conference,* 99, Doc. WCIT12/DT/1-E [online] Available from: http://www.soumu.go.jp/main_content/000188223.pdf [Accessed 28 August 2013].

ITU (International Telecommunication Union). 2013. *Fifth World Telecommunications/ICT Policy Forum* [online] Available from: http://www.itu.int/en/wtpf-13/Pages/default.aspx [Accessed 29 August 2013].

ITU-SG (International Telecommunication Union Secretary-General), 2013.*Report for the Fifth World Telecommunication/Information and Communication Technology Policy Forum 2013* [online] Available from: http://www.itu.int/md/S13-WTPF13-C-0003/en [Accessed 29 August 2013].

ITU-T (International Telecommunication Union Telecommunication Standardization Sector), 2013. International Internet Connectivity, *ITU-T Study Group 3 Special Projects and*

Issues [online] Available from: http://www.itu.int/ITU-T/studygroups/com03/iic/index.html [Accessed 29 August 2013].

ITU-T (International Telecommunication Union Telecommunication Standardization Sector), 2013a. *International Internet Connection. Supplement 2: Guidelines for Reducing the Costs of International Internet Connectivity.* Rec. D.50 Supplement 2, May 2013.

ITU-T (International Telecommunication Union Telecommunication Standardization Sector), 2013b.The Mobile Money Revolution: Part 2 Financial Inclusion Enabler, *ITU-T Technology Watch* [online], 6 June 2013. Available from: http://www.itu.int/oth/T2301000020/en [Accessed 21 June 2013].

Jackson, J.H., 2003. Sovereignty—Modern: A New Approach to an Outdated Concept. *American Journal of International Law,* vol. 97, pp. 782–802.

Johnson, D., R., Crawford, S., P. and Palfrey, J. G., 2004. The Accountable Internet: Peer Production of Internet Governance. *Virginia Journal of Law & Technology,* 9(9), pp. 1–33.

Hafner, Katie. 1998. *Where Wizards Stay Up Late: The Origins Of The Internet.* Simon & Schuster.

Kampfner, J., 2013. Prism surveillance: spies thrive in the Internet's legal free-for-all, *The Guardian* [online], 12 June 2013. Available from: http://www.guardian.co.uk/commentisfree/2013/jun/12/prism-surveillance-internet-william-hague [Accessed 15 June 2013].

Karimi, F., 2013. Facebook, Microsoft disclose information on user data request, *CNN* [online], 15 June 2013. Available from: http://edition.cnn.com/2013/06/15/politics/data-tech-giants/index.html?hpt=hp_t1 [Accessed 15 June 2013].

Kaul I., Grunberg I. and Stern M.A., (eds), 1999. *Global Public Goods International Cooperation In The 21St Century,* The United Nations Development Programme (UNDP), New York and Oxford: Oxford University Press.

Keating, D., 2013. US promises to provide EU information on Prism, *Europeanvoice.com* [online], 14 June 2013. Available from: http://www.europeanvoice.com/article/2013/june/us-promises-to-provide-eu-information-on-prism/77547.aspx [Accessed 15 June 2013].

Kennedy, S., 2006. The political economy of standards coalitions: explaining China's involvement in high-tech standards wars. *Asia Policy,* 2 (July), pp. 41–62.

Khalil, A, 2012. Internet freedom not to be curbed: UN telecoms head, *AFP* [online], 3 December 2012. Available from: http://www.google.com/hostednews/afp/article/ALeqM5gJvqyLxxnGbfnmLjWbiBJtopMmGA?docId=CNG.b93152338931f5ba637dce59fa389a5e.31 [Accessed 20 August 2013].

Kisrawi, N., 2006. *Comment on "The Continued Transition of the Technical Coordination and Management of the Internet Domain Name and Addressing System"* [online] Available from: http://www.ntia.doc.gov/legacy/ntiahome/domainname/dnstransition/comments/dnstrans_comment0081.htm [Accessed 29 August 2013].

Klein, H., 2005. Understanding WSIS: An Institutional Analysis of the UN World Summit on the Information Society. *Information Technology and International Development,* Special Issue on WSIS, 1(3–4), pp. 3–13.

Klein, M., 2009. *Wiring Up The Big Brother Machine...And Fighting It.* Charleston: BookSurge Publishing.

Kleinwächter, W., 2000. ICANN between technical mandate and political challenges. *Telecommunications Policy, 24*(6–7), pp. 553–563.

Kleinwächter, W., 2001. *Governance in the Information Age.* Aarhus: Aarhus University Press.

Kleinwächter, W., 2002. From Self-Governance to Public-Private Partnership: The Changing Role of Governments in the Management of the Internet's Core Resources. *Loyola of Los Angeles Law Review, 36,* 1103.

Kleinwächter, W., 2004. Beyond ICANN Vs ITU? How WSIS tries to enter the new territory of Internet governance. *Gazette, 66*(3–4), pp. 233–251.

Kleinwächter, W. (ed.), 2007. *The Power of Ideas: Internet Governance in a Global Multi-stakeholder environment.* Berlin: Marketing fur Deutschland GmbH.

Kleinwächter, W., 2008. Internet governance and the Information Society. Global Perspectives and European Dimensions. *In:*W. Benedek, V. Bauer, & M. C. Kettemann (eds.) *Internet Governance and the Information Society: Global Perspectives and European Dimensions.* Utrecht: Eleven International Publishing, pp. 79–92.

Kleinwächter, W., 2009. The history of Internet governance. *In:* C. Möller and A. Amouroux (eds.) *Governing the Internet: freedom and regulation in the OSCE region,* Vienna: Organization for Security and Cooperation in Europe, pp. 41–90.

Kleinwächter, W., 2011a. *Internet Principle Hype: How Soft Law is Used to Regulate the Internet* [online], 25 July 2011. Available from: http://news.dot-nxt.com/2011/07/27/internet-principle-hype-anon [Accesses 18 July 2013].

Kleinwächter, W., 2011b. Editorial. *MIND Paper Series,* No. 2, September 2011. Berlin: Internet& Gesellschaft Colaboratory.

Kleinwächter, W., 2012. Es herrscht kalter Krieg (Interview), *Das Netz 2012–Jahresrückblick Netzpolitik,* 1, pp. 15–17 [online]. Available from: http://irights.info/wolfgang-kleinwaechter-%E2%80%9Ees-herrscht-kalter-krieg [Accessed 23 July 2013].

Kleinwächter, W., 2013. Internet Governance Outlook 2013: "Cold Internet War" or "Peaceful Internet Coexistence"? *CircleID* [online], 3 January 2013. Available from: http://www.circleid.com/posts/20130103_internet_governance_outlook_2013/ [Accessed 23 July 2013].

Klensin, J., 2003. Role of the Domain Name System (DNS), *Network Working Group, The Internet Society* [online] Available from: http://www.ietf.org/rfc/rfc3467.txt [Accessed 27 June 2012].

Klimburg, A., 2011. Mobilising Cyber Power, *Survival,* 53(1), pp. 41–60.

Klimburg, A., 2013. The Internet Yalta, *Centre for a New American Security* [online] Available from: http://www.cnas.org/theinternetyalta [Accessed 23 July 2013].

Kohl, U., 2013. Google: the rise and rise of online intermediaries in the governance of the Internet and beyond (Part 2). *International Journal of Law and Information Technology,* 21(2), pp. 185–210.

Koppell, J. G. S. (2005). Pathologies of Accountability: ICANN and the Challenge of "Multiple Accountabilities Disorder." *Public Administration Review, 65*(1), 94–108.

Königsgruber, R., 2010. A political economy of accounting standard setting. *Journal of management and governance.* 14(4), pp. 277–95.

Krahmann, E., 2008. Security: Collective Good or Commodity? *European Journal of International Relations,* 14(3), pp. 379–404.

Krisch, N., 2010. *Beyond Constitutionalism: The Pluralist Structure of Post-National Law.* Oxford: Oxford University Press.

Kruger, L.G., 2013. Internet Governance and the Domain Name System: Issues for Congress, *Congressional Research Service* [online], 13 April 2013. Available from: http://www.fas.org/sgp/crs/misc/R42351.pdf [Accessed 6 June 2013].

Kuehn, A. and Mueller, M., 2012. *Profiling the Profilers: Deep Packet Inspection and Behavioral Advertising in Europe and the United States* [online]. Available from: http://dx.doi.org/10.2139/ssrn.2014181 [Accessed 20 August 2013].

Kulesza, J., 2012. *International Internet Law.* New York: Routledge.

Kummer, Markus. 2007. "The Debate on Internet Governance: From Geneva to Tunis and Beyond." *Information Polity* 12 (1) (January 1): 5–13.

Kummer, M., 2013. *Multistakeholder Cooperation: Reflections on the emergence of a new phraseology in international cooperation* [online] Available from: http://www.internetsociety.org/blog/2013/05/multistakeholder-cooperation-reflections-emergence-new-phraseology-international [Accessed 29 August 2013].

Kunigami, A. and Navas-Sabater,ka J., 2010. Options to increase access to telecommunications services in rural and low-income areas. *World Bank Working Paper,* vol. 178. Washington D.C: World Bank.

Kurbalija, J. 2012. *An Introduction to Internet Governance.* Geneva: DiploFoundation.

de La Chapelle, B., 2011. Multistakeholder Governance. *MIND Paper Series,* No. 2, September 2011. Berlin: Internet& Gesellschaft Colaboratory.

de La Chapelle, B., 2013. The Multi-stakeholder model of Internet Governance, *Guarder.net* [online], August 2013. Available from: http://www.guarder.net/kleinwaechter/images/lecturenotes/2013/Chapelle.pdf [Accessed 20 August 2013].

Landler, M., and Stelter, B., 2009. Washington taps into a potent new force in diplomacy, *The New York Times* [online], 16 June 2009. Available from: http://www.nytimes.com/2009/06/17/world/middleeast/17media.html [Accessed 28 August 2013].

Lane, J.-E., 2013. On the Growth in Normativity in International Relations. *Journal of Politics and Law,* 6(1), pp. 15–23.

Latour, B. and Woolgar, S., 1979. *Laboratory life: the construction of scientific facts.* Beverly Hills: Sage.

Le Monde, 2013. Prism: les Européens obtiennent des informations, *Le Monde* [online], 14 June 2013. Available from: http://www.lemonde.fr/europe/article/2013/06/14/prism-les-europeens-obtiennent-des-informations_3430566_3214.html [Accessed 15 June 2013].

Lessig, L., 1999. Open code and open societies: values of Internet governance. *Chicago-Kent Law Review,* 74(3), pp. 1405–20.

Lessig, L., 1999a. *Code and Other Laws of Cyberspace.* New York: Basic Books.

Levi-Faur, D., 2002. New Regimes, New Capacities: The Politics of Telecommunications Nationalization and Liberalization. *In:* L. Weiss (ed.) *States in the Global Economy: Bringing Domestic Institutions Back In,* Cambridge: Cambridge University Press.

Levi-Faur, D., 2005. The Global Diffusion of Regulatory Capitalism. *The Annals of the American Academy of Political and Social Science,* vol. 598, pp. 12–32.

Lewis, R., 2003. *Letter form Rusty Lewis to Paul Twomey* [online], 30 July 2000. Available from: http://www.icann.org/en/news/correspondence/lewis-to-twomey-13oct03-en.htm [Accessed 19 June 2013].

Liddicoat, J., Doria, A., 2012. *Human Rights and Internet Protocols* [online]. Available from: https://www.internetsociety.org/sites/default/files/Human%20Rights%20and%20Internet%20Protocols-%20Comparing%20Processes%20and%20Principles.pdf Page 7 [Accessed 20 August 2013].

Liebowitz, S.J. and Margolis, S.E., 1990. The fable of the keys. *Journal of Law and Economics,* 33(1), pp. 1–25.

Livingston, E., 1987. *Making sense of ethnomethodology.* London: Routledge.

Loo, B P., 2004. Telecommunications reforms in China: towards an analytical framework. *Telecommunications Policy,* 28(9), pp. 697–714.

Lynch, G., and Burstein, D., 2012. WCIT collapses: US, UK, allies refuse to sign treaty after Africa wins floor vote, *CommsDay.com* [online], 14 December 2012. Available from: http://www.commsday.com/uncategorized/wcit-collapses-us-uk-allies-refuse-to-sign-treaty-after-africa-wins-floor-vote [Accessed 29 August 2013].

Lynn, S., 2002. President's Report: ICANN—The Case for Reform, *ICANN* [online] Available from: http://archive.icann.org/en/general/lynn-reform-proposal-24feb02.htm [Accessed 9 September 2013].

Mac Síthigh, D., 2013. App law within: rights and regulation in the smartphone age. *International Journal of Law and Information Technology,* 21(2), pp. 154–186.

MacAskill, E., 2010. Hillary Clinton attacks release of US embassy cables, *The Guardian* [online], 29 November. Available from: http://www.theguardian.com/world/2010/nov/29/clinton-reacts-us-embassy-cables [Accessed 20 August 2013].

MacAskill, E., 2010a. Julian Assange like a hi-tech terrorist, says Joe Biden, *The Guardian* [online], 19 December. Available from: http://www.theguardian.com/media/2010/dec/19/assange-high-tech-terrorist-biden [Accessed 20 August 2013].

MacLean, D., 2004. *Internet governance: a grand collaboration: an edited collection of papers contributed to the United Nations ICT Task Force Global Forum on Internet Governance, New York, March 25–26, 2004.*New York, United Nations Information and Communications Technologies Task Force.

Maguire, J.S., 2008. *Hanging out and the mall: the production of a teenage social space.* Saarbrücken: VDM Verlag.

Major, P., 2011. *IGF 2.0.* Presented at the 3rd meeting of the Working Group on Improvements to the IGF, Geneva: UNCSTD.

Malcolm, J., 2008. *Multi-Stakeholder Governance and the Internet Governance Forum.* Perth: Terminus Press.

Marlin-Bennett, R., 2001. ICANN and democracy: contradictions and possibilities. *Info, 3*(4), pp. 299–311.

Marsden; C.T., 2008. Beyond Europe: The Internet, Regulation, and Multistakeholder Governance—Representing the Consumer Interest? *Journal of Consumer Policy,* 31(1), pp. 115–132.

Marsden; C.T. 2011. *Internet Co-Regulation: European Law, Regulatory Governance and Legitimacy in Cyberspace.* Cambridge: Cambridge University Press.

Martin, L. 1999. The Political Economy of International Cooperation. *In:* I. Kaul, I. Grunberg and M.A. Stern (eds) *Global Public Goods International Cooperation In The 21St Century,* The United Nations Development Programme (UNDP), New York and Oxford: Oxford University Press, pp. 51–64.

Mathiason, J. 2009. *Internet Governance: The New Frontier of Global Institutions.* London: Routledge.

Mayer-Schoenberger, V. and Ziewitz, M., 2007. Jefferson Rebuffed—The United States and the Future of Internet Governance. *The Columbia Science and Technology Law Review,* vol. 8, pp. 188–228.

McAfee, 2010. In the Crossfire—Critical Infrastructure in the Age of Cyber War, A global report on the threats facing key industries [online] Available from: http://www.mcafee.com/us/resources/reports/rp-in-crossfire-critical-infrastructure-cyber-war.pdf [Accessed 20 August 2013].

McCarthy, K., 2012. Verisign loses dot-com piggybank, *.nxt* [online], 30 November 2012. Available from: http://news.dot-nxt.com/2012/12/06/verisign-loses-dot-com-piggyba [Accessed 8 June 2013].

McCarthy, K., 2013. Living in a talk-shop bubble, *dot-next.com.* [online], 28 February 2013. Available from: news.dot-nxt.com/2013/02/28/living-talk-shop-bubble [Accessed 9 September 2013].

McDowell, R.M., 2012. The U.N. Threat to Internet Freedom, *Wall Street Journal,* [online], 21 February. Available from: http://online.wsj.com/article/SB10001424052970204792404577229074023195322.html [Accessed 26 July 2013].

McKinsey Global Institute, 2011. *Internet Matters: The Net's Sweeping Impact on Growth, Jobs and Prosperity.* [online] Available from: http://www.mckinsey.com/mgi/publications/internet_matters/pdfs/MGI_internet_matters_full_report.pdf [Accessed 30 October 2011].

McLaughlin, L. and Pickard, V., 2005. What Is Bottom-up About Global Internet Governance? *Global Media and Communication,* 1(3), pp; 357–373.

Mello, J. P., 2012. Opponents say ITU treaty threatens Internet freedom, *PCWorld* [online], 12 December 2012. Available from: http://www.pcworld.com/article/2020469/opponents-say-itu-treaty-threatens-internet-freedom.html [Accessed 20 August 2013].

Mena, S. and Palazzo, G., 2012. Input and Output Legitimacy of Multi-Stakeholder Initiatives. *Business Ethics Quarterly,* 22, pp. 527–556.

Merriam-Webster, 2013. The Merriam-Webster Dictionary [online]. Available from: http://www.merriam-webster.com/dictionary/ism [Accessed 29 August 2013].

Miller, C.R. and Shepherd, D., 2004. *Blogging as social action: a genre analysis of the weblog* [online] Available from: http://blog.lib.umn.edu/blogosphere/blogging_as_social_action_a_genre_analysis_of_the_weblog.html [Accessed 23 August 2013].

Molière, 1670. *The Middle Class Gentleman.* Gutenberg.org [online] Available from: http://www.gutenberg.org/files/2992/2992-h/2992-h.htm [Accessed 9 September 2013].

Morris, I., 2011. *Why the West Rules—For Now.* London: Profile Books.

Mueller, M., 1999. ICANN and the Internet Governance: Sorting through the debris of "self-regulation." *Info, 1*(1), 497–520.

Mueller, M., 2002. Competing DNS Roots: Creative Destruction or Just Plain Destruction? *Journal of Network Industries,* 3(3), pp. 313–334.

Mueller, M., 2002a. *Ruling the Root: Internet Governance and the Taming of Cyberspace.* Cambridge: MIT Press.

Mueller, M., 2009. ICANN Inc: Accountability and Participation in the Governance of Critical Internet Resources, *Korean Journal of Policy Studies,* 24(2), pp. 91–116.

Mueller, M., 2010. *Networks and States: The Global Politics of Internet Governance.* Cambridge: MIT Press.

Mueller, M., 2013. *Are we in a Digital Cold War?* Presentation delivered at the GigaNet workshop "The Global Governance of the Internet: Intergovernmentalism, Multistakeholderism and Networks", Graduate Institute, Geneva, Switzerland (17 May), [online] Available from: http://www.internetgovernance.org/wordpress/wp-content/uploads/DigitalCold War31.pdf [Accessed 23 July 2013].

Mueller, M., 2013a. Has the USA Run Out of Ideas About Internet Governance? (Part 2), *Internet Governance Project* [online], 18 June 2013. Available from: http://www.internet governance.org/2013/06/18/has-the-usa-run-out-of-ideas-about-internet-governance-part-2/ [Accessed 19 June 2013].

Mueller, M., Mathiason, J. and Klein, H., 2007. The Internet and Global Governance: Principles and Norms for a New Regime. *Global Governance,* 13(2), pp. 237–254.

Mueller, M.and Asghari, H., 2012. Deep packet Inspection and Bandwidth Management: Battles over BitTorrent in Canada and the United States. *Telecommunications Policy,* 36(6), pp. 462–475.

Mueller, M. and Kuehn, A., 2013. *Einstein on the Breach: Surveillance Technology, Cybersecurity and Organizational Change.* Paper presented at the 12th Workshop on the Economics of Information Security (WEIS 2013), Georgetown University, Washington, D.C. June 11–12, 2013 [online] Available from: http://weis2013.econinfosec.org/papers/MuellerKuehnWEIS2013.pdf [Accessed 20 August 2013].

Mueller, M., Kuehn, A. and Santoso, S., 2012. Policing the Network: Using DPI for Copyright Enforcement. *Surveillance and Society,* 9(4), pp. 348–364.

Mueller, M., Schmidt, A. and Kuerbis, B., 2013. Internet Security and Networked Governance in International Relations. *International Studies Review,* 15(1), pp. 86–104.

Müller, J., Bohlin, E., Karpakka, J., Riis, C. and Skouby, K. E., 1993. Telecommunications Liberalization in the Nordic Countries. *Telecommunications Policy,* 17(8), pp. 623–630.

Muller, J.Z., 2002. *The Mind and the Market.* Capitalism in Modern European Thought. New York: Alfred A. Knopf.

Musil, S., 2013. Iran develops software to control social networks, *CNET* [online], 6 January 2013. Available from: http://news.cnet.com/8301-1023_3-57562295-93/iran-develops-software-to-control-access-to-social-networks/ [Accessed 15 June 2013.

National Security Agency, 2013. *The National Security Agency: Missions, Authorities, Oversight and Partnerships* [online], 9 August 2013. Available from: http://www.nsa.gov/public_info/_files/speeches_testimonies/2013_08_09_the_nsa_story.pdf [Accessed 13 August 2013].

Negro, G., 2011. Internet Regulation in China, *China Media Observatory Newsletter,* 15(1), pp. 2–6.

Nietzsche, F., 2013. Untimely Meditations, Cambridge Texts in the History of Philosophy [Kindle Edition], Cambridge: Cambridge University Press. First published in 1874–1876.

Noam, E., 2013. *Presentation at the workshop "The Future of Internet Governance after Dubai: Are We Heading to a Federated Internet?",* Columbia Institute for Tele-Information (CITI), 20 June 2013. Available from: http://www8.gsb.columbia.edu/citi/thefutureofthe internet [Accessed 29 August 2013].

Nothias, J-C., 2012. The Hypocrisy Threatening the Future of the Internet, *The Global Journal* [online], 22 November 2012. Available from: http://theglobaljournal.net/article/view/904/ [Accessed 16 July 2013].

Nothias, J-C., 2012a. The Battle for the Future of the Internet?, *Huffington Post* [online], 2 December 2012. Available from: http://www.huffingtonpost.com/jeanchristophe-nothias/internet-governance_b_2227820.html [Accessed 16 July 2013].

Nothias, J-C., 2013. And Now the Second Battle of the Internet. *Huffington Post* [online], 13 June 2013. Available from: http://www.huffingtonpost.com/jeanchristophe-nothias/internet-governance_b_3435812.html [Accessed 15 June 2013].

Nyswander Thomas R., 2013. Securing Cyberspace Through Public-Private Partnership—A Comparative Analysis Of Partnership Models. Thesis [online] Available from: http://csis.org/files/publication/130819_tech_summary.pdf [Accessed 25 August 2013].

O'Neil, L., 2012. Internet freedom debate intensifies at UN conference, *CBCNews Your Community Blog,* [online], 5 December 2012. Available from: http://www.cbc.ca/newsblogs/yourcommunity/2012/12/internet-freedom-debate-intensifies-at-un-conference.html [Accessed 20 August 2013].

OMB (U.S. White House Office of Management and Budget), 2012. *Fiscal Year 2011.* Report to Congress on the Implementation of The Federal Information Security Management Act of 2002.

Open Technology Institute and the Center for Democracy and Technology, 2013. Letter to the House Energy and Commerce Committee [online], 10 April. Available from: https://www.cdt.org/files/file/CDT-OTI_NetGovernanceBill.pdf [Accessed 30 July 2013].

Ostrom, E., 1990. *Governing the commons: the evolution of institutions for collective action.* Cambridge: Cambridge University Press.

OED (Oxford English Dictionary), 2002. *The Compact Oxford English Dictionary* (2nd edition). Oxford: Oxford University Press.

Palfrey, J. G., 2004. The End of the Experiment: How ICANN's Foray into Global Internet Democracy Failed. *SSRN Scholarly Paper,* No. ID 487644. Rochester, NY: Social Science Research Network.

Pauwelyn, J., 2011. The Rise and Challenges of "Informal" International Law-making. *In:* S. Muller, S. Zouridis, M. Frishman and L. Kistemaker (eds.) *The Law of the Future and the Future of Law.* Oslo: Torkel Opsahl Academic Epublisher, 2013, pp. 125–141.

Payne, E., 2013. Morales challenges U.S. after Snowden rumor holds up plane in Europe, *CNN* [online], 4 July 2013. Available from: http://edition.cnn.com/2013/07/04/world/americas/bolivia-morales-snowden/index.html?hpt=hp_t3 [Accessed 14 July 2013].

Penaloza, L., 1998. Just doing it: a visual ethnographic study of spectacular consumption behavior at Nike Town. Consumption, *Markets and Culture,* 2(4), pp. 337–401.

Peter, I., 2013. *E-mail to the Internet Governance Caucus mailing list* [online], 1 March 2013. Available from: http://igcaucus.org/[Accessed 9 September 2013].

Pfanner, E. 2012. U.S. Rejects Telecommunications Treaty. *The New York Times* [online], 13 December, available at http://www.nytimes.com/2012/12/14/technology/14iht-treaty14.html?_r=0 [Accessed 9 September 2013].

Phrontistery. 2013. The Phrontistery. Available at: http://phrontistery.info/isms.html [Accessed 29 August 2013].

Pogge, T., 1994. Cosmopolitanism and Sovereignty. *In:* C. Brown (ed.) *Political Restructuring in Europe: Ethical Perspectives.* London: Routledge, pp. 85–118.

Posner, M.H., 2011. *Conversations With America: The State Department's Internet Freedom Strategy,* Interview by Philip J. Crowley[online], 18 February. Available from: http://www.state.gov/j/drl/rls/rm/2011/157089.htm [Accessed 13 August 2013].

Post, D.G., 1996. Governing cyberspace. *Wayne Law Review.* 43(1), pp. 155–71.

Postel, J. 1996. "Draft Specifications for Administration and Management of gTLDs". Internet Draft. Network Working Group, IETF.

Powell, W.W., 1990, Neither Market nor Hierarchy: Network Forms of Organization, *Research in Organizational Behavior,* 12, pp. 295–336.

Qiu, J.L., 2003. The Internet in China: data and issues. Paper presented at the Annenberg Research Seminar on International Communication, Los Angeles, 1 October 2003. Available from: http://arnic.info/Papers/JQ_China_and_Internet.pdf [Accessed 20 August 2013].

Radu, R. 2013. Negotiating meanings for security in the cyberspace. *Info.* 15 (6), forthcoming.

Rafanell, I., 2013. Micro-situational foundations of social structure: an interactionist exploration of affective sanctioning. *Journal for the Theory of Social Behaviour.* 43(2), pp. 181–204.

Rasmussen, T., 2007. Techo-politics, Internet Governance and Some challenges Facing the Internet, *Oxford Internet Institute,* Research Report [online] Available from: http://www.media.uio.no/prosjekter/internettiendring/downloads/RasmussenTechno-politics.pdf [Accessed 25 August 2013].

Raz, J., 1994. *Ethics and the Public Domain.* Oxford: Clarendon Press.

Reed, C., 2012. *Making Laws for Cyberspace.* Oxford: Oxford University Press.

Reidenberg, J.R., 1998. Lex Informatica: The Formulation of Information Policy Rules Through Technology, *Texas Law Review,* 76(3), pp. 553–584.

Rezwan 2007. Globalization of Internet: The next billion users are combing with a challenge, *The third World View* [online], 26 January 2007. Available from: http://rezwanul.blogspot.ch/2007/01/globalization-of-internet-next-billion.html [Accessed 27 June 2013].

Ringmar, E., 2007. *A blogger's Manifesto: Free Speech and Censorship in the Age of the Internet.* London: Anthem Press.

Rollnick, R., 2002. China concerned at electronic threats to moral standards, *Earth Times News Service* [online], 14 January 2002. Available from: http://www.earthtimes.org/jan/telecommunicationchinajan14_02.htm [Accessed 27 June 2013].

Rosen, S., 2010. Is the Internet a positive force in the development of civil society, a public sphere, and democratization in China? *International Journal of Communication,* vol. 4, pp. 509–516.

Rosenau, J.N. and Singh, J.P. (eds.), 2002, *Information Technologies and Global Politics: The Changing Scope of Power and Governance,* Albany: State University of New York Press.

Rosenau, J.N. and Czempiel, E.O. (eds.), 1992. *Governance Without Government: Order and Change in World Politics.* Cambridge: Cambridge University Press.

Russia, 2011. *CWG-WCIT12 Contribution 40* [online], 30 March 2013. Available from: http://files.wcitleaks.org/public/Russia%2040.pdf [Accessed 17 July 2013].

Sacks, H., 1972. An initial investigation of the usability of conversational data for doing sociology. *In:* D.N. Sudnow (ed.) *Studies in social interaction.* New York: Free Press, pp. 31–74.

Saez, C., 2013. US Defender Of Internet Freedom, Keen On Protecting IP Rights, *Intellectual Property Watch* [online], 8 March 2013. Available from: http://www.ip-watch.org/2013/03/08/us-as-defender-of-internet-freedom-keen-on-protecting-ip-rights [Accessed 15 June 2013].

Savage, C., Wyatt, E. and Baker, P., 2013. U.S. Confirms that it Gathers Online Data Overseas. *The New York Times* [online], 6 June 2013. Available from: http://www.nytimes.com/2013/06/07/us/nsa-verizon-calls.html?_r=0 [Accessed 8 June 2013].

Scharpf, F. W., 1997. *Games real actors play: Actor-centered institutionalism in policy research.* Boulder: Westview Press.

Schegloff, E.A., 2007. *Sequence organization in interaction: a primer in conversation analysis,* vol. 1. Cambridge: Cambridge University Press.

Schiller, D. 2000. *Digital Capitalism: Networking the Global Market System.* Cambridge: MIT Press.

Schiller, D., 2013. Masters of the Internet, *Le Monde Diplomatique* [online], February 2013. Available from: http://mondediplo.com/2013/02/15internet [Accessed 16 July 2013].

Schmidt A., 2004. Hegemonie durch Technologie – Strategien zur Instrumentalisierung von Informationstechnologien in globaler Politik – Überlegungen amerikanischer Think Tanks. Unpublished thesis.

Schmidt, A., 2012. At the boundaries of peer production: The organization of Internet security production in the cases of Estonia 2007 and Conficker, *Telecommunications Policy,* 36(6), pp. 451–61.

Schmidt, A., 2013a. The Estonian Cyberattacks. *In:* J. Healey (ed.), *The Fierce Domain—Conflicts in Cyberspace 1986–2012,* Washington, D.C: Atlantic Council.

Schmidt, A., 2013b (forthcoming). Hierarchies in networks—Emerging hybrids of networks and hierarchies for producing Internet security. *In:* J. Kremer & B. Müller (eds), *Cyber Space and International Relations—Theory, Prospects and Challenges (Working title).* New York: Springer.

Schneier, Bruce, 2013. Has U.S. Started an Internet War?, *CNN* [online], 18 June 2013. Available from: http://edition.cnn.com/2013/06/18/opinion/schneier-cyberwar-policy/index.html [Accessed 19 June 2013].

Scholte, J. A., 2011. *Building Global Democracy.* Cambridge: Cambridge University Press.

Schütz, A., 1953. Common-sense and scientific interpretation of human action. *Philosophy and Phenomenological Research,* 14(1), pp. 1–38.

Schwöbel, C.E.J., 2011. *Global Constitutionalism in International Legal Perspective,* Leiden: Martinus Nijhoff.

Scott, J.C., 1998. *Seeing like a state: how certain schemes to improve the human condition have failed.* New Haven: Yale University Press.

Senn, M., 2011. *Non-State Regulatory Regimes.* Berlin: Springer Verlag.

Shanghai Cooperation Organization, 2009. *Agreement among the member states of the Shanghai Cooperation Organization on cooperation in the field of international information security* [online] Unofficial translation available from: http://media.npr.org/assets/news/2010/09/23/cyber_treaty.pdf [Accessed 24 July 2013].

Shapiro, A. 2000. *The Control Revolution: How the Internet is Putting Individuals in Charge and Changing the World We Know.* New York: PublicAffairs.

Sharrock, W., 2004. What Garfinkel makes of Schutz: the past, present and future of an alternate, asymmetric and incommensurable approach to sociology. *Theory and Science,* 5(1). Available from http://theoryandscience.icaap.org/content/vol5.1/sharrock.html [Accessed 24 August 2013].

Sherman, S. and Westland, J.C., 2009. *Red Wired: China's Internet Revolution,* London: Marshall Cavendish.

Shirk, S. L., 2010. *Changing media, changing China.* Oxford and New York: Oxford University Press.

Shore, M., Du, Y. & Zeadally, S., 2011. A Public-Private Partnership Model for National Cybersecurity, *Policy & Internet,* 3(2).

Sidnell, J., 2010. *Conversation analysis: an introduction.* Chichester: Wiley-Blackwell.

Singh, P. J. 2005. The US factor in the WSIS needs highlighting as much as the Tunisian factor. *www.worldsummit2003.de.*

Simon, C., 2006. *Launching the DNS War: Dot-Com Privatization and the Rise of Global Internet Governance.* PhD dissertation at the University of Miami, Coral Gables, FL.

Simon, H.A., 1953. Notes on the observation and measurement of power. *Journal of Politics,* 15(4), pp. 500-16.

Singh, P. J., 2005. The US factor in the WSIS needs highlighting as much as the Tunisian factor, *www.worldsummit2003.de* [online] Available from: http://www.worldsummit2003.de/en/web/812.htm [Accessed 9 September 2013].

Singh, P. J., 2012. Hyping one threat to hide another. *The Hindu* [online], 28 November 2012. Available from: http://www.thehindu.com/opinion/lead/hyping-one-threat-to-hide-another/article4140922.ece [Accessed 16 July 2013].

Slaughter, A.M. and Zaring, D., 2006. Networking Goes International: An Update. *Annual Review of Law and Social Science,* 2, pp. 211–229.

Slaughter, A.M., 2004. *A New World Order.* Princeton: Princeton University Press.

Slaughter A.-M. and Hale, T.N., 2011. Transgovernmental Networks. *In:* M. Bevir (ed.) *Handbook of Governance,* Thousand Oaks: SAGE.

Smartling 2012. Say Hello to the Global Web, *Smartling.com* [online] 20 April 2012, Available from: http://www.smartling.com/globalweb#people-online [Accessed 27 June 2013].

Sourdis, I., 2007. *Designs and algorithms for packet and content inspection.* Delft: TU Delft.

Sowell, J.H., 2012. Empirical studies of bottom-up Internet governance. Paper presented at Telecommunications Policy Research Conference, George Mason University School of Law, Arlington, VA [online] Available from: http://ecir.mit.edu/images/stories/sowell-tprc2012-camera.pdf [Accessed 20 August 2013].

Spar, D.L., 1999. The public face of cyberspace. *In:* Kaul I., Grunberg I. and Stern M.A., (eds), *Global Public Goods International Cooperation In The 21St Century,* The United Nations Development Programme (UNDP), New York and Oxford: Oxford University Press, pp. 344–363.

Starr, P., 2005. *The creation of the media: Political origins of modern communications.* New York: Basic Books (AZ).

Strange, S., 1996. *Retreat of the State,* Cambridge: Cambridge University Press.

Suchman, L., 1987. *Plans and situated actions: the problem of human-machine communication.* Cambridge: Cambridge University Press.

Sutherland, E., 2012. Corruption in telecommunications: problems and remedies, *Info,* Vol. 14 Iss: 1, pp. 4–19.

Sylvan, D., 2012. "Hi-tech hermeneutics": combining rigor and alternative epistemologies of social science. *In:* R. Marlin-Bennett (ed.) *Alker and IR: global studies in an interconnected world.* London and New York: Routledge, pp. 178–89.

Tai, Z., 2006. *The Internet in China: Cyberspace and civil society.* Routledge, New York.

Tan, Z., 1999. Regulating China's Internet: Convergence toward a coherent regulatory regime. *Telecommunications Policy,* 23(3–4), pp. 261–276.

Tan, Z A., Mueller, M. and Foster, W., 1997. China's new Internet regulations: two steps forward, one step back. *Communications of the ACM,* 40(12), pp. 11–16.

Taubman, G., 1998. A Not-So World Wide Web: The Internet, China, and the Challenges to Nondemocratic Rule, *Political Communication,* 15(2), pp. 255–272.

Tech Freedom et al., 2012. *Declaration of Internet Freedom* [online], 4 July. Available from: http://declarationofinternetfreedom.org/ [Accessed 20 August 2013].

Telecommunications, National, and Information Administration. 1998. "Management of Internet Names and Addresses". Statement of Policy 980212036-8146-02. Washington, DC: US Department of Commerce.

Teubner, G., 2004. Societal Constitutionalism: Alternatives to State-Centred Constitutional Theory? *In:* C. Joerges, I.J. Sand, G. Teubner (eds.) *Transnational Governance and Constitutionalism.* Oxford: Hart, pp. 3–28.

The Economist, 2011. In Praise of Chaos: Governments' Attempts To Control The Internet Should Be Resisted, *The Economist* [online], 1 October. Available from: www.economist.com/node/215311011 [Accessed 23 July 2013].

The Economist, 2012. A Digital Cold War?, *The Economist* [online], 14 December. Available from: http://www.economist.com/blogs/babbage/2012/12/internet-regulation [Accessed 29 August 2013].

Thorne, S., 2013., *Sara Thorne English Language* [online] Available from: http://sarathorne englishlanguage.com/2013/05/31/ism-and-ist-helpful-suffixes/ [Accessed 29 August 2013].

Touré, H., 2012. *ITU Secretary-General's Report for the Fifth World Telecommunication/Information and Communication Technology Policy Forum 2013.* Geneva: International Telecommunications Union (ITU).

Touré, H., 2012a. *Statement from Dr Hamadoun I. Touré, Secretary General of the ITU* [online], 13 December 2012. Available from http://www.itu.int/en/wcit-12/Pages/statement-toure.aspx [Accessed 5 September 2013].

Townes, Miles. 2012. "The Spread of TCP/IP: How the Internet Became the Internet." *Millennium—Journal of International Studies* (July 11). doi:10.1177/0305829812449195.

Trautmann C., 2011. Multistakeholderism Needs Fundamental and Decisive Legitimation. *MIND Paper Series,* No. 2, September 2011. Berlin: Internet& Gesellschaft Colaboratory.

Tribe, L.H., 2011. *The Stop Online Piracy Act (SOPA) Violates the First Amendment.* [online] Available from: http://www.netcoalition.com/wp-content/uploads/2011/08/tribe-legis-memo-on-SOPA-12-6-11-1.pdf [Accessed 12 July 2013].

UNGA (UN General Assembly), 1999. *Developments in the field of information and telecommunications in the context of international security.* Resolution A/RES/53/70. 4 January 1999.

UNGA (UN General Assembly), 2011. *Information and communications technologies for development.* A/RES/65/141. 2 February 2011.

UNGA (UN General Assembly), 2012. *Information and communications technologies for development.* A/RES/67/195. 5 February 2012.

UN Human Rights Council, 2012. P*romotion, protection and enjoyment of human rights on the Internet,* Resolution A/HRC/20/L.13. 29 June 2012.

UN SG (UN Secretary-General), 2011. *Public policy issues pertaining to the Internet.* Report A/66/77. 4 May 2011.

UNSG (United Nations Secretary-General), 2009. Enhanced cooperation on public policy issues pertaining to the Internet. *Report of the Secretary-General,* E/2009/92.

UN Special Rapporteur on Freedom of Expression, 2011.Promotion and protection of the right to freedom of opinion and expression. Report A/HRC/17/27. 16 May 2011.

UN Special Rapporteur on Freedom of Opinion and Expression, OSCE Representative on Freedom of the Media, OAS Special Rapporteur on Freedom of Expression and the ACHPR Special Rapporteur on Freedom of Expression and Access to Information, 2011. Joint declaration on freedom of expression and the Internet. 1 June 2011.

US Census Bureau, 1997. *Computer Use in the United States. U.S Department of Commerce.* Available from: www.census.gov/hhes/computer/publications/ [Accessed 9 September 2013].

US Congress, 2012. *Report to Congress of the US-China Economic and Security Review Commission,* 112th Congress, 2nd session, November 2012.

US Department of Commerce, 2012. *Department of Commerce Approves Verisign-ICANN .com Registry Renewal Agreement* [online], 20 November 30, 2012. Available from: http://www.ntia.doc.gov/press-release/2012/department-commerce-approves-verisign-icann-com-registry-renewal-agreement [Accessed 8 June 2013].

US Department of State, 2006. *Global Internet Task Force Strategy: A Blueprint for Action.* [online] Available from http://2001-2009.state.gov/g/drl/rls/78340.htm [Accessed 10 August 2013].

US G.P.O. (United States Congress House Committee on Commerce Subcommittee on Oversight and Investigations), 1999. *Domain name system privatization, is ICANN out of control?: hearing before the Subcommittee on Oversight and Investigations of the Committee on Commerce, House of Representatives, One Hundred Sixth Congress, first session, July 22.*

US House of Representatives, Energy and Commerce Committee, 2013. *Fighting for Internet Freedom: Dubai and Beyond* [online], 5 February 2013. Available from: http://

energycommerce.house.gov/hearing/fighting-for-internet-freedom-dubai-and-beyond [Accessed 26 July 2013].

US House of Representatives, 2013. *Bill HR 1580 to affirm the policy of the United States regarding Internet governance,* 15 May 2013.

US White House Press Office, 2013. Joint Statement by the Presidents of the United States of America and the Russian Federation on a New Field of Cooperation in Confidence Building, *The White House* [online], 17 June 2013. Available from: http://www.whitehouse.gov/the-press-office/2013/06/17/joint-statement-on-a-new-field-of-cooperation-in-confidence-building [Accessed 18 June 2013].

Van Huijstee, M., 2012. *Multistakeholder initiatives, A strategic guide for civil society organizations* [online] Available from: http://papers.ssrn.com/sol3/papers.cfm?abstract_id=2117933 [Accessed 23 July 2013].

Vanderbilt, T., 2008. *Traffic: why we drive the way we do (and what it says about us).* New York: Knopf.

Van Eeten, M. J. and Mueller, M., 2012. Where Is the Governance in Internet Governance? *New Media & Society,* 15(5), pp. 720–736.

Verisign, 2013 *The Domain Name Industry Brief* [online], April 2013. Available from: http://www.verisigninc.com/en_CH/why-verisign/research-trends/domain-name-industry-brief/index.xhtml?loc=en_CH [Accessed 27 June 2013].

Verveer, P., 2013. *Comments made at the workshop The Geopolitics of Internet Governance, Internet Society* [online], 23 May 2013. Available from: http://new.livestream.com/internetsociety/geopolitics [Accessed 4 June 2013].

Von Arx, K., 2003. ICANN—Now and Then: ICANN's Reform and Its Problems. *Duke Law & Technology Review, 2*(1), pp. 1–22.

Walden, Ian (Ed.), 2009. *Telecommunications Law and Regulation.* Oxford: Oxford University Press.

Waters, T.W., 2009. The Momentous Gravity of the State of Things Now Obtaining: Annoying Westphalian Objections to the Idea of Global Governance. *Indiana Journal of Global Legal Studies,* 16(1), pp. 33–58.

Waz, J. and Weiser, P., 2012. Internet Governance: The Role of Multistakeholder Organizations. *Journal of Telecommunications & High Technology Law,* 10(2), pp. 331–350.

Weber, M., 1920. Basic sociological terms. Translated by A.M. Henderson and T. Parsons. *In:* G. Roth and C. Wittich (eds.), 1978. *Economy and society: an outline of interpretive sociology.* Berkeley: University of California Press, pp. 3–62.

Weber, R.H., 2008. Transparency and the governance of the Internet. *Computer Law and Security Report,* 24, pp. 342–348.

Weber, R.H., 2009. *Shaping Internet Governance: Regulatory Challenge.* Zurich: Schulthess.

Weber, R.H., 2009a. Internet Corporation for Assigned Names and Numbers. *In:* C. Tietje and A. Brouder (eds.). *Handbook of Transnational Economic Governance Regimes.* Leiden: Martinus Nijhoff, pp. 612–614.

Weber, R.H., 2010. New Sovereignty Concepts in the Age of Internet? *Journal of Internet Law,* August issue, pp. 12–20.

Weber, R.H., 2011, Accountability in the Internet of things. *Computer Law & Security Review,* 27, pp. 133–138.

Weber, R.H., 2012. Corporate social responsibility as new challenge for the IT industry. *Computer Law & Security Review,* 28, pp. 634–640.

Weber, R.H., 2012a. Future Design of Cyberspace Law. *Journal of Politics and Law,* 5(4), pp. 1–14.

Weber, R.H., 2013. Responsibilities of Business as New Topic in Internet Governance Debates. *Journal of International Law,* May issue, pp. 3–12.

Weber, R.H., 2013a. International Governance in a new media environment. *In:* M.E. Price, S.G. Verhulst and L. Morgan (eds.). *Routledge Handbook of Media Law.* London: Routledge, pp. 361–372.

Weber, R.H., 2013b. The legitimacy and accountability of the Internet's governing institutions, *In:* Brown, Ian (ed.), *Research handbook on governance of the Internet.* Northampton: Edwrd Elgar, p. 101.

Weber, R.H. and Grosz, M., 2009. Legitimate governing of the Internet. *International Journal of Private Law,* 2, pp. 316–330.

Weber, R.H. and Gunnarson, R.S. 2012. A Constitutional Solution for Internet Governance. *The Columbia Science and Technology Law Review,* XVII, pp. 1–254.

Weber, R.H. and Heinrich, U.I., 2011. IP Address Allocation through the Lens of Public Goods and Scarce Resource Theories. *Scripted,* 8(1), p. 83.

Weiner, J.B., 2000. *From Sustainable Development to Sustainable Governance* [online], 24 April 2000. Available from: http://law.duke.edu/news/papers/sustgov3wiener.pdf [Accessed 20 August 2013].

Weller, D. and Woodcock, B., 2013. Internet Traffic Exchange: Market Developments and Policy Challenges. *OECD Digital Economy Papers,* No. 207, Paris: OECD Publishing.

Wentworth, S., 2013. Testimony. Hearing: Fighting for Internet Freedom, Dubai and Beyond, *U.S. House of Representatives Committee on Energy and Commerce's Subcommittee on Communications and Technology* [online], 5 February 2013. Available from: http://docs.house.gov/meetings/IF/IF16/20130205/100221/HHRG-113-IF16-Wstate-ShipmanWentworthS-20130205.pdf [Accessed 16 July 2013].

Westby, J., 2012. Google's Media Campaign Against the UN Slapped Down. *Forbes* [online], 4 December 2012. Available from: http://www.forbes.com/sites/jodywestby/2012/12/04/googles-media-campaign-against-the-un-slapped-down/ [Accessed 16 July 2013].

WGIG (Working Group on Internet Governance), 2005. *Background Report.* June 2005.

WGIG (Working Group on Internet Governance), 2005. *Report of the Working Group on Internet Governance.* [online], June 2005. Available from: http://www.wgig.org/docs/WGIGREPORT.pdf [Accessed 23 July 2013].

WGIGF (Working Group on Improvements to the Internet Governance Forum), 2011. *Working Group on Improvements to the Internet Governance Forum.* Report A/66/67 E/2011/79, 4–29 July 2011.

WGIGF (Working Group on Improvements to the IGF, 2011. *Questionnaire on improvements to the Internet Governance Forum (IGF). Compilation of contributions* [online] Available from: www.unctad.info/en/cstdWG/ [Accessed 9 September 2013].

White House—National Security Council, 1998. *The Clinton Administration's Policy on Critical Infrastructure Protection: Presidential Decision Directive 63* [online] Available from: http://clinton4.nara.gov/WH/EOP/NSC/html/documents/NSCDoc3.html [Accessed 29 August 2013].

White House, 2009. *Remarks by the President on securing our nation's Cyber Infrastructure.* [online], 29 May 2009. Available from: http://www.whitehouse.gov/the_press_office/Remarks-by-the-President-on-Securing-Our-Nations-Cyber-Infrastructure [Accessed 20 August 2013].

White House, 2011. I*nternational Strategy for Cyberspace* [online], 16 May 2011. Available from: http://www.whitehouse.gov/sites/default/files/rss_viewer/international_strategy_for_cyberspace.pdf [Accessed 20 August 2013].

White House, 2013. *Executive Order—Improving Critical Infrastructure Cybersecurity.* [online], 12 February 2013. Available from: http://www.whitehouse.gov/the-press-office/2013/02/12/executive-order-improving-critical-infrastructure-cybersecurity [Accessed 20 August 2013].

Whittaker, Z., 2013. Amid NSA spying scandal, the gloves are off for EU's justice chief, *ZDNet* [online], 21 June 2013. Available from: http://www.zdnet.com/amid-nsa-spying-scandal-the-gloves-are-off-for-eus-justice-chief-7000017132/ [Accessed 29 June 2013].

Wiener, N., 1948. *Cybernetics: or control and communication in the animal and the machine.* Cambridge: MIT Press.

Owens, W.A., Dam, K.W. and Lin, H.S. (eds.), 2009. *Technology, Policy, Law, and Ethics Regarding U.S. Acquisition and Use of Cyberattack Capabilities.* Washington, D.C.: National Academic Press.

Winchester, N.B., 2009. Emerging Global Environmental Governance. *Indiana Journal of Global Legal Studies,* 16(1), pp. 7–23.

WCIT (World Conference on International Telecommunications), 2012. *Third series of texts submitted by Editorial Committee to the Plenary Meeting* (Document 65-E). [online], 13 December 2012. Available from: http://files.wcitleaks.org/public/S12-WCIT12-C-0065!!MSW-E.pdf [Accessed 23 July 2013].

WCIT (World Conference on International Telecommunications), 2012a. *Informal discussions on route* (Document DT 46 rev.1), 7 December 2012.

Wouters, J. and Ramopoulos, T., 2012. The G20 and Global Economic Governance: Lessons from Multilevel European Governance? *Journal of International Economic Law,* 15(3), pp. 751–775.

WSIS (World Summit on the Information Society), 2003. *Declaration of Principles—Building the Information Society: a global challenge in the new Millennium.* Document WSIS-03/GENEVA/DOC/4-E [online], 12 December 2003. Available from: http://www.itu.int/wsis/docs/geneva/official/dop.html [Accessed 29 August 2013].

WSIS, 2003a. *Plan of Action,* Document WSIS-03/GENEVA/DOC/5-E [online], 12 December 2003. Available from: http://www.itu.int/wsis/docs/geneva/official/poa.html [Accessed 29 August 2013].

WSIS, 2005. *The Tunis Agenda for the Information Society.* Document WSIS-05/TUNIS/DOC/6(Rev. 1)-E [online], 18 November 2005. Available from: http://www.itu.int/wsis/documents/doc_multi.asp?lang=en&id=2316|0 [Accessed 29 August 2013].

WTO Council for Trade in Services, 2011. Communication from the European Union and the United States: Contribution to the Work Programme on Electronic Commerce, paper S/C/W/338, 13 July 2011.

WTO Council for Trade in Services, 2012. Communication from Australia: Suggestions on ICT principles, paper S/C/W/349, 26 September 2012.

WTPF (World Telecommunication Policy Forum), 2013. *Dialogue captured from the real time transcription during the WTPF meeting* [online] Available from: http://www.itu.int/en/wtpf-13/Documents/16%20May%20PM%20WTPF%20final%20file.docx [Accessed 20 August 2013].

WTPF (World Telecommunication Policy Forum), 2013a. IPv4 and IPv6 Issues. *WTPF Backgrounder* [online] Available from: http://www.itu.int/en/wtpf-13/Documents/backgrounder-wtpf-13-ipv4-ipv6-en.pdf [Accessed 29 August 2013].

Wu, T.S., 1997. Cyberspace Sovereignty—The Internet and the International System. *Harvard Journal on Law and Technology,* 10, pp. 647–666.

Wu, W., 1996. Great leap or long march: some policy issues of the development of the Internet in China. *Telecommunications Policy,* 20(9), pp. 699–711.

Xue, H., 2004. Voice of China: A Story of Chinese-Character Domain Names, *The Cardozo Journal of International & Comparative Law.* 12, p. 559.

Yang, G., 2003. The Internet and civil society in China: A preliminary assessment. *Journal of Contemporary China,* 12(36), pp. 453–475.

Yang, G. 2009. *The power of the Internet in China: Citizen activism online.* New York: Columbia University Press.

Zhao, Y., 2000. Caught in the Web: the public interest and the battle for control of China's information superhighway. *Info,* 2(1), pp. 41–66.

Zheng, C., 1993. CDN Special Issue on Networking in China, *CDN* [online], 11 July 1993. Available from: http://www.sdsc.edu/~zhengc/93trip.html [Accessed 27 June 2013].

Zhou, J., 2000. Beijing Lodges Complaint Over Domain Names, *South China Morning Post* [online], 4 November 2000. Available from: http://www.webmasterworld.com/forum32/8.htm [Accessed 24 June 2013].

Zhu, J.J. and Wang, E., 2005. Diffusion, use, and effect of the Internet in China. *Communications of the ACM,* 48(4), pp. 49–53.

Zittrain, J., 1999. ICANN: Between the Public and the Private Comments before Congress. *Berkeley Technology Law Journal,* 14, p. 1071.

Zittrain, J., 2003. Internet filtering in China, *Internet Computing,* 7(2), pp. 70–77.

Contributors

Nicolas Adam is a researcher at the Centre for Research on Integration and Globalization (CEIM, Centre d'études sur l'intégration et la mondialisation). His research is related to the telecommunication sector and the role of ICANN (Internet Corporation for Assigned Names and Numbers). He is also interested in the sociology of technologies and in the analysis of institutions involved in the global governance of the information and communication technologies. He completed a Master program with a thesis on the emergence and development of ICANN that emphasized competing norms and principles. He now studies the links between competing normative systems and the development of coalitions of actors in the domain of Internet governance.

Jean-Marie Chenou is a PhD candidate and teaching assistant at the Institut d'Etudes Politiques et Internationales at the University of Lausanne. He is also a member of the Centre de Recherche Interdisciplinaire sur l'International (CRII). He is currently a visiting fellow at the Department of Business and Politics of the Copenhagen Business School, with a scholarship from the Swiss National Foundation for Scientific Research. He is working on transnational elites and Internet governance and specializing in International Political Sociology. Prior to starting his PhD, he has worked as an adjunct professor in the Universidad del Rosario and Universidad Externado in Bogotá, Colombia.

Biel Company Pérez is a PhD candidate at the Internet Interdisciplinary Institute (IN3) of the Open University of Catalonia (UOC). He pursued law studies at the Pompeu Fabra University in Barcelona, where he obtained a Law Degree and a Masters in Legal Sciences, and at the University of Geneva, where he specialized in international and comparative law. He has also been a visiting researcher at the Max Planck Institute for Comparative Public Law and International Law in Heidelberg, where he participates in the "International Public Authority 3+" project. He also collaborates with the UOC's "InterDret" research group and with the Centre d'études sur l'intégration et la mondialisation (CEIM) of the Université du Québec à Montréal. He is interested in international legal theory and political philosophy, and his research focuses on the relationship between legitimacy and juridicity in global Internet governance.

Avri Doria is a member of the UNCSTD WG on Enhanced Cooperation and serves on the 2013 ICANN Accountability and Transparency Review Team. She was chair of the ICANN GNSO Council, was chair of the Civil Society Internet Governance Caucus (IGC) and was a member of the UN Working Group on Internet Governance (WGIG). She spent 5 years working for the IGF Secretariat and currently is a volunteer researcher for the Association for Progressive Communications (APC) and VP of Policy and Governance for dotgay LLC. As a technologist she has been involved in the development of Internet protocols and architectures for over 30 years, is a participant in the IETF, and past chair of the IRTF Routing Research Group. Ms. Doria is a member of the faculty of the International Summer Schools on Internet Governance. In the past she held an Adjunct Professor appointment at Luleå Technology University. Ms. Doria has a BA from the University of Rhode Island, an MA from the University of Chicago in Philosophy and an MA from Rhode Island College in Counseling Psychology. Full details can be found at http://psg.com/~avri/resume.html.

Richard Hill is the principal of Hill & Associates in Geneva, Switzerland. He has an extensive background in information systems, telecommunications, negotiation, mediation, and conflict management. Richard was the Secretary for the ITU-T Study Groups dealing with numbering and tariffing issues, network operations, and economic and policy issues; he was the Secretary for the preparatory process for the 2012 World Conference on International Telecommunications and headed the secretariat team dealing with substantive issues at the Conference. He is a Centre for Dispute Resolution (CEDR) accredited mediator. He has published papers on mediation and computer-related intellectual property issues and the standard reference book to X.435. He was also Department Head, IT Infrastructure Delivery and Support, at Orange Communications (a GSM operator). He previously was the IT Manager at the University of Geneva. Richard holds a Ph.D. in Statistics from Harvard University and a B.S. in Mathematics from M.I.T.

Anne-Claire Jamart is a doctoral student at Cornell Law School in the US. She is currently a junior visiting fellow at the Programme for the Study of International Governance at the Graduate Institute, in Geneva. Her dissertation focuses on the emerging notion of internet freedom and its role in internet governance. Prior to resuming her studies, Anne-Claire clerked at the Conseil d'Etat in Paris. She also practiced corporate and finance law in the London office of Fried Frank. She earned a Juris Doctor from Cornell Law School, a Maîtrise en droit from Université Panthéon-Sorbonne and a Master in European Law from the College of Europe.

Andreas Kuehn is a PhD student and Fulbright Scholar at the School of Information Studies at Syracuse University, Syracuse, NY, United States. Currently, he is a visiting student at Cornell University's Department of Science and Technology Studies. His research is informed by Information Science and Science & Technology Studies literature to examine emerging issues in Internet Governance and Cybersecurity Policy, particularly privacy, security and surveillance. He is currently focusing on the use of deep packet inspection in online copyright enforcement, behavioral targeting, and cybersecurity and its effects on Internet Governance. He worked in various technology and policy positions for the Austrian Ministry of Finance, the Swiss E-Government-Institute, the Swiss OFCOM, the Malaysian National Advanced IPv6 Centre of Excellence, and several international corporations. In 2009, the Austrian Computer Society awarded him an eGovernment Innovation Award for his research on multidisciplinary actor coordination and collaboration in e-government. Kuehn holds an MSc in Information Systems from the Department of Informatics at the University of Zurich, Switzerland.

Gianluigi Negro holds a B.A. and M.A. in *Language Economics and Legal Institutions of East Asia* from Ca' Foscari University. He obtained a second master in *Global Management: Society and Institutions of the Contemporary China* from Roma Tre University. In 2008 he worked at the General Consulate of Italy in Guangzhou. His second professional experience in China was at the China-Italy Chamber of commerce as Publications & Media Executive in 2010. Since September 2011 he is PhD candidate at Università della Svizzera Italiana (USI), Faculty of Communication Sciences and editor assistant at China Media Observatory (USI). Mr. Negro's research focuses on the Internet in China and its impact on the nascent Chinese civil society.

Roxana Radu is a PhD candidate in International Relations/Political Science at the Graduate Institute of International and Development Studies in Geneva (Switzerland) and a research fellow at the Center for Media and Communication Studies (CMCS), Central European University, Budapest (Hungary). Prior to starting her PhD, she worked as a program coordinator and researcher at CMCS, where she focused on cybersecurity, e-government and e-participation, and on (new) media regulation in transitional societies. In 2011, Roxana took part of the Next Generation Leadership programme of the Internet Society (ISOC) and was awarded the 2012 and 2013 ISOC Ambassadorship to the Internet Governance Forum. Her current research focuses on new modes of governance for global internet policy-making.

Michèle Rioux is Director of the Centre for Research on Integration and Globalization (CEIM, Centre d'études sur l'intégration et la mondialisation) and professor at the department of political science at Université du Québec à Montréal (Canada). Her research and publications are mainly focused on international political economy, integration and globalization processes, the ICT sector, competition policy, and labour governance. She recently published with C. Deblock *De la nationalisation du monde à la globalisation* (PUL-Verbatim, Québec).

Andreas Schmidt researches organizational and political aspects of Internet security at the Faculty of Technology, Policy and Management at Delft University of Technology. He currently writes up the results of his PhD research project on the role of technical communities in Internet security governance and previous Internet security incidents. Andreas holds a Master degree in Political Science, and Medieval and Contemporary History. He is a member of the German Research Foundation's research network on "Digital citizens and their identity." Before joining TU Delft, Andreas worked as a business consultant with a focus on identity management and enterprise IT security. Recently published or accepted peer-reviewed articles have covered the organization of Internet security production, the Estonian cyberattacks, networked governance in International Relations, and emerging hybrids of networks and hierarchies.

David Sylvan is Professor of International Relations and Political Science at the Graduate Institute of International and Development Studies in Geneva. He has been a faculty member since 1991. Dr. Sylvan previously taught at the University of Minnesota and at Syracuse University. He works on international political economy issues (notably on world cities); on international relations theory (particularly on the rules of the Westphalian system); on foreign policy analysis (writings on the continuity of US policy toward client states and enemies); and on methodology (qualitative methods; computational models). He recently co-authored *US Foreign Policy in Perspective* (2009). He received his PhD from Yale University.

Rolf H. Weber is ordinary Professor for Civil, Commercial and European Law at the University of Zurich, Switzerland, and a Visiting Professor at the University of Hong Kong. His main fields of research are Internet and Information Technology Law, International Business Law, Media Law, Competition Law and International Financial Law. He is director of the European Law Institute and the Center for Information and Communication Law at the University of Zurich. Since 2008, Rolf H. Weber is member of the Steering Committee of the Global Internet Governance Academic Network (GigaNet) and of the European Dialogue on Internet Governance (EuroDIG) and since 2009 he is member of the High-level Panel of Advisers of the Global Alliance for Information and Communication Technologies and Development (GAID). Besides, he is engaged as an attorney-at-law. His research focus lies on the mentioned regulatory topics; the publication list is available at http://www.rwi.uzh.ch/lehreforschung/alphabetisch/weberr/person.html.

List of Abbreviations

ACLU	American Civil Liberties Union
ARPANET	The Advanced Research Projects Agency Network
ASCII	American Standard Code for Information Interchange
BRICS	Brasil, Russia, India, China and South Africa
ccNSO	Country Code Names Supporting Organisation
ccTLD	Country Code Top-Level Domain
CERTs	Computer Emergency Response Teams
CIIP	Critical Information Infrastructure Protection
CIRP	Council for Internet-Related Policies
CoE	Council of Europe
CSIRTs	Computer Security Incident Response Teams
CSTD	UN's Commission on Science and Technology for Development
CSISAC	Civil Society Information Society Advisory Council
DoD	US Department of Defense
DNS	Domain Name System
DNSSEC	Domain Name System Security Extensions
EP3R	European Public Private Partnership for Resilience
ETNO	European Telecommunication Network Operators' association
EU	European Union
GAC	ICANN's Governmental Advisory Committee
GDP	Gross Domestic Product
G8	Group of 8
gTLD	generic Top-Level Domain
IAB	Internet Architecture Board (ISOC)
IANA	Internet Assigned Numbers Authority
IBSA	India, Brazil and South Africa
ICANN	Internet Corporation for Assigned Names and Numbers
ICT	Information & Communication Technology
ICTs	Information & Communication Technologies
IDN	Internationalized Domain Name
IEEE	Institute of Electrical and Electronics Engineers
IEG	Informal Experts Group
IESG	Internet Engineering Steering Group (ISOC)
IETF	Internet Engineering Task Force (ISOC)
IGF	Internet Governance Forum
IGOs	Inter-governmental Organizations
IP	Internet Protocol
IPv4	Internet Protocol version 4
IPv6	Internet Protocol version 6
IRTF	Internet Research Task Force (ISOC)
ISOC	Internet Society
ISPs	Internet Service Providers

ITRs	International Telecommunication Regulations
ITU	International Telecommunication Union
IXPs	Internet Exchange Points
NAFTA	North American Free Trade Agreement
NSA	US National Security Agency
NTIA	US National Telecommunication Industry Association
OECD	Organization for Economic Cooperation and Development
OSCE	Organization for Security and Co-operation in Europe
OSS	Open Source Software
PIPA	Protect Intellectual Property Act
PPP	Public-private partnership
PRC	People's Republic of China
RCTU	Russia China Tajikistan Uzbekistan
SCO	Shanghai Cooperation Organization
SOPA	Stop On-Line Piracy Act
TCP/IP	Transmission Control Protocol/Internet Protocol
TLD	Top-Level Domain
UDHR	Universal Declaration of Human Rights
UN	United Nations
UNESCO	United Nations Educational, Scientific and Cultural Organization
UNGA	United Nations General Assembly
US	United States
WCIT	World Conference on International Telecommunications
WGIG	Working Group on Internet Governance
WIPO	The World Intellectual Property Organization
WSIS	World Summit on the Information Society
W3C	World Wide Web Consortium
WTO	World Trade Organization
WTPF	World Telecommunication/ICT Policy Forum
WTDC	World Telecommunication Development Conference

List of Figures and Tables

Preface and Acknowledgements

The unprecedented growth and the fast development of the Internet have prompted new forms of interaction and collective action, generating a series of institutional changes, innovations and challenges. Following the World Conference on International Telecommunications (WCIT) in Dubai, the role and relevance of intergovernmental organizations in Internet governance, as well as the promises and limitations of multistakeholderism, have been more stringently questioned. Complementing the policy discussions around ITU's World Technology Policy Forum, we organized a two-day expert workshop in Geneva on 17–18 May 2013, bringing together Internet Governance stakeholders to reflect on current governance practices, challenges and scenarios for the future.

Jointly organized by the Programme for the Study of International Governance (PSIG) of the Graduate Institute of International and Development Studies and the Global Internet Governance Academic Network (GigaNet), the workshop on "The Global Governance of the Internet: Intergovernmentalism, Multistakeholderism and Networks" covered a wide range of issues related to the evolution of Internet governance, from the current implementations of the multistakeholder model to the principles that might inspire collective action in the field in the coming years. The present volume is inspired by the array of perspectives represented at the workshop, and draws on the paper presentations and roundtable discussions held in Geneva. We are particularly indebted to Professor Thomas Biersteker, Director of PSIG, and to Professor Milton Mueller, Chair of GigaNet, for their invaluable support throughout this collaborative process. We would also like to thank all the contributors to the Geneva workshop for the richness of the debates.

The volume explores the consequences of recent events in the field of global Internet policy and possible ways forward following the 2012 World Conference on International Telecommunications (WCIT-12). It offers expert views on transformations in governance, on the future of multistakeholderism and on the increasing significance of cybersecurity issues. The book provides a comparative and interdisciplinary perspective at the crossroads of international relations, international law and communication studies, which is further strengthened by the varied backgrounds of the contributors. It addresses not only researchers interested in the evolution of new forms of transnational networked governance, but also practitioners who wish to get a scholarly reflection on current regulatory developments. It notably provides first-hand accounts on the role of the WCIT-12 in the future of Internet governance.

Roxana Radu, Jean-Marie Chenou and Rolf H. Weber

Introduction

Jean-Marie Chenou / Roxana Radu

Global Internet Policy: a Fifteen-Year Long Debate

What do the Internet user from 1997 and the one from 2013 have in common? In terms of user experience, certainly not much. Accessing 100 000 websites with a 33.6 Kbps dial-up modem was very different from today's experience. However, some of the underlying questions about the regulation of the network remain the same. Which institutions should be in charge of the governance of the Internet? Where should their legitimacy come from? How should users participate in the governance of the network? What role, if any, should the ITU play? What role, if any, should the US government play? These questions have been left only partially answered by the evolution of global Internet governance. A complex framework of institutions and fora has been created. The number of actors aware of, and involved in, the regulation of the network has increased dramatically. Yet, almost 15 years after the creation of the Internet Corporation for Assigned Names and Numbers (ICANN), the World Conference on International Telecommunications (WCIT) failed to reach a consensus on new telecommunication regulations because of divergences on Internet governance issues.

Transnational regulation that occurs outside of the intergovernmental sphere (Graz and Noelke 2008; Hall and Biersteker 2002), informal international lawmaking (Pauwelyn 2011) or public-private partnerships are epitomes of modern-day governance. Instances of contestation over what is to be regulated in the public domain, are, however, not unique to the Internet. Complementing broader paradigm shifts in telecommunication regulation (Irion and Radu 2014), hybrid forms of governance give rise to public policies building on or as a result of private efforts. For the largest part of the 1990s, technical innovations were fused with a relatively widespread belief in the potential of new technologies to empower individuals, able to drive, alter or restructure political makeovers using mobile phones, new media or social networks (Grossman 1996; Shapiro 2000; add more). Albeit in less visible ways, certain states, intergovernmental organizations and private bodies were also empowered to act globally, as we discuss below.

Before the authorization of commercial activities on the Internet in 1992 and before the democratization of Internet usage, the political stakes of Internet regulation were low. Ad-hoc solutions and institutional bricolage were still accepted by Internet users. However, the situation changed rapidly around the mid-1990s, and global Internet governance became a debated matter. The last 15 years have witnessed an increase in the demands for a more efficient, accountable, transparent, legitimate and democratic Internet governance. These demands translated in diverging views on the respective role of intergovernmental organizations, national governments (especially the US), private sector, civil society, the technical and academic communities, and other stakeholders, in the management of the network. From time to time (see below and timeline in Annex 1), these diverging views inspire conflicting positions and generate moments of crisis. Although crises are necessary for evolution and change, some unresolved issues cause stalemates and prevent the creation of a comprehensive Internet governance framework.

The purpose of this book is to analyse what constitutes Internet governance nowadays, what the main sources of divergences in Internet governance are, and ways forward that can be envisioned for different aspects of global Internet policy. The introduction provides a general framework in which particular issues addressed by individual chapters are located. To show how the WCIT failure—or success, opponents may argue—derives from structural controversies that have only partly been addressed within the current governance framework, we identify the underlying questions that have constantly re-emerged in global Internet politics over the last fifteen years.

1. Internet Governance in the 1990s and the Creation of the ICANN

The very first attempts to institutionalize Internet governance in the mid-1990s already addressed the core issues that are still discussed today. The proposals by the "technical community" (e.g. Postel 1996) stemmed from the idea that the network could be self-regulated by its users, and particularly those with sufficient technical knowledge. In these documents, Internet governance was envisaged mostly as the technical issue of allocation of unique domain names and Internet Protocol (IP) addresses. Other aspects were bound to be "determined, and coordinated, by contractual agreements between private interests" (Postel 1996: Abstract). Reactions from intellectual property owners, intergovernmental organizations, and some states proved that a broader base was needed in order for a governance system in the making to obtain some legitimacy and acceptance. For example, the issue of trademarks in Internet domain names was completely ignored by the technical community despite its growing commercial and political salience. As a result, an International Ad Hoc Committee (IAHC) tried to design a governance system that took into account the varied interests of what was going to become the "stakeholders" of Internet governance (IAHC 1997). The IAHC gathered individuals from various intergovernmental organizations such as the International Telecommunication Union and the World Intellectual Property Organization, the US National Science Foundation[1], trademark interests representatives, and intellectual property owners. The focus on trademarks in domain names illustrates concerns of the late 1990s that became of lesser importance over the years. However, the attempt to gather several stakeholders and to root the legitimacy of Internet governance in the United Nations (UN) system has constantly influenced the debates in the following years. The proposed institutionalization of Internet governance foresaw an overarching role for the International Telecommunication Union (ITU), the specialized agency which had been in charge of the regulation of most telecommunication networks since its creation in 1865.

While the IAHC's proposal solved some legitimacy issues, it failed because of another fundamental aspect of Internet global policy. The IAHC failed to acknowledge the special relationship between the Internet and the US. The Internet was largely seen as a US invention (Abbate 1999; Hafner 1998; for a discussion of this argument, see Townes 2012 and Chapter 4 by Hill in this volume). In 1997, more than half of Internet users were based in the US[2]. The project of creating a new governance system backed by the ITU and located outside the US triggered strong reactions by US Internet entrepreneurs and by the US administration (Mueller 2002a). The US Department of Commerce started its own process of consultations in order to design a private and bottom-up regulation system for Internet domain names. This process explicitly excluded intergovernmental organizations and (other) national governments from the management of Internet names and addresses (NTIA 1998).

The creation of the Internet Corporation for Assigned Names and Numbers (ICANN) was the final step of the process lead by the US Department of Commerce. The creation of the ICANN, although more successful than earlier attempts, did not put an end to the debates around the core questions of legitimacy and respective roles of the US and the UN system in Internet governance. First, the creation of the ICANN left a number of stakeholders marginalized. The debates that led to the creation of the ICANN involved only a small number of individuals and organizations, mostly from the US National governments from developing countries were excluded from the negotiations. The most significant attempt to internationalize the debates and to include civil society actors, the International Forum on the White Paper, was by-passed in the final stages of the creation of the

---

1 The National Science Foundation had been in charge of the network for several years until its commercialization.

2 According to the US census bureau, there were more than 40 million Internet users in the US in 1997. The total number of Internet users worldwide was at the same time estimated around 70 to 76 million by companies like Reuters and IDC (Internetworldstats 2013; US Census Bureau 1997).

ICANN. As a result, a "dominant coalition" of stakeholders designed the ICANN as the central element of an Internet governance system that excluded many stakeholders (Mueller 2002a). The legitimacy of the ICANN was fragile from the start because of the limited participation of a wide range of stakeholders. Another major critique to the ICANN was the relationship between the corporation and the US Department of Commerce. While this relationship has evolved towards greater autonomy of the ICANN, the successive Memoranda of Understanding and the Affirmation of Commitment have always been criticized as an illegitimate supervision of the ICANN by the US Department of Commerce (e.g. Singh 2005, Weber & Gunnarson 2012). The lack of legitimacy of the ICANN triggered a number of procedures, and even threatened its existence (United States Congress 1999). The large scholarly literature that was critical of the ICANN certainly played a role in raising awareness on this issue (Froomkin 2000; Kleinwächter 2000; Mueller 1999; Zittrain 1999).

Second, the creation of a private sector-led governance system outside traditional organizations raised some issues of transparency and accountability. If the ICANN was to manage some of the critical resources of the Internet, who was it accountable to? And how could its operations be supervised? The ICANN structure gave way to a number of broader questions related to the legitimacy of a governance system. Transparency was seen as an important aspect of the organization's legitimacy. One of the most discussed aspect of the ICANN by-laws before their adoption was the inclusion of transparency procedures and participation mechanisms. A suit was even successfully filed against the ICANN for its lack of transparency procedures (ICANN 2002b). Accountability was also a major issue, with concerns about democratic procedures within the ICANN (Koppell 2005; Marlin-Bennett 2001).

Third, the issue of participation is closely related to the lack of legitimacy of the institution. Who were the stakeholders? Where were the stakeholders represented? And in what proportion with regards to other stakeholders? Marginalized actors such as civil society organizations, individual users and developing countries governments were represented in peripheral bodies whereas the representative of the "dominant coalition" controlled the core of the organization. A global membership was foreseen in the by-laws but was never implemented. The relative failure of ICANN global elections in 2000 illustrated the difficulty to implement meaningful participation mechanisms (Palfrey 2004).

Finally, one of the most debated issues related to the ICANN has been the evolving role of the Governmental Advisory Committee (GAC). The GAC was originally designed as an advisory body that would act only upon the request of the Board. The GAC gathers representatives of national governments and intergovernmental organizations. The original role of the GAC was consistent with the idea of the US Department of Commerce to limit the role of national governments in the management of the network. However, non-US governments required to be taken on board. Their presence, as well as their struggle to become more influential within the institution, drew the attention of many observers and the ICANN became the nexus of the political conflict between diverging views on the role of governments in Internet governance. That is why the ICANN became the symbolic locus of Internet governance struggles for several years. National governments, and especially developing countries' governments managed to impose a deep reform of the ICANN that favored the GAC over other bodies (see below). However, some governments wanted to go further than influencing a private sector-led organization, they wanted the Internet governance system to acknowledge the privileged role of national governments and ensure that governments had the final say in global Internet policy.

The lack of legitimacy undermined the work of the ICANN. At the beginning of the 2000s, the need for more inclusion of national governments and a new repartition of roles among stakeholders seemed necessary. A report by ICANN president Stuart Lynn entitled "ICANN—The case for change" (Lynn 2002) paved the way for a deep reform of the organization in order to strike a new balance between public and private governance and to gain some legitimacy at a global level. One of the main change in the ICANN structure was the strengthening of the role of the GAC. Developing countries saw the GAC as the policy forum of Internet governance while the other bodies of the organization were to be in charge of technical matters. The result of the reform process was embodied by the new by-laws of the corporation that entered into force on December 15, 2002 (ICANN 2002a). The resulting ICANN has been described as an ICANN 2.0 and as a public-private partnership (Froomkin 2002; Kleinwächter 2002; von Arx 2003). The reform also triggered the creation of an At-Large Advisory Committee. The At-Large Advisory Committee was designed to include the "community of individual Internet users" (ICANN At-Large Community 2013) and to strengthen the participation of civil society in Internet governance.

Despite the reform, the ICANN continued to be criticized by marginalized actors. While the ICANN took the form of a more classical public-private partnership rather the rather undefined structure of 1998, it still clashed with the traditional "one state, one vote" principle of intergovernmental organizations. The board remained the central body of the corporation and the ICANN still largely escaped the control of national governments (Mathiason 2009).

Thus, the evolution of the ICANN did not completely solve the issues of participation and legitimacy that had emerged at the time of its creation. The changing international context of the early 2000s favored a continuing debate on the role of national governments in Internet governance. Discourses about cybersecurity became more important in the context of the terrorist attacks in the US and in Europe; the consequences of the Dotcom crisis undermined the confidence in the self-governance of the private sector; and the rise of emerging economies, as illustrated by the increase in the number of Internet users in these countries, strengthened their position in global Internet politics. At the eve of the World Summit on the Information Society (WSIS), the legitimacy of the ICANN system was still debated.

2. The WSIS and the Post-WSIS Environment

The World Summit on the Information Society (WSIS), which took place in two phases in Geneva and Tunis in 2003 and 2005, had a much broader mandate than the limited issue of Internet governance. However, because of the tensions around the ICANN system and the increasing importance of the network for the "information society", Internet governance made gradually its way to the top of the agenda of the conference. The first phase of the Summit evidenced the strong dissensions about global Internet governance. The debate rapidly became very polarized between supporters of the ICANN and advocates of change (Kummer 2007). Since no consensus was going to be reached during the first phase of the Summit, the idea emerged to create a working group dedicated to the issue between the two phases in order to build a consensus before the second phase.

A Working Group on Internet Governance (WGIG) was appointed by the UN Secretary-General in November 2004. Its mandate was perceived differently by supporters of the status-quo and advocates of change. Whereas the former saw the WGIG as an information forum about Internet governance issues, the latter expected the designing of a new governance system. The WGIG held a series of consultations and produced a report that largely inspired the articles on Internet governance of the Tunis Agenda for the Information Society (WSIS 2005). Once again, the negotiations did not permit to solve core issues such as the role of the UN system and national governments in Internet governance. The Tunis Agenda carefully acknowledged the work of existing institutions, while recalling the role of governments and intergovernmental organizations in Internet governance policy-related issues. Rather than cutting short the issues, the WSIS promoted further dialogue.

Despite this limited success, the WSIS marked the accession of Internet governance to the core issues of global politics and played a crucial role in raising the level of awareness and knowledge among stakeholders. Moreover, the WSIS is a landmark in the history of global Internet policy for two main reasons. First, the

WGIG was formed as a multistakeholder group and it provided a definition of Internet governance as a multistakeholder process. As such, the WGIG sanctioned multistakeholder governance as a guiding principle for future debates. Second, the Tunis Agenda remains the document of reference for current discussions. It created the two fora, whose relationship is currently at the heart of the debates: the Internet Governance Forum and the Enhanced Cooperation process.

The first references to the inclusion and participation of the different stakeholders in the governance of the Internet dates back to 1997 (IAHC 1997). The US Department of Commerce also claimed that the legitimacy of the future ICANN would derive from the participation of "key" stakeholders (NTIA 1998). However, it is during the WSIS that multistakeholderism became a guiding principle of global Internet policy. The selection of the WGIG members sought a balance between three main stakeholders: the private sector, civil society, and governments (Flyverbom 2011), although governmental representatives represented the most numerous group (Mathiason 2008). More importantly, the WGIG famously defined Internet governance as:

> "the development and application by Governments, the private sector and civil society, in their respective roles, of shared principles, norms, rules, decision-making procedures, and programmes that shape the evolution and use of the Internet" (WGIG 2005, §10).

This definition was adopted by the WSIS even if the document; in its different paragraphs, refers to other stakeholders such as intergovernmental organizations, international organizations, and the academic and technical communities within these groups.

In spite of the reluctance of some actors, "multistakeholderism" (see Doria in this volume for a discussion of the use of -ism) rapidly became successful as a guiding principle for Internet-related policy. Early adopters included the supporters of the ICANN, who saw a legitimization of the ICANN model in the use of the principle within the UN context. Much like Molière's middle-class gentleman[3], the ICANN had been doing multistakeholderism without knowing it. It then could claim to be the multistakeholder organization par excellence. Other Internet governance bodies also labeled their practices as multistakeholderism. Western governments saw in the multistakeholder model a way to promote the delegation of authority and a way to improve self-regulation and the limited state intervention that they had been implementing in various sectors, and especially in the telecommunication sector since the 1980s. Civil society organizations and some governments in-

[3] In this classic French play, Mr. Jourdain suddenly discovers the definition of prose, and that he had been speaking prose without knowing it for 40 years. He then brags about his newly-acquired knowledge in front of his wife and his maid (Molière, 1670).

terpreted multistakeholderism as participatory democracy and hailed the effort to improve democratic processes in global governance. Only some non-Western governments and some critical factions within civil society criticized multistakeholderism as a pejoration of democratic practices compared with traditional intergovernmentalism.

Since the WSIS, multistakeholderism gained momentum. The use of the word and of multistakeholder practices spread throughout the institutions of Internet governance. Every organization involved in Internet governance now claims to promote mutlistakeholder practices. Even formerly reluctant actors now embrace the multistakeholder model. A new interpretation, not much represented during the WSIS, consider multistakeholder dialogue as a valuable, or even necessary, step before decision-making, the latter remaining in the hands of national governments. There is not much disagreement about multistakeholderism as a principle any more, but conflicting views about its implementation and about the "respective roles" of each stakeholder group remain.

At a more concrete level, the WSIS launched two tracks of dialogue in order to improve Internet governance. First, the UN secretary-General was asked to create an Internet Governance Forum (IGF), envisioned as a "multistakeholder policy dialogue" (WSIS 2005) with the mandate to serve as a coordination, advisory and reflexion body for all actors involved in Internet governance. The first IGF was organized in 2006 and has been convened on a yearly basis since[4]. The success of the global annual meeting has fostered the creation of a number of national and regional IGFs. The IGF has been recognized by most stakeholders as a necessary space of dialogue (Working Group on Improvements to the IGF 2011). However, as the end of the second five-year mandate of the IGF is coming to an end in 2015, appraisals of the forum have raised some issues.

The lack of decision-making power of the IGF has been identified as conductive to real dialogue, but undermining the concrete outcomes of the forum (Major 2011). Some participants suggested that the forum should be able to make recommendations (Working Group on Improvements to the IGF 2011). Other more critical observers pointed to the risk of "inward focus" (McCarthy 2013) and even to the risk of "navel-gazing" (Peter 2013). The general opinion is that the IGF needs improvement and a renewed energy in order to fulfil its role as the most important multilateral, multistakeholder, democratic and transparent forum on Internet governance. The future of the IGF is closely related to the future of the other track of dialogue created by the WSIS: the Enhanced Cooperation process.

The Tunis Agenda had two very different interpretations of the Enhanced Cooperation process. The paragraph 69 of the Tunis Agenda reads:

---

4 For an overview of the thematic areas discussed at the IGF, see Kurbalija (2012, pp. 27–28).

> "We further recognize the need for enhanced cooperation in the future, to enable governments, on an equal footing, to carry out their roles and responsibilities, in international public policy issues pertaining to the Internet, but not in the day-to-day technical and operational matters, that do not impact on international public policy issues" (WSIS 2005).

For some stakeholders, an active participation to the IGF met the conditions for an enhanced cooperation. This is why most of the report of the stakeholders to the UN Secretary-General mentioned their efforts in the IGF as their contribution to an enhanced cooperation in Internet governance (UNSG 2009). However, the Economic and Social Council of the United Nations confirmed the interpretations of others stakeholders, who understood the IGF and Enhanced Cooperation as two different processes. Each side tried to impose its conception of Enhanced Cooperation. Again, the stakes behind the separation or the unification of both processes were about the role of the UN system in Internet governance. A UN-driven Enhanced Cooperation process would strengthen the intergovernmental aspect of Internet governance and might eventually lead to profound reforms since most of the UN members, and especially emerging powers, are discontent with the existing Internet governance system. A continuation of the Enhanced Cooperation process within the IGF would strengthen the multistakeholder model of governance and would protect the existing system from significant reforms.

Discussions about the principle of multistakeholder governance and about the respective roles of the different stakeholders were particularly heated around the time of the extension of the IGF mandate for another five years. This period coincided with the debates around the Indian proposal to the UN General Assembly for the creation of a Council of Internet-Related Policies that aimed to transform Internet governance in a significant way. Against this background, the World Conference on International Telecommunications became a forum, where the diverging positions of the different actors on the unresolved issues of Internet governance were expressed.

3. The WCIT and the Post-WCIT Environment

While the last 15 years have witnessed the development of a complex institutional framework in order to address Internet governance issues, some fundamental questions are yet to be answered. Multistakeholderism has been established as a model of governance, adopted by numerous institutions and organizations involved in global Internet politics and sanctioned in the Tunis Agenda. However, the interpretation and implementation of this common base is still debated, as illustrated by the negotiations of the 2012 World Conference on International Telecommunications (WCIT-12).

The structural shifts undergone by the telecommunication sector in the past four decades have also been reflected in the changing role of the ITU, which is currently challenged by a diffuse network of governors and regulation frameworks. Following the WSIS, the ITU also entrusted the WSIS Action Line C5 on building confidence and security in ICTs and initiated a Global Cybersecurity Agenda in 2007. The decision to hold the meeting to amend the International Telecommunication Regulations (ITRs) dates back to 2006, when the ITU proposed the update of the 1988 treaty to reflect the changes in the international telecommunications environment, in accordance with the ITU Constitution (ITU 2006). The ITRs serve as a global treaty binding signatories to comply with general principles for worldwide interconnection and interoperability, and facilitating the availability of international telecommunication services and networks.

With more than 1600 delegates from 151 member states gathered in Dubai between 3 and 14 December 2012, the ITRs revision talks highlighted a series of underlying tensions between different stakeholders envisioning different degrees of state involvement in Internet regulation. Discussion at WCIT-12 also covered, among others, fostering transparency and competition for international mobile roaming charges, reducing electronic waste, increasing accessibility to international telecommunication services for the disabled, or facilitating access to international optical fiber networks for landlocked and small island developing states. Amid these issues, the ITU Secretary General Hamadoun Touré repeatedly stated that WCIT-12 would not address the Internet (e.g. Touré 2012a), yet among the 1275 revision proposals submitted by member states, there were a number of documents making direct reference to the Internet. Among the most controversial of these was the one by Russia, including the following provision: "Member States shall have equal rights to manage the Internet, including in regard to the allotment, assignment and reclamation of Internet numbering, naming, addressing and identification resources and to support for the operation and development of the basic Internet infrastructure" (ITU 2012).

The talks around amending the ITRs were greatly contested for increasing the jurisdiction and legal control of the ITU over the Internet (Blackman 2013). WCIT-12 included, apart from the revision of the treaty, discussions around the adoption of a non-binding resolution for fostering an enabling environment for the greater growth of the Internet, which affirmed a strong and continuous role for the ITU in Internet governance, stating that "all governments should have an equal role and responsibility for international Internet governance" (for a discussion of the implications of this amid contestation by civil society and private sector, see the chapters by Jamart and Weber in this volume).

The US voiced concerns that the revised ITRs aim to replace the multistakeholder model of Internet governance[5] and pose threats to an open Internet. A broad coalition of non-state actors, including civil society organizations and large Internet companies, mobilized against WCIT-12. These stakeholders questioned not only the legitimacy of the ITU to oversee security issues, in particular in the context of the provisions regarding cybersecurity (Art. 5A) and unsolicited bulk electronic communications (Art. 5B), but also the fact that participation in the discussions was relatively limited (observation and advisory role) and voting was restricted to states only.

The new Article 5A binds states to "endeavour to ensure the security and robustness of international telecommunication networks", which raised concerns about limitations on content that signatory countries might pursue, thus legitimizing potential infringements on human rights. In this case, the negotiations revealed older tensions between the approach of Russia, China vs. US on information security, which have also surfaced in other UN fora, such as the UN General Assembly (Radu 2013; see also Jamart in this volume). The revised article 5B of the treaty, stating that "Member States should endeavour to take necessary measures to prevent the propagation of unsolicited bulk electronic communications and minimize its impact on international telecommunication services", was questioned with regard to possible attempts to limit freedom of expression. Similar concerns also surround the wording of the preamble, which contains a provision upholding the right of access of member states to international telecommunication services. At the same time, the preamble makes reference to the commitment of member states to upholding human right obligations in the implementation of the new ITR[6].

Given these fault lines, consensus was impossible to reach at WCIT-12, and majority voting showcased the emergence of dissenting positions. As shown in Table 1 below, out of the 144 delegations with voting rights, 89 were in favour (including Russia, China, Arab states, Iran, Brazil, Argentina, Mexico, Indonesia, South Korea, Turkey, and many African states) and 55 against (including US, UK, Canada, EU states, Australia, Japan, India, Kenya), yet other states might join the new treaty later. The revised 2012 ITRs take effect on 1 January 2015 and the current situation allows for both the 1988 and the 2012 ITRs to be in force.

5 "We cannot support a treaty that is not supportive of the multistakeholder model of Internet governance", Mr. Kramer, head of the US delegation, stated at WCIT-12 (Pfanner 2012).

6 Paragraph 2 of the Preamble reads: "Member States affirm their commitment to implement these Regulations in a manner that respects and upholds their human rights obligations".

Table 1: Vote of national delegations at the WCIT-12

Signatories of 2012 ITRs	Non-signatories of 2012 ITRs
Afghanistan, Algeria, Angola, Argentina, Azerbaijan, Bahrain, Bangladesh, Barbados, Belize, Benin, Bhutan, Botswana, Brazil, Brunei Darussalam, Burkina Faso, Burundi, Cambodia, Cape Verde (Republic of), Central African Republic, China, Comoros (Union of the), Congo (Republic of the), Cote d'Ivoire, Cuba, Djibouti, Korea (Democratic People's Republic of), Dominican Republic, Egypt, El Salvador, Gabon, Ghana, Guatemala, Guyana, Haiti, Indonesia, Iran, Iraq, Kazakhstan, Kirghizstan, Kuwait, Lesotho, Lebanon, Liberia, Libya, Jamaica, Jordan, Malaysia, Mali, Mauritius, Mexico, Mozambique, Morocco, Namibia, Nepal, Niger, Nigeria, Oman, Qatar, Panama, Papua New Guinea, Paraguay, Rwanda, Russian Federation, Saint Lucia, Saudi Arabia (Kingdom of), Senegal, Sierra Leone, Singapore, Somalia, South Africa, South Sudan, Sri Lanka, Sudan, Swaziland, Tanzania, Thailand, Trinidad and Tobago, Togo, Tunisia, Turkey, United Arab Emirates, Uganda, Ukraine, Uruguay, Uzbekistan, Venezuela, Vietnam, Yemen, Zimbabwe	Albania, Andorra, Armenia, Australia, Austria, Belarus, Belgium, Bulgaria, Canada, Chile, Cyprus, Colombia, Costa Rica, Croatia, Czech Republic, Denmark, Estonia, Finland, France, Gambia, Georgia, Germany, Greece, Hungary, India, Ireland, Israel, Italy, Japan, Kenya, Latvia, Lithuania, Lichtenstein, Luxembourg, Malawi, Malta, Marshall Islands, Moldova, Mongolia, Montenegro, Norway, New Zealand, Netherlands, Peru, Philippines, Poland, Portugal, Serbia, Slovakia, Slovenia, Spain, Sweden, Switzerland, United Kingdom, United States of America

Source: ITU

The split in the votes was associated with a 'digital Cold War' (The Economist 2012), with countries divided into two camps led by the US and Russia[7]. Similar grouping of states could also be observed five months after WCIT, on 16–18 May, when the ITU hosted in Geneva the World Telecommunication/ICTs Policy Forum (WTPF)[8], a meeting facilitating views exchange and information sharing on emerging telecommunication/ICT policy and regulatory matters between member states and sector members. The role of WTPF is to prepare reports and adopt opinions by consensus, without any binding commitments. Around this meeting, the ITU convened an Informal Experts Group (IEG)—with membership open to all stakeholders—which approved, during the preparatory process, the text of the draft opinions to the report of the ITU General Secretary, to be discussed in Geneva. The report focused on the following themes: development and diffusion of ICTs globally, the multistakeholder model, Internet Protocol (IP)-based networks and management of Internet resources, international public policy issues and the management of Internet resources, role of administrations of member states in the management of internationalized (multilingual) domain names. Six draft opinions

---

7 For a thorough analysis of the Cyber Cold War metaphor, see Mueller (2013).

8 ITU World Telecommunication/ICT Policy Forum (WTPF) was established by the 1994 Kyoto Plenipotentiary Conference and is covered by the provisions of Resolution 2. The 2013 meeting was preceded by a Strategic Dialogue session, *Building our Broadband Future,* held on 13 May.

to the report of the Secretary-General were discussed, including support for multistakeholderism and enhanced cooperation[9].

Against this background, current discussions about the implementation of the Enhanced Cooperation process, the WSIS+10 events and other UN-related debates addressing Internet governance are perceived as potential battlefields for the definition of future Internet governance mechanisms. Advocates of a greater role for the ITU and other intergovernmental bodies feel that the time has come for their ideas to prevail, after 15 years of relative failure. On the contrary, supporters of the status-quo fear that Internet governance might change radically in the coming years. The present volume aims to present a more balanced picture. A middle-ground position already existed during the WCIT (see Weber in this volume). Only a critical assessment of the current situation in Internet governance and an informed discussion on future institutions and principles can prevent stalemates and never-ending debates in the coming years. This assessment involves a reflection on the respective role of different types of actors and institutions in Internet governance. It also involves a an informed discussion on the potential of multistakeholder governance (the crucial character of participation and inclusion and the potential legitimacy issues of international negotiations being discussed without multistakeholder participation), but also a critical appraisal of the shortcoming of the multistakeholder model. Finally, an analysis of the salience of cyber-security issues, notably the issue of surveillance, is necessary. This broad perspective on Internet governance echoes the debates of the last fifteen years and addresses crucial elements of the current discussions in a post-WCIT environment.

4. Organization of the Volume

The book analyses the current model of Internet governance and explores possible future developments based on the norms and principles discussed after WCIT. A timely contribution to both scholarly and policy discussions around the changing roles of intergovernmental organizations, states, private actors and communities, the volume focuses, in a twofold manner, on types of interactions and relationships shaping the global governance of the Internet. First, it aims to shed light on the current system through an overview of different governance models and the

9 Opinion 1: Promoting Internet Exchange Points (IXPs) as a long term solution to advance connectivity; Opinion 2: Fostering an enabling environment for the greater growth and development of broadband connectivity; Opinion 3: Supporting Capacity Building for the deployment of IPv6; Opinion 4: In Support of IPv6 Adoption and Transition from IPv4; Opinion 5: Supporting Multi-stakeholderism in Internet Governance; Opinion 6: On supporting operationalizing the Enhanced Cooperation Process.

institutional history of Internet governance. Second, it underscores the shortcomings of the existing system and discusses possible directions of development likely to shape future modes of Internet governance. Finally, it builds on the geopolitics of Internet governance and cybersecurity to evaluate change in the realm that most directly affects state sovereignty and modes of organization in the digital world.

The book has been structured into three parts, which combine the perspectives of scholars and policy practitioners, including policy-makers and activists.

Actors, institutions and principles of Internet governance

The first part of the volume concentrates on the context of developments affecting global Internet policy-making: where do emergent types of governance come from and how do they differ other issue domains? Which problems and institutional predispositions explain their diffusion? Which historical examples and precursors are relevant and what can we learn from them? Are there new principles emerging for Internet governance? This section comprises three chapters placing global Internet policy-making at the center of governance transformations, closely following key trends over the past five decades.

Building on a broad literature in international relations theory, David Sylvan discusses, in the first chapter, four ways in which governance can occur: constraint or inducement; rhetoric acts; frameworks and habituation; and routine, everyday practices. While all these modes shape the evolution of Internet governance, moving from the global to the local level brings us closer to the 'governor-ness' of the network, transitioning from political authority to the equally-important authority of daily practices. This chapter looks at localized interactions between users recreating the Internet every day, independent of the high-stake decisions taken in different regional or global fora.

In chapter two, Michèle Rioux, Nicolas Adam and Biel Company explore how regulatory shifts and institutional trajectories have molded the evolution of telecommunications governance, and the specificity of Internet policy-making in this context. At the intersection of market forces and state power, the co-existence of different sites of governance in the international arena shapes Internet policy-making in unprecedented ways. This analysis reveals the challenges of decision-making in a diffuse network of actors, the role of institutional predispositions and the ensuing continuous rivalry between the ITU and ICANN. Rather than a reform of the governance system, we observe an interplay between traditional actors and new ones and contestation over the extent to which the fragmentation of ICT governance is desirable.

Anne-Claire Jamart's chapter examines the emergence of Internet principles and Internet freedom, in the broader context of intergovernmental proposals to further regulate the global network of networks. The tensions between different groupings of states reveal fundamental divergences over basic understandings of human rights and their applicability to the Internet. The evolution of the Internet freedom discourse, eagerly promoted by the US Secretary of State Hillary Clinton, points out how multistakeholderism was upheld as a principle and reveals the authority derived from reframing issues. Jamart assesses the suitability of a global constitutionalism framework, drawing attention to legitimacy issues and the institutionalization of power.

Multistakeholderism and its limits

Part two of the volume focuses on the limitations of the multistakeholder model and the emergence of new concepts that might structure future debates on Internet governance. It asks questions such as: what are the shortcomings of the multistakeholder model? How can accountability be implemented in such model? What concepts could replace multistakeholderism as principles of Internet governance?

Richard Hill's chapter makes a broad claim about the global communication and information system evolving in the shadow of US dominance. Investigating the situation of developing countries and related concerns regarding access to and affordability of Internet, he argues that the insistence on US control is an illustration of traditional colonialism fused with techno-imperialism, transpiring into different venues of decision-making. Hill's analysis reminds us that multistakeholderism can disguise and preserve the privileged position of particular state actors.

Discussing international treaty-making and the multistakeholder approach, Rolf Weber explores the conditions that need to be met for a multistakeholder governance model to be accountable and legitimate. He argues that power distribution is desirable in Internet governance but that it is under threat because of the rise of a new cyber-sovereignty approach, epitomized by the position of some countries during the WCIT. Drawing upon the concept of cosmopolitanism, he argues for network structures and for the inclusion of human rights in future Internet governance debates.

Examining the uses and abuses of the governance model most often applied to internet governance, Avri Doria argues that multistakeholderism might become another vaguely-defined -ism rather than an empowerment tool for civil society. Drawing upon the models of the ICANN, the IETF, and the IGF, she documents the implementation and shortcomings of the multistakeholder model. She concludes that the multistakeholder model should aim at participatory democracy, through an enhanced participation of stakeholders, an improved cooperation and trust among stakeholders and an unambiguous commitment from the different actors.

Internet security between competition and cooperation

The last section of the book focuses on areas of Internet governance in which emerging norms and principles do not override traditional institutions and state-centred policy-making. It addresses Internet security and the role of global powers in the governance of the Internet. It looks at the types of political objectives pursued by global powers in Internet policy-making, as well as the long-term implications for cybersecurity governance. Are we at the eve of a digital cold war or are we witnessing new governance models in the making? Three chapters provide answers to these questions, using specific examples of security-related policies that expose national interest and sovereignty concerns.

Chapter 7 by Gianluigi Negro discusses the assertiveness of China in the decision-making processes related to the domain name system (DNS). Currently registering the largest number of Internet users in the world, China had a rapid shift from inward looking-policies to global ICT governance and currently asserts itself in management of the internationalized domain name system, in contesting the US dominance over root servers and in supporting an equal role of states in global Internet policy-making.

Andreas Kuehn focuses on the implications of US cybersecurity programs for global Internet governance. He shows how national policies in cybersecurity matters might curtail the space for multistakeholderism. Drawing upon the example of the US Einstein program, he shows that crucial issues for the network are shifting to private agreements between great powers and private firms, to the detriment of globally-negotiated agreements. He concludes that this removal from the public debate particularly affects the political space of civil society actors.

While public-private partnerships (PPPs) have become the prevalent organizational mode in security matters, the rise of bottom-up Internet security communities might contribute to overcome some of the limitations of the PPP model in terms of accountability and legitimacy. Andreas Schmidt discusses network approaches to Internet security and elaborates upon the concept of security communities. His chapter suggests shifts in relational dynamics, bringing us back to the importance of day-to-day interactions, as explained by Sylvan in Chapter 1.

Together, these chapters demonstrate the variety and variability of the current modes of Internet governance, and consider the highly contingent nature of the interplay between global and national policies, private initiatives and everyday orderings. The conclusion analyses the risks of increased tensions in Internet governance, both between states and non-state actors and between institutions, and discusses the ways forward. It asks whether the multistakeholder model is coming to a more advanced stage where issues of accountability and democratic legitimacy are fully addressed. It also explores the possibility of analysing the recent developments as the end of the post-WSIS era in Internet governance.

Annex 1: Timeline of major Internet governance events

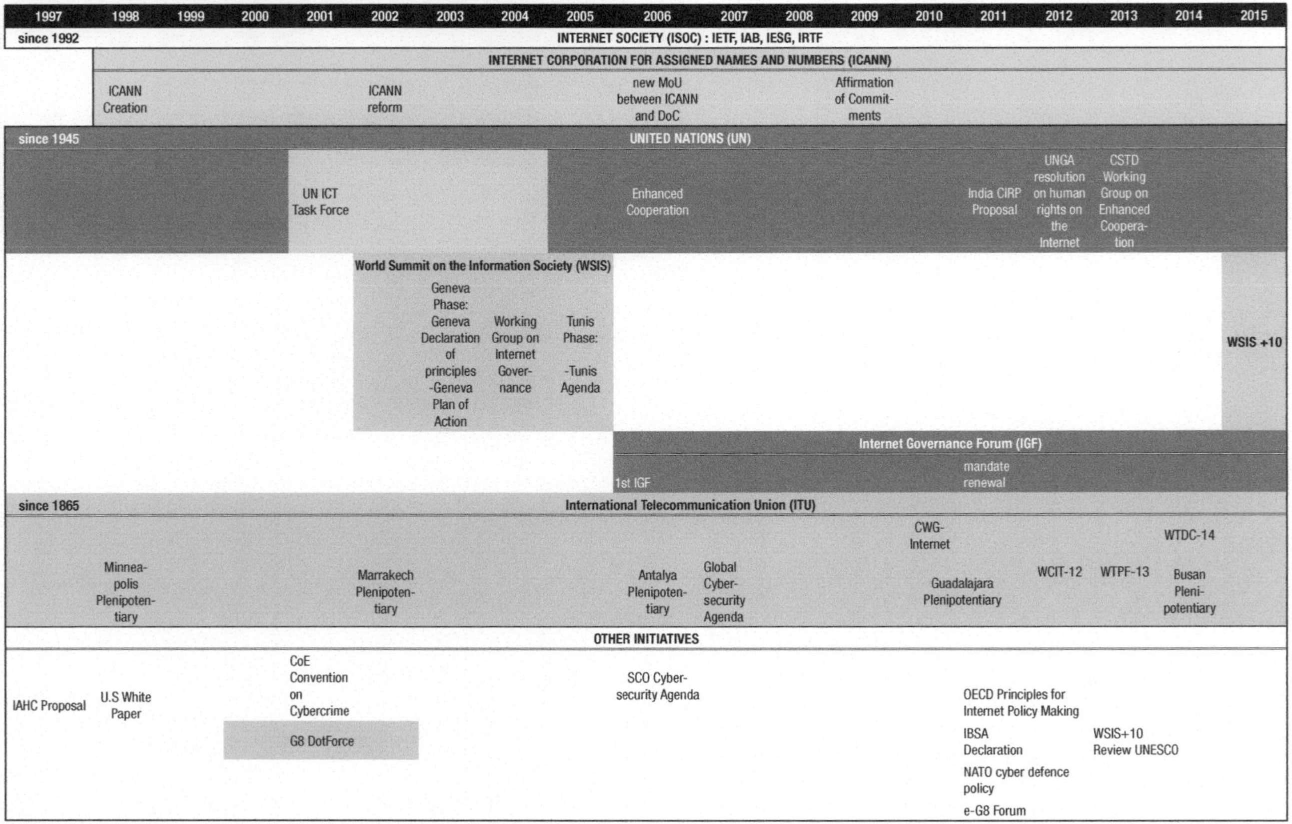

Part 1.
Actors, Institutions and Principles of Internet Governance

David Sylvan

Chapter 1
Global Internet Governance: Governance without Governors

The purpose of this paper is to discuss different ways by which governance can occur, both in general and with respect to the Internet in particular. My argument will be that although Internet governance is often conceived as a matter of designing or strengthening frameworks within which various activities will be facilitated, there is in fact another type of governance, based on everyday orders and "bottom-up" coordination. This type of governance is ubiquitous and is only affected indirectly by framework-related design or redesign; the prevalence of this sort of "governance without governors" thus helps explain why classic attempts at Internet governance have succeeded or failed.

The structure of this paper is simple. I begin by defining the concept of governance, discussing what I believe to be at the core of the concept. Four types of governance are then presented, with particular attention paid to their differences as well as to their applicability across numerous domains, including, but not limited to, the Internet. At this point, it becomes possible to classify types of governance by their "governor-ness." The final section of the paper focuses on Internet governance and discusses the prevalence, or lack thereof, of each of the four types of governance in this domain. My argument, as sketched in the preceding paragraph, implies that if we want to understand how Internet users' actions are governed, we would do well to spend less time on standards, or persuasion, or laws, and more on what users do on an everyday basis.

1. Definition

What is governance? Although there are many distinct uses of this term in different scholarly and policy literatures, one definition that captures much of what is meant by many authors comes from 1940s work in "cybernetics" (e.g., Wiener 1948; cf. Deutsch 1963). This word was an anglicization of the Greek word κυβερνήτης, steersman, which, through its latinization, was at the origin of the French gouverneur and its English cognate. What is significant about Wiener's work is that he immediately separated out the intention of the steerer (I will use this awkward word to avoid unwanted connotations) from the steering itself. In this sense, a thermostat is a steering device: it switches on or off a heating or cooling apparatus as a way of maintaining temperature at a particular level. To be sure, the thermostat was designed by an engineer, but it was also installed by a construction worker, who in turn was obeying the orders of a contractor and ultimately a client; and it can subsequently, for many years, be switched on or off, as well as have its target temperature adjusted, by any number of users. In this sense, it is more confusing than illuminating to concentrate on who the steerer may be and what he/she wants to happen. Rather, we can cut to the heart of the matter by looking at the act of steering itself.

From this perspective, we can define governance (whether of the Internet or of other domains) as "procedures that influence others' actions." Each of the terms here is worth noting. First, "actions." When governance takes place, particular actions do or do not occur, perhaps in alternative ways. Whether the governance in question is of "common pool resources" (Ostrom 1990) or of international relations ("global governance": Barnett and Duvall 2005), governance involves a relation between actions of various sorts and particular antecedent conditions. Without a focus on somebody doing something or failing to do something else, there is no point in talking about governance.

Second, "others". Actions are carried out by one or more agents, whether individuals or collective entities. In many cases, it matters enormously who those agents may be, and much effort in designing governance structures goes into imagining how particular agents will respond to certain states of affairs.

Third, "influence." This is a key issue. Whichever actions we are talking about must have been influenced in one way or another, else nothing was actually governed. Here it is useful to borrow from Weber's definition of power (1920): actions are influenced insofar as they would not have occurred—at least in the way they occurred, or when they occurred, or where they occurred—in the absence of whatever it was that influenced them. To assess whether or not actions were influenced, one therefore needs to engage in a sort of counterfactual analysis, figuring out what would have happened otherwise. When the actions in question pertain to the Internet, with millions of users, counterfactual analysis in turn involves specifying default patterns of behaviour.

Fourth, "procedures." What exactly is it that influences actions? Rules, whether or not in the form of laws, are often referred to in the governance literature (see, for example, almost any issue of the journal Global Governance); so too are decisions, norms, or for that matter, various actions. The common element to these various phenomena is a series of steps followed in a particular order: for example, enacting a rule, budgeting for its enforcement, and enforcing it; or deciding to do something, carrying out that decision, reevaluating it, and so forth. (Note that each of the steps in the above examples is itself decomposable into a series of more fine-grained steps, etc.) A rule that is never promulgated or implemented cannot influence actions. Similarly, a rule that is implemented with a different series of steps each time can only with difficulty be characterized as the same rule.

It should be apparent from this discussion that governance need not be aimed at to exist. Rules can be drafted and implemented in order to carry out particular goals; but they may instead influence other actions by agents whom no one thought about when the rules were being considered. Of course, the converse is also true: the fact that certain individuals or organizations may aim at influencing particular actions by others need not mean that they perforce succeed in that aim. In other words, there may not be a link between governance and the intentions of those whose procedures in fact govern. This, as we shall see, provides an important wedge between governors and governance.

2. Four Modes of Governance

There are four ways in which governance can occur. The first, in keeping with the Weberian take on influence (cf. Simon 1953; Dahl 1957; Alker 1973), involves constraint and/or inducement: individuals or other agents are rewarded or punished if they behave in certain ways. This requires either a transfer of resources to effectuate rewards, or an enforcement mechanism to carry out punishments. Note that either reward or punishment may occur in a centralized or a decentralized fashion (for example, compare the Security Council voting sanctions with the World Trade Organization's members being authorized to impose countervailing duties) by individual or collective actors; note also that constraints and inducements can be carried out by private actors as well as public ones (e.g., the way that a business might offer discounts to potential customers on certain products).

From the standpoint of social theory, constraints and inducements are quintessential means by which power is exercised. Those who control violence, whether as private actors or as state officials executing laws are similar in this respect to those who control resources such as money or commodities, whether or not they are the legal owners of those resources. Of course, neither inducement nor reward may be the immediate aim of acting in certain ways, and both politics and economic life are replete with examples of how certain actions, via their inducement/reward consequences, led to outcomes which had not been intended. Since states, via their ability to outlaw certain types of behaviour, are in a good position to inflict punishments, it is no surprise that governance of various domains is often conceived as involving, at least at some point, action by one or more states, or procedures that involve state-like action. Interestingly, although the same can be said about business actors, via their ability to mobilize and distribute resources for reward, they tend to be thought of more as affected by governance than as key agents of governance (for a discussion on the respective role of states and private actors in Internet governance, see Weber in this volume).

The second way by which governance can occur is through rhetoric or acts of modeling. What I mean by this is that one agent, A, convinces another, B, to act in a particular way, either by providing information or making arguments, or alternatively by serving as a source of emulation. In these situations, A neither constrains B by punishment nor induces B by reward; rather, A's rhetoric convinces B, or B models its actions after what A does. An example of rhetoric at work is the way in which scientific evidence persuaded states around the world to ban chlorofluorocarbons (CFCs) in the Montreal Protocol; a long-standing example of modeling is the way in which states act to change domestic legislation to follow the "best practices" of other states (the International Labour Organization organizes much of its staff work along these lines; cf. Eagleton-Pierce 2013, on symbolic power in the World Trade Organization).

It might be argued that rhetoric, and perhaps modeling, is effective only insofar as the convinced or copying agent B imagines it will face a better future, or alternatively will avoid a worse future, by acting in this way. That may well be the case, but it does not perforce mean that B thinks its better future will come from agent A, or that its avoided worse future would involve a punishment by A. Put differently: B may well operate by a utilitarian calculus, but that calculus is influenced by A's words or its deeds generally, not by hopes or fears of what A will do to B. We can, if we wish, say that A is exercising rhetorical power over B, or that A is in a Gramscian sense hegemonic with respect to B, but this is different from power (or wealth) as usually understood. Not all persuasive actors are necessarily wealthy or militarily strong, and so however common this form of governance may be, it is already useful as a corrective to any temptation to focus on international organizations or sovereign states.

So far, we have been looking at procedures which are commonly actions. The third mode of governance concentrates on other kinds of procedures: those which involve setting up frameworks or otherwise facilitating habituation. Agents, in the face of these frameworks, find themselves in an environment structured to facilitate certain types of behaviour (but not to reward that behaviour, or to punish alternative behaviours, or to persuade them to adopt that behaviour); often, they develop habits of engaging in the specific behaviour (cf. Hopf 2010). A classic example of frameworks and habituation, regarding wheeled transportation, is the use of lane dividers, curbs, traffic signals, and so forth. These establish an environment in which drivers stay in certain lanes while avoiding others; stop, go, and turn in particular places and at certain times; and otherwise conform their actions to the environment. Indeed, for most drivers, such conformity is typically a habit and only rarely a matter of conscious decision. Of course, the physical environment in which wheeled transportation is governed may be authorized statutorily, through the traffic code, but the laws in question rarely specify such details as the painting of arrows in a lane, or the height of a curb, or whether an intersection has a stop sign, a traffic light (much less the number of seconds the light is red as opposed to green), or nothing at all (cf. Vanderbilt 2008). Similarly, the traffic code, as pertaining to a particular location and a particular time, may be enforced by the police ("went through a red light"), but the (often correct, at least in some jurisdictions) presumption is that most of the time, drivers will simply obey signals, conform to painted lane lines, and so forth.

Frameworks and habituation, as a mode of governance, should be distinguished from the means by which they were established. Actors may set up frameworks by themselves, or in collaboration with others; any agreements may take the form of standards, or of more detailed specification of the environment in which actions will occur. Interestingly, some frameworks can become so ubiquitous and habituation so strong that "lock-in" results, with alternatives being shunned as strange or unusable (this was notoriously the case with the QWERTY keyboard, designed originally to slow down typing speeds as a way of reducing key jams: David 1985; see also Liebowitz and Margolis 1990). Similar claims have been made about the difficulty of updating or otherwise changing many of the standards elaborated, notably, by private or mixed private-public bodies such as the Institute of Electrical and Electronics Engineers (IEEE) (Kennedy 2006; Königsgruber 2010). Given these claims, and given that debates over frameworks are common for many domains of activity (everything from electronic equipment to accounting standards), it should be expected that this type of governance is most commonly associated with governance more generally (and, as discussed below, with Internet governance in particular)—and this regardless of whether the frameworks in question are conceived of as akin to standards, or infrastructure, or as networks with particular properties (Chiariglione 2000).

Although debates over frameworks are often in the news, frameworks themselves work for the most part in the background, in a low-key way. The fourth mode of governance is still lower key. Routine procedures, through unremarkable forms of adjustment, are quotidian ways in which agents' actions are influenced. When individuals adjust their behaviour to others', in order to solve problems, or to accomplish tasks, or only to socialize, they are influencing the actions by which those phenomena (problem solving, task accomplishment or socializing) unfold and are contoured. For example, workplace activities such as completing a sale or carrying out an inspection involve concatenated, mutually adjusted action by two or more agents. So too do family chores, or many aspects of negotiation, or conversation, whether face-to-face or over the telephone (Sacks 1972). As these examples make clear, routine interaction is a mode of governance present in almost every domain of activity. Business, politics, schooling, and relations among friends or family members, tourism, even brief encounters between strangers at traffic crossings: all are marked by routine interactions and unremarkable forms of coordination. Sociologists refer to this as forms of everyday order (Schütz 1953; Garfinkel 1967; Livingston 1987; Sharrock 2004), and it arguably captures the meaning of steersmanship better than any other type of governance, precisely because of its routine and unremarkable workings (when sailing a boat, for example, one is constantly adjusting the helm, trimming the sail, etc., even when maintaining the same tack).

How different are routine interactions from frameworks, at least as regards governance? To say that the former are lower-level and far more common than the latter, while true, tells us little. A better way of getting at the difference is to consider a concrete phenomenon, say international multilateral negotiations. Such negotiations in fact display all four modes of governance. As is well known, states affect each other's behaviour by rewards and, from time to time, threats; they also are influenced by arguments (whether by other states or by non-state actors, such as scientific experts) and occasionally model their behaviour after each other. Moreover, negotiations are strongly affected by the framework within which they take place: rules such as who is allowed to participate or mediate, and what concessions they can legally make; standards by which offers may be assessed or ranked; and even the physical environment (e.g., the shape of the table; whether the venue is in the middle of a busy city or isolated in the countryside). All of these are of potentially great importance. However, we know from microsociology that negotiations, like all conversational interactions, involve extensive connections between each interlocutor's statements. Take a simple exchange between two individuals, A and B. After A has spoken, B has the obligation, in responding, to connect what he/she says to what A said, if only to explain why what A said is unacceptable. Moreover, B's speech opens up certain possibilities for A in his/her rejoinder, while rendering other possibilities more difficult. These forward- and backward-looking connections between a statement and the statements that precede or follow it (the technical term in conversation analysis is "adjacency pair") are one illustration of just how collaborative conversation is—even when the interlocutors are strongly disagreeing with each other—and of the joint work necessary for it to take place (Sacks 1972; Schegloff 2007; Sidnell 2010). None of the details of this collaboration is determined by frameworks, and although power or wealth can certainly affect which actors are most likely to get their way in negotiations, they tell us little about the nature of any agreement, qua the details of content. Obviously, interlocutors can be and are convinced by arguments, but how the convincing works depends much on conversational interlocking (Sylvan 2012). In this sense, the first three modes of governance depend for their efficacy on everyday order (de Certeau 1984; Latour and Woolgar 1979; Rafanell 2013).

It is possible to array the four modes of governance in terms of what we might call "governor-ness": how closely each resembles the stereotype of a powerful official governing in a "L'Etat c'est moi" fashion. Consider two dimensions: the extent to which procedures aim at influencing others' actions, and the extent to which those executing the procedures are highly ranked on some power or status scale.

Table 2: Types of governance by rank and intentionality

		Rank/status of procedural executor	
		Lo	Hi
Intentionality of influence	Lo	Routine interactions/ coordination	Rhetoric/ modeling
	Hi	Frameworks/habituation	Constraint/ inducement

As can be seen from this table, the modes of governance vary from high "governor-ness" (constraint/inducement) to low (routine interactions/coordination). Neither rhetoric nor frameworks are really at the other end of the scale from constraint, even if both appear less centralized. It is routine interactions which represent the purest examples of governance without governors. This is, in a sense, a hypothesis which can be tested by looking at Internet governance.

3. Internet Governance

The Internet dates from the late 1970s[1]; the first uses of the term "governance" as applied to the Internet follow by some 15 years[2]. This lag, in accordance with the typical focus of governance discussions on frameworks, and to a lesser degree on constraint/inducement, should immediately raise flags, since the obvious question is how the Internet was governed given the relative paucity of standards and

1 This date is roughly midway between alternative candidates: the first ARPANET link began in 1969; after multiple networks had been created, the term "Internet" was coined in 1974; TCP/IP protocols were authorized as the sole protocol in ARPANET in 1983; and around the time that ARPANET was linked with NSFNET in the late 1980s, the resulting (and expanding) worldwide TCP/IP network came to be known as the Internet.

2 Searches using both Google Scholar and Google Books (via its Ngram viewer) indicate that the phrase "Internet governance" started to be used in academic and technical writing, and in books and monographs, in 1995–96.

the near-absence of laws in the early years. The typical answer, of course, is that the Internet was indeed governed by frameworks—protocols, in particular, but also computer code which was widely accepted—with the earliest actors receiving indirect state support (e.g., Post 1996; Lessig 1999; Hill in this volume). However, this answer is problematic, because it implies either that in the early days of the Internet it was governed only to a slight degree, and hence that there were Internet-related actions which were not influenced by particular procedures (what would those actions have been?); or that as the number of interacting users grew massively, nothing changed appreciably in the way their actions were influenced. This dilemma suggests that the Internet was governed, from its earliest days, without governors. To see this, consider in turn each of the four modes of governance.

Constraint and inducement played a notable, though relatively minor, role in the Internet from its origins to the present day. Some laws extended copyright or anti-pornography or anti-hate speech statutes to information uploaded to or downloaded from various computer sites (or, in some cases, to modifications of computer-related hardware); other laws prohibited unauthorized access to servers or networks. Punishments provided for by these laws were in some cases criminal penalties, in others, civil damages. As regards inducements, some countries subsidized the construction of network-related infrastructure in rural or poorer areas; in other cases, private companies provided financial incentives to buy their products.

These various examples illustrate just how few are the number of Internet-related activities influenced by punishments or rewards. While, at the limit, millions of people might from time to time download copyrighted material, such actions not only represent a tiny fraction of those people's Internet-related activities, but the fact that downloads have continued in the face of potential punishment indicates that the chances of getting caught are infinitesimally small—and hence that the actions in question are not really influenced by state-mandated constraints. In this respect, as with most criminal laws, the purpose of legally-authorized punishments is less to regulate activity (most people do not think every day of whether or not they should commit a murder, a burglary, or some other crime) than to stigmatize it symbolically.

On the other hand, financial inducements could affect many Internet-related actions, but only, of course, if they rewarded many different types of actions, which is not the case. This limitation is due to the simple fact that most Internet-related actions by users are not commercial in nature. If one is able to afford access to a device which in turn connect to the Internet, there are numerous activities in which one can engage, only a few of which involve purchasing a commodity. Obviously, this percentage is higher for Internet Service Providers (ISPs) and some web sites, but even then, few concrete activities (as opposed to the organization's potential raison d'être) are actually pursued or eschewed for financial reasons or, for that matter, from fear of criminal prosecution or civil pursuit. In short, constraints and inducements represent a relatively minor form of Internet governance.

The second type of governance, rhetoric and modeling, is slightly more prevalent than rewards and punishments regarding the Internet. Users clearly model their behaviour on other that of other users, system administrators do the same, and website design (and indeed content, such as privacy notices) displays considerable convergence. Moreover, at least with regard to certain norms of courtesy, as well as for lawmakers considering legislation, arguments occasionally do change minds. However, since much Internet-related activity does not involve real-time interactions (e.g., Skype calls, or instant messaging, or multiplayer games are all interactive in real time; by contrast, Facebook postings and email exchanges are non-real-time interactive; online shopping and video downloads are non-interactive), the opportunities for influencing such activity by modeling or even convincing by various rhetorical means are limited. An example of rhetoric and modeling which illustrates this point comes from a study of conferences involving Network Operator Groups (NOGs): "a substantive amount of the conference content relates to peering and routing. Conference content comprises tutorials, vetted conference presentations, and perhaps most importantly, hallway conversations during the coffee breaks. For new network operators, the tutorials are often an introduction to best practices" (Sowell 2012, p. 9). In other words, network operators learn from each other when they are face-to-face, i.e., not interacting via the Internet. Similarly, legislators can be convinced to pass constraining laws, and experts to promulgate standards, by rhetorical means, but those means only affect Internet-related activity via the laws and the standards, not in their own right.

This last point suggests a difference between rhetoric and modeling, at least as they pertain to Internet governance. Modeling, unlike rhetoric, can operate without real-time interaction. The problem is that the resultant behaviour (say the choice of a user name, or the colour scheme or menu structure of a given site) is in a sense one-shot: it sets the environment within with Internet-related actions take place, but not the actions themselves (the same goes for hacking, or for virus-writing). For that, we have to turn to the third type of governance.

As mentioned earlier, frameworks and habituation have received far more attention than other modes of Internet governance. The standard story goes something like this: actions such as linking a server, or connecting to, the web involve the use of domain names, the transmission of data using the TCP/IP protocol, a browser which interprets HTML, and so forth. Each of these aspects builds on an architecture and a set of standards enshrined by various framework-related entities: ICANN, the W3C, and so forth. That architecture and those standards, in turn, are computer code: they specify how to take text, sounds, images, or other materials, convert them to strings of 1s and 0s, transmit them to various computers, reassemble them, and display them. The code is instantiated in programs of various sorts, including operating systems, and often hard-wired onto computer chips[3]. Frameworks, in the end, turn out to be code instantiated across millions of computing devices—which is one reason why it is so easy to hack into networks, or to surveil their users (Hill in this volume, sect. 4).

This is an elegant story, and it obviously can be retold for various types of Internet-related activities. Whenever one user is interacting with another, or with a computer program, that interaction is structured by the computer code that makes it possible. However, to go from this observation to the claim that the actual substance of the interactions is influenced by that code, via its widespread adoption as a standard, is quite different. Consider, first, that frameworks operate by channelling activities and that the channelling becomes second nature through a process of habituation. Thus, for example, a curb makes it difficult to drive on a sidewalk and almost immediately, a motorist develops habits of keeping a distance between her vehicle and the curb. What exactly are the Internet-related activities analogous to this sort of channelling cum habit? One such activity might be the practice of cc'ing addressees on emails, an activity greatly facilitated by the design of email clients and the decentralized way in which emails (and indeed, all other data transmissions) are sent. The problem with this example, though, apart from the not insignificant point that cc'ing is not in fact a habit for most users, is that there is no evidence to support the claim that including addressees on emails is an activity which the standards of the Internet channel, as opposed to facilitate. One could, I suppose, argue the converse side of the question: it is difficult, if not impossible, to specify a particular route that an email would follow, but there is no evidence that Internet code writers wanted to keep users from specifying particular routes, as opposed simply to building robustness and decentralization into the network.

However, the biggest problem with the standards claim is that it has little to do with the substance of the vast majority of the Internet-related actions carried out by various persons. To see this, consider a basic distinction: between an action and a type of action. Actions are recognizable sequences of behaviours: I put up a tent pole, you shake my hand, she writes a message. Types of actions are categories which can be attributed to multiple actions: I can greet you by shaking hands, or by smiling and asking how you are doing, or by nodding, or waving, or saying "hi". For certain types of actions, the multiple ways of performing those actions differ from each other only trivially: for example, not driving onto the curb by, say, aiming at an imaginary line a few meters from the curb, versus drifting toward the curb then jerking the steering wheel away, versus asking the front seat passenger

[3] I have adapted this story from Lessig (1999a), though he somewhat conflates the values inherent in the software engineering process in that era with the actual instructions written in the code.

to call out whenever the car gets too close to the curb. These obviously are different actions, with some far safer than others, but the difference between them, qua carrying out "not driving onto the curb," are of negligible importance. But this is not true of all actions. For example, the action "not going to war" is very different depending on whether it is instantiated by a policy of friendship and one of barely thwarted aggression. Similarly, and lest one imagine that this is a matter of non-actions as opposed to actions, the action "staying in touch" is often significantly different if it is carried out by a daily phone call rather than by having coffee once every twelve months, or of a friend stopping by one's house rather than a government agent barging into an office. The point is simply that for many actions, knowing the type to which it belongs tells us little or nothing about the substance of those actions.

This is definitely the case when it comes to most Internet-related actions. To be sure, some of those actions often differ only trivially for a given type—one thinks of the difference between logging into an account by keying information, as opposed to touching an icon on a smartphone—but the converse is much more common. Consider, for example, the action of registering with a website. This action is of course facilitated and to a great degree standardized by the long-prevalent use of usernames and passwords to characterize computer accounts, but that does not mean that there are not multiple, and quite distinct, ways of furnishing this information. Does one use a pseudonym or one's own name, a single email address or multiple such addresses across sites, a simple or a complicated password? Does one register regardless of the owner of the site (commercial, say, or a forum), or the nature of the network (e.g., public WiFi) on which one is accessing the site? Each of these choices (or habits, as the case may be) arguably results in a substantively different action, as can easily be seen by reflecting on the ways in which users will subsequently interact with the sites in question.

This non-determination of substance by type is not only more common, but is most likely the norm, when the Internet-related actions in question are not with a machine (as is the case when one registers on a website) but with other human beings. Thus, interactions using Skype, or instant messaging, or email, or posting comments on blogs, though clearly enabled and constrained by the protocols permitting the establishment of those services (and of course the more detailed code distinguishing one Voice over IP (VoIP), or Instant Messaging (IM), or email service, or comment submission mechanism from another), have an enormous range of substance which knowledge of the standards in question tell us nothing about, just as knowing that two people were talking on the telephone tells us nothing about what they said to each other. Even social interactions of a more asymmetrical nature, such as updating a Facebook page in response to what someone else did online or sending a tweet as a response to someone else's tweet, have levels of substance undetermined by the type of Internet action they happen to be[4]. Hence, most user actions, and almost all user social interactions, cannot be said to be governed by frameworks[5].

By contrast, the fourth type of governance is present in practically every type of social interaction among users—and, as we will see below, even in many of the interactions that users have with machines. The argument here is straightforward: when a user interacts online with another user (even if in an insulting way), each is contouring her behaviour to the other. They are, in the simplest sense, carrying out procedures which influence each other. Of course, those procedures are not usually thought of in a formal way, since they are substantive and highly local; nonetheless, what a user does in this respect is clearly a sequence of steps. If two people are having an email exchange and A sends a message asking a question about what B said, B will (normally) respond not only to the substance of the question but to the fact that the question referred to what B had said previously. That is, A reads what B said, refers to what B said, then poses his question. If one of those three elements were missing, B would not feel nearly as constrained to answer A, at least in relatively short order[6].

When A and B influence each other in this fashion, they are not only affecting their actions at that moment but are building up precedents, habits, and repertoires of interaction patterns for future interactions, both between them and with other people. This is why even asymmetrical or time-lagged interactions, such as over Facebook, also are forms of local order: people respond not only directly to what others did regarding them, but to various interactions they previously had or are currently

4 It could be argued that this claim is misleading, since the type of action in question is not "posting a comment on a blog" but "flaming someone" or "trolling someone". However, quite apart from the fact that it is unlikely code was actually written to enable flaming or trolling, or that such behavior is, for almost everyone, not at all habitual, the same point about type and substance applies: there are all sorts of ways to troll people, people whom one can troll, and so forth. Put differently, social action has a highly localized quality: what a given person is doing, at that time, vis-a-vis another specific person (cf. on indexicality Garfinkel 1967; and Barnes and Law 1976).

5 This raises a more subtle point. Much of the literature on Internet governance is implicitly premised on the idea that the actions supposedly influenced by procedures of various sorts are actions carried out by actors other than end-users: ISPs, cloud services, equipment manufacturers, and so forth. While in one sense this focus is understandable, since many standards are in fact written with intent of affecting the behavior of those sorts of actors, in another sense the focus is somewhat curious, akin to studying the governance of markets without looking at consumers, or the governance of the commons without looking at those who use the commons.

6 If A had not read what B wrote, his citation would be perceived as non-germane, thereby reducing B's obligation to answer. If A did not cite B, his question could be perceived as rude, again reducing B's obligation to respond. And, obviously, if A did not pose a question, B would not have to respond to it.

having (or may even hope to have) with third parties. By extension, when individuals interact with machines (e.g., uploading photos, or even coming up with new passwords), they engage in behaviour they already learned, or modify behaviour from earlier interactions. Obviously, the machines do not modify their behaviour (though the programmers can and do rewrite code in light of user complaints), but the humans in question are influenced in their actions very much the same way as when one person interacts with another (though cf. Suchman 1987). In this way, the Internet displays local order whenever human beings act in it; such actions re-create the Internet every day, both maintaining and changing it.

Consider the practice of commenting in blogs. This was originally a capability built into early blogging software, but it has subsequently taken on a variety of forms (conversational, critical, etc.) which have in turn led to efforts by some bloggers to avoid comments. Those efforts have spurred both criticisms and defences, so that by now, there are families of norms on the activity of commenting, something which has now begun to colonize other domains of activity, such as music production and consumption. Indeed, commenting norms have begun to be connected to ongoing and long-standing debates about freedom of speech, tolerance, the value of participation, democracy in the workplace, and so forth (Miller and Shepherd 2004; BBC News 2007; Ringmar 2007). While these debates are of great potential significance, it is worth noting that they continue to be driven forward in everyday practice, when individuals make comments on each other, react to those comments, react to the reactions, etc. In other words, even though the practice and norms of commenting have long since escaped their blogging birthplace, they continue to evolve (e.g., as in the development of topics that stem from user-defined threads).

What is striking about routine interaction and coordination is not only its ubiquity and the relatively limited notice that it has received among students of governance, but the fact that it is only related tangentially to other modes of governance. It is clear that constraints and inducements have little to no effect on users' localized interactions: one may indeed be afraid to say or do something, but that fear has little to do with how what one does online influences those with whom one is interacting. Users do interact with each other rhetorically and model their behaviour on what they perceive others to be doing; however, most of the time, when one actor locally reacts to what another is doing, it has little to do with being convinced, or simply with copying the other. Similarly, and as we saw above, standards are for the most part substance-less, so there is relatively little connection between everyday order and infrastructure, at least as regards types of Internet governance (cf. the interesting literature on how consumers remake the physical space of shopping malls, thereby counteracting architects' and developers' visions: Penaloza 1998; Maguire 2008).

A good case in point about the tangential relation between the first three types of governance and the fourth has to do with users' dissemination of copyrighted material. As is well-known, various governments have tried different means of limiting or downright eliminating such dissemination. Laws have been passed providing for penalties to users found to have downloaded or uploaded copyrighted material; other laws have been passed making it easy to shut down companies or arraign individuals alleged to have facilitated such dissemination; and yet other laws have been passed making it possible for users to be barred from Internet connections if they are accused on more than two occasions of being involved with the dissemination of copyrighted material. For years, companies and governments have put forward arguments equating file-sharing with theft, or piracy; how-to questions about downloading in various user forums have been met with anger or eviction from the forum. Infrastructure-related actions, such as requirements that manufacturers build copy restrictions into hardware, or take down files, or block certain Internet Service Providers, have also proliferated, as have the development of legal streaming or downloading sites. Nonetheless, these various governance attempts appear to have governed remarkably little: activities of sharing files of copyrighted material appear to be as prevalent now as when the Napster case first brought the matter to public attention (cf. Aguiar and Martens 2013). Similar results could apply to numerous other activities that have been the focus of concerted efforts by various authorities and standard-setting bodies; it appears that most types of governance in fact govern very few activities.

This last point means that to an important extent, everyday Internet governance is orthogonal to most conscious attempts at governance by governments, or standard-setting organizations, or activists of various stripes. Of course, such attempts can, from time to time, influence users' activities, even if that influence is not always positive (cf. Scott 1998). However, routine interactions are both so common and so far under the radar that they will continue more or less regardless of what is done "higher up." For hundreds of millions of users around the world, the Internet is indeed governed without governors. Perhaps the time has come to spend less of our time studying laws, money, arguments, or standards, and more time studying our fellow users.

Michèle Rioux in collaboration with Nicolas Adam and Biel Company Pérez

Chapter 2
Competing Institutional Trajectories for Global Regulation—Internet in a Fragmented World

At the 2012 World Conference on International Telecommunications (WCIT-12) convened by the International Telecommunication Union (ITU) saw discussions stalled over the role of governments and their power to regulate cyberspace. Western powers (55) rallied behind a "hands off approach" or multistakeholder approach to Internet regulation, whereas many other states (89) pled in favour of greater government control and increased ITU oversight of Internet governance. This collision between two institutions, the ITU and ICANN (Internet Corporation for Assigned Names and Numbers), is a revealing case of the many controversies that are shaping the debates and realities of institutional life and evolution facing globalization and technological changes. It certainly illustrates a strong competition amongst sites of governance that accompanies important underlying structural changes affecting the world economy. This rivalry involves the ITU, one on the oldest international organizations, created in 1865, and one of the youngest global private regulatory bodies, ICANN, which was created in 1998. The rivalry clearly favours ICANN because it is global and private, two conditions required to fit with digital capitalism.

While the world moves on and changes radically, institutions are often "backward" and "slow", and are sometimes unable to adjust to change as they reflect, at a specific point in time, equilibria and compromises. With new issues emerging and new actors asserting themselves, new governance frameworks are developed. Nowadays, they often aim at establishing a transnational—or a global—regulatory system of rules replacing old international regimes, which are increasingly out of touch with new challenges. Transnational regulatory frameworks are being built in different sites and spaces, a process involving an increasing number of actors, notably the private sector and civil society but even, at times, national states and international organizations engaging in new forms of diplomacy.

This process of institutional emergence is challenging traditional forms of regulation and institutions, especially the role and activities of the ITU and of states, which were based, until the end of the 20th century, on monopolistic regulation at the national level. Recent events signify that the issue of "international regime" vs.

"multistakeholder global governance" opposing the ITU and ICANN is a controversial one that must be contextualized in terms of the historical evolution of this sector, taking into consideration the structural changes induced by globalization and technological changes as well as broader transformations in the regulation models. The telecommunication sector has undergone radical transformations in the 20th century. It was also at the core of very significant innovations that had transformative effects on economic, political and social life. In this chapter, we argue that these transformations have translated into a shift from an international telecommunication regime centred on the ITU to a more diffuse and complex network of global and transnational governance frameworks which reflect the emergence of a global networked capitalism that, so far, has benefited corporate agents and sometimes, quite paradoxically, old and revamped monopolies that have restructured to adapt to new conditions.

The "regulation" of the information and communication technologies (ICTs) sector, and more generally, of the information society, is constituted by an ever-growing (and dynamic) array of practices, instruments and forums, which allows for forum shopping, shifting, and interlinking. Paradoxically, the global digital world is matched by a patchwork of regulatory agencies. This chapter will attempt to explain the current fragmentation/segmentation of the Internet universe in three worlds of institutions or rationales of regulation, and will discuss global Internet governance in terms of the competing institutional trajectories that are a reflection of these three overlapping worlds. First, we introduce the recent events opposing the ITU to ICANN. Second, we link these events to the historical transformations of the telecommunication sector. Third, we introduce a theoretical approach that situates those competing sites of governance in three distinct models.

1. ITU vs. ICANN—the ITU Looking for its Significance in a World Global Internet Governance

The Internet, like globalization, transformed the world of nation-states into a complex and heterogeneous network of actors interacting within a new form of global diplomacy that has a significant transnational dimension (Kleinwächter 2004). It is no surprise that some states are reacting to the hegemonic powers of the US government and global firms—many from the US—shaping global Internet governance (see also chapter 4 in this volume). In the 1990s, engineers and technical experts were the most important actors establishing the "rules of the game", managing the Internet through institutions such as ICANN, which became one of the first truly global private Internet governance bodies. Until the creation of ICANN in 1998, the Internet had been governed through a set of "organically developed Internet institutions", which emerged around the so-called "Internet community", such as the IETF and ISOC (Mueller 2010, p. 217). DNS and IP address policies, as well as root management were centralized in ICANN, a private self-regulatory alternative to the international public model represented by the ITU. The ITU had indeed few comparative advantages.

It is now common to characterize the relationship between the ITU and other organizations related to the regulation of ICT networks and services as an adversarial one (Kleinwächter 2004). As Van Eeten and Mueller stated, global Internet governance is going through a period of rivalry between the ITU and ICANN (van Eeten & Mueller 2012, p. 5). It is quite remarkable to note that these two organizations represent two different paradigms of regulation: intergovernmentalism (centred on nation-states and international cooperation) and multistakeholderism (based on global governance structured and influenced by a plurality of competing actors and sites of governance with very different amounts of authority and influence). More than a decade after the World Summit on the Information Society (WSIS), the struggle between these organizations continues. ITU organized the WSIS, a process by which it was decided to leave ICANN do its work. Neither at WSIS nor at the United Nations (UN) was there ever a consensus on the role of public regulation in relation to Internet, and only an advisory role for governments was developed in ICANN through the Government Advisory Council (GAC). Yet, many countries are questioning the legitimacy of ICANN[1], and this is mostly due to the link between ICANN and the United States.

The intergovernmentalist side demands that ICANN's public policy authority be transferred to an ad hoc or already existing intergovernmental organization, the ITU being an obvious candidate. The global powers which support this option, notably China, Russia and Brazil, demand an international convention formally delegating authority over Internet governance, in a narrow sense, in the name of the international community—be it to ICANN or to the ITU or an equivalent of it. Such a convention would also lay out an international legal framework for the exercise of such regulatory functions, including some oversight institution—presumably the ITU (also discussed by Jamart in Chapter 3).

What is at stake is the influence and authority over a narrow yet crucial set of regulatory functions, currently performed by ICANN: 1) policy authority over the Do-

[1] In 2005 Brazil stated, in a preparatory committee for the second phase of the WSIS, that "[o]n Internet governance, three words tend to come to mind: 'Lack of legitimacy'. (…) [O]nly one nation decides on behalf of us all." Brazil's Statement On Internet Governance to the WSIS Prepcom III (September 20th, 2005) Geneva. Available at: http://gnso.icann.org/mailing-lists/archives/ga/msg02745.html (Last accessed on 6/9/2013).

main Names Space (DNS); 2) authority to define IP addresses allocation policies; and 3) the management of the root zone servers (Mayer-Schoenberger and Ziewitz 2007, p. 192–3). These are the only regulatory functions with a global reach centralized in ICANN and providing the ability to decide which device can connect to Internet. Since the WSIS, they are characterized as *Internet governance in a narrow sense,* as opposed to *Internet governance in a broad sense,* which covers the rest of Internet-related regulatory issues[2]. Generally, but not strictly, this controversy aligns Western industrialized countries, led by the United States, the American ICT business or private sector and some of its civil society organizations, on one side, and emerging global powers and developing countries, on the other.

The United States have adopted and promoted a new model of governance by delegating policy authority over unique identifiers and the root server system to a private self-regulatory organization (Hill in this volume; Cogburn et al. 2005, Drezner 2004, Benkler 2000, Froomkin 2000, Goldsmith 2000). ICANN was established as a non-profit corporation based in California, and thereby subjected to US and California laws. Through its creation, the US constituted a transnational/global regime that effectively prevented Internet governance from being taken over by a traditional, intergovernmental international regime and reasserted and secured US control over unique identifiers and root server system policies. This strategy was a way to avoid the ITU control over the Internet, a strategy of regime shifting also illustrated in other domains of global ICT governance, as in the case of the Basic Telecommunications Agreement at the World Trade Organization (WTO). The latter contributed decisively to the gradual decay of the international telecommunications regime and of the ITU itself as a result of the growing regulatory competition in the sector (Holitscher 2005).

What happened at the ITU? Reforms were discussed and the WSIS process was established in order to face the new global challenges of the emerging information society. The WSIS provided a hybrid

solution involving a process of multistakeholderism within the logic of intergovernmentalism. On the one hand, this implicitly meant the acceptance of ICANN and of the Internet governance scheme being developed outside of ITU and UN control. On the other hand, it allowed the UN and the ITU to develop a voice and a role in Internet governance, notably with the creation of the Internet Governance Forum (IGF). While the WSIS served as a bridge between the two sides, it also

[2] Paragraph 34 of the Tunis Agenda adopted a *broad* understanding in its "working definition" of Internet governance as: "(…) the development and application by governments, the private sector and civil society, in their respective roles, of shared principles, norms, rules, decision-making procedures, and programmes that shape the evolution and use of the Internet." See *Tunis Agenda for the Information Society,* Tunis, 18 November 2005 (WSIS-05/TUNIS/DOC/6[Rev. 1]-E).

clearly confirmed *par défaut* the authority of ICANN. The WSIS distinguished between the "day-to-day" operations of the Internet and the "international public policy issues pertaining to the Internet", situating only the latter within the purview of the "sovereign right of states"[3]. Moreover, it acknowledged, reaffirmed and consolidated multistakeholderism as a legitimizing principle for Internet governance within an international organization, and explicitly recognized and assigned "roles and responsibilities" to several kinds of actors or stakeholder categories. It established the IGF, which constitutes one of the main pillars of multistakeholderism in Internet governance in a broad sense (Doria in this volume; Malcolm 2008). It also strengthened the principle of multilateralism and called for the opening of an "enhanced cooperation process", an expression transplanted from European Union Law making reference to the coexistence of different rhythms and depths in institutional integration in different policy areas and thereby suggesting further intergovernmentalism[4].

Since then, there are debates on what multistakeholderism is exactly. The multistakeholder model has been identified with network governance and, in terms of regulatory theory, it has been conceptualized as a form of co-regulation (Marsden 2008; Marsden 2011; Kleinwächter 2001)[5]. What underlies such different approaches is the broad notion of involvement or inclusion of multiple stakeholders, i.e. of interested parties in the policy-making process. Minimal conceptions would limit such involvement to rather robust and inclusive participatory structures in essentially state-regulatory processes, but this conception is difficult to distinguish from participation *tout court*. A more ambitious conception defines it as "the coming together of different interest groups on an equal footing, to identify problems, define solutions and agree on roles and responsibilities for policy development, implementation, monitoring and evaluation" (Banks 2005, p. 85). The idea that stakeholders' involvement may go beyond mere participation and that non-state

---

3 This distinction between policy and technical governance functions is neither new nor unproblematic. At its best, it points out that a certain degree of consensus over the principles that must frame certain governance functions must be isolated from the broader political debate, excluding certain kinds of considerations.

4 Governments in the multistakeholder side have started interpreting the mandate for "enhanced cooperation" in a way that makes it extensive to all stakeholders, as a sort of intensification of the multistakeholder principle and not specifically of intergovernmental aspect. This seems to go, however, against the letter of the Tunis Agenda, which paragraph 69 states that "enhanced cooperation is needed to enable governments, on an equal footing, to carry their responsibilities in international public policy issues pertaining to the Internet" (Touré 2012, p. 14)

5 It has been conceptualized in the context of intergovernmental institutions as a neo-corporatist evolution of *tripartism* or *trilateralism,* historically developed by International Labor Organization and extended to other regimes and institutional forms within the UN, as well as in the UN Summits (McLaughlin and Pickard 2005).

actors may collectively assume regulatory functions within co-regulatory systems is what defines this more robust model of concerted policy-making.

At least discursively, the difference between these organizations and governance models has become more visible in the way in which they understand stakeholder involvement in the global Internet public policy making and, more specifically, in the way in which the contribution of governments should be institutionalized. This shows that, beyond the state, the regulatory debate on ICT and Internet governance more generally is framed, at least since the WSIS, in terms of governance in a narrow sense, i.e. *governance* as opposed to *government* (Rosenau & Czempiel 1992). The consensus on the need to redefine the respective roles and responsibilities of the actors involved in global ICT policy development, with respect to those they used to play in the traditional, essentially intergovernmental international telecommunications regulatory model, clearly situates the debate within the governance conceptual framework. This also reflects a widespread reluctance to centralize in any way the distributed institutional architecture that has so far characterized global ICT governance in general (Drake 2008).

The latest episodes of the ICANN-ITU dispute at the World Conference on International Telecommunications held in Dubai on December 2012, and ITU's Fifth World Telecommunication/ICT Policy Forum (WTPF-13) of May 2013 crystallized the debate between the two conceptions of global Internet governance. There is persistent disagreement on the weight the multilateral principle should be given within such model, i.e. on how to institutionalize the international public component of the co-regulatory or hybrid governance system[6].

[6] The 5th WTPF drew significant attention as the 2010 ITU Plenipotentiary Conference of Guadalajara had decided that it would address "Internet Protocol (IP)-based Networks" and it was held a few months after the WCIT-12. The WTPF debated a report of the ITU Secretary General which was based on the contributions of an Informal Expert Group (IEG) that included 6 opinions. The WTPF did approve the opinions by consensus. Two of them, opinions 5 and 6 are particularly relevant for the ITU-ICANN debate. A draft opinion 7, submitted by Brazil and not through the IEG-Secretary General report, was not approved. Opinion 6, on "Enhanced Cooperation Process", did not meet resistance and reaffirmed the need for enhanced cooperation to enable governments to develop international Internet-related public policy. Opinion 5, on "Supporting multi-stakeholderism in Internet governance" was somewhat more controversial. The United States, RIPE-NCC (Réseaux IP Européens Network Coordination Centre) and ISOC supported the opinion as it had been drafted in the Secretary General's report, while India, Brazil and Russia proposed to amend it to emphasize the need for coordination and cooperation amongst organizations. It is worth noting that, when Brazil proposed draft Opinion 7, on "The Role of Governments in the Multi-stakeholder Framework for Internet Governance" calling for international organizations and especially the ITU to assist developing countries in the fulfillment of their roles and responsibilities in international Internet-related public policy making, Russia explicitly called for international rules for the Internet, and the issue was deferred to other pertinent venues,

The consensus around the multistakeholder model seems to have consolidated, but the struggle and the public discourse on global Internet governance continue to unfold in the same terms (see also Chapter 6). The rejection of the new International Telecommunication Regulations can be interpreted as the result of the US strategy to avoid international control over ICANN and its governance functions. Still, more significantly, the failure to agree on new ITR means that the slow but constant erosion of the international telecommunication regime and its marginalization in a new world of global governance continues. As Drake recalls, ICANN is a departure from the old international regime that was best represented by the ITU[7]. But one must not forget that the ITU has been transformed as well by changes brought by globalization and technological advances.

2. The Origin of a Global Internet Governance—the Slow and Silent Surrender of the International Regime

The ITU is the oldest international organization and we can recall that the international regime it governs is itself the result of the merging of multiple telecommunication technology-specific regimes and international organizations. Yet, the merger or convergence of services and networks that is now occurring pushes the ITU in a peripheral position. The repositioning of the ITU within global ICT network governance is the result of structural economic and regulatory changes that took place between 1970 and 1997.

From a sector based on national telecommunication networks and services, the telecommunication sector has become a global multi-sector communications network. Traditional boundaries based on geographic national and sub-national systems interconnected at the ITU, as well as boundaries separating sectors that are now converging into one single integrated information and communications network, constituting the basis for the emergence of a global networked economy

amongst which the ITU Council Working Group on Internet Related Public Policy Issues was mentioned.

7 Drake says of ICANN that: "(…) it has operated under contracts, memoranda of understanding, and now a joint project agreement with the US Department of Commerce. ICANN represents a complete departure from the tradition of intergovernmental, sovereignty-based governance that preceded it, and its contested performance of key functions such as the governance of the domain name system (DNS) and other core resources in the service of an amorphously defined transnational 'Internet community' and other stakeholders has been a constant source of friction with many governments, most notably in the developing world" (2008, pp. 25–26).

and society[8]. This transformation was the result of a technological revolution culminating in the emergence of the Internet, accompanied by significant changes in ideas pertaining to telecommunication regulations which allowed for competition and trade to unfold (or gain momentum) in new networks and services. The institutional basis onto which new networks and services could be developed came to be in direct contradiction with the international regime and national regulatory approaches that characterized the most part of the 19th and 20th centuries. The main difference relates to competition, now one of the core principles guiding the organization of the global electronic communication sector, while the core organizational principle of the telecommunication regime was the implicit consensus on monopoly provision of telecommunications services.

Our historical approach is based on the following overlapping chronology: 115 years of a stable international regime (European model—hegemony), followed by 30 years of erosion (1970–97), characterized by the strategic diffusion of institutional change by the US. From 1995 onwards, re-regulation takes central stage: markets need institutions and rules to function and to provide public goods, thus this period involves a transatlantic dialogue/clash as well as a debate over regulation and over the division of labour between the diverse sites of governance involved in global internet policy.

2.1. The Old Compromise—Network of National Monopolistic Networks and... no Competition

What is called "telecommunication" is the continuing advancement of communicative technology[9]. From the beginning, there were very complex debates on the economic, social and political organization of information flows and communication devices. Yet, telecommunication has traditionally been considered to be a natural monopoly, which called for regulation of private monopolies or direct public ownership, as well as regulation of service providers and vertically-integrated equipment makers. There was also a clear preference expressed towards the sepa-

[8] The economic importance of global networks and services is enormous. Its strategic importance for the competitiveness of other sectors is well recognized. This sector also plays a crucial role in shaping new social and political relations based on information, communication and knowledge networks and services and in the development key infrastructure elements of economic strategies of states and firms.

[9] Telegraphy made its modern day political appearance in 1792 when an optical telegraphy network helped Napoleon to gain a strategic advantage. The advent of electric telegraph, then radiotelegraph and eventually the telephone changed the rate of messaging, the speed with which messages arrived at destination, and the range of such messages, which completely changed international relations.

ration of content industries, on the one hand, and networks operators and service providers, on the other. Interdependence of national telecommunication systems was the subject of intense and elaborate interstate negotiations on joint provisions of services, and interconnection schemes and standards, which, notably, provided for joint service provisions. Strong regulation was also put in place to build sector barriers between this sector and others, which now form the ICT sectors. In the end, it led to the organization of an international network of national networks of strongly regulated national telecommunication monopolies, as shown in Figure 1 below.

Figure 1:
International network of national monopolistic networks (1865–1970)

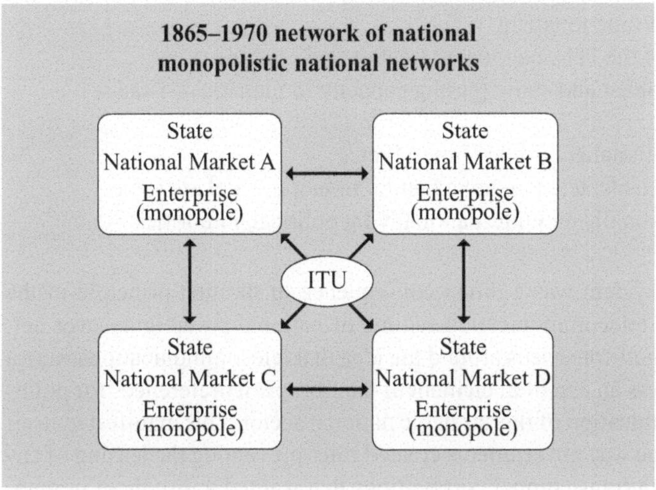

For the best part of its 148 years of operation, the ITU succeeded in the monumental task of maintaining participating members under an international telecommunication regime. This "regime", like all regimes, was based on shared broad principles. It had the dual purpose of growth and protection of national telecommunication system, and was never in the business of global public policy-making. Drake summarizes the principles as follows: national sovereignty, network interconnection and joint service provisioning (2008, p. 124). The ITU was created on the basis of the internationalization processes of bilateral treaties signed by European governments that had set up ministries (or agencies) purporting to be in charge of developing Posts, Telegraphs, and Telephones (PTT) policies and controlling national public monopolies (or regulated monopolies in some countries such as the US) that provided domestic telecommunications. International prices were fixed, compensation schemes were developed and a strict *no competition policy* was adopted. As such, it was a multi-level governance scheme that preserved simple interdependence of national monopolistic systems and networks. The main characteristics of this well ordered international regime are listed in Figure 2 below.

Figure 2: Characteristics of the international regime

Main Characteristics

- European model (hegemony)
- Public network under political control of the state (or... independent regulation of private monopoly)
- Sovereignty (managing international interdependence)
- No free trade, no competition
- Solidarity and functionalism
- Central role of the ITU, negotiated treaties and consensus
- Efficiency: Robust and static (strong capacity to manage resistance and changes)
- Tension: exeptionalism of the United States
- Implicit consensus: telecom are a natural monopoly and are to be organized nationally and internationally by political authorities

This monopolistic system was a direct consequence of the first principle of the ITU's international telecommunication regime of national sovereignty over networks. Yet, the implicit consensus around the idea that telecommunications were a natural monopoly was an essential element of the European preferences for political control and organization of this strategic national sector. This manifested itself most forcefully in the way governments created rules preventing the leasing of circuits for the growing transnational corporations that wanted to use them in innovative ways and/or at lower costs. As we mentioned, this principle flowed through to the two other constitutive principles of the regime: inter-national network interconnection, and inter-network joint service provisioning (services jointly provided would see fixed revenues shared between the two carriers involved).

Even though US policy preferences for private monopolies brought in a regime of *exceptionnalisme* (since private monopolies were given more recognition as part of the deal to bring the US into the ITU), European preferences largely dominated. "Special arrangements" did not really shake the regime. AT&T's approach to joint service provisioning—supported by the "domestic ITU" of the US (the Federal Communications Commission)—directly challenged the old order. It adopted its own rates and accounting models, and sought to negotiate bilateral "special arrangements". There were also challenges emerging from the growing pressures from economic globalization, more precisely the integration of production, financial, trading and distribution through international firms and transnational corporate networks. Yet, the international regime was robust, in spite of the compromises and accommodations made for the US within the ITU and despite transnational private pressures. Once the debate on the monopolistic organization of the system emerged, the erosion of the system started. This process began with the issues surrounding innovative equipment and services in relation to the control of domestic and international telecommunication by AT&T and the Bell system.

2.2. Erosion of the International Regime

In the first phase of institutional changes, from the 1970s until the end of the 1990s, competition was introduced through deregulation, privatization and liberalization, removing existing political and legal obstacles to market access in the telecommunications sector. There was, first of all, the distinction between old (voice) and new (data processing and other "value-added") services. This distinction was important as most new services were evolving outside the scope of monopolistic telecommunications market regulations, i.e. in a competition-based market environment. This created a pressure that ultimately led to the liberalization of all services and the death of the monopolistic network and public services. It was not only a question of integrating new technology into the regime, but also a challenging political move as this specific technological change came with new governance models bridging across nations and sovereignties and across old industrial sector divides.

As computerization met the growth of transnational activities in the 1980s and internet-working developed computer-to-computer or host-to-host communication, the global telecommunication backbone could no longer be based solely on interconnected national systems. "In-house" communication possibilities, such as the ones which would come to define, airlines and financial systems, offered advantaged that rendered obsolete the conception of telecommunication as a public utility provided on national monopolist terms. Telecommunication was to become, in the emerging ubiquitous computing era, more and more a matter of private efficiency-enhancing necessity. Transnational corporations (TNC) could not be contented with occasional, ultra-regulated, and expensive "leased circuits". While pressure from private multilateral associations was nothing new, the arrangements constituting the old order—standardization at gateway points, joint accounting and provisioning schemes—could not possibly be maintained. The regulation which had been acceptable in a certain technological age simply could not match the emerging one. New commercial routes were in the making. Figure 3 below illustrates their complexity.

Figure 3: New commercial routes

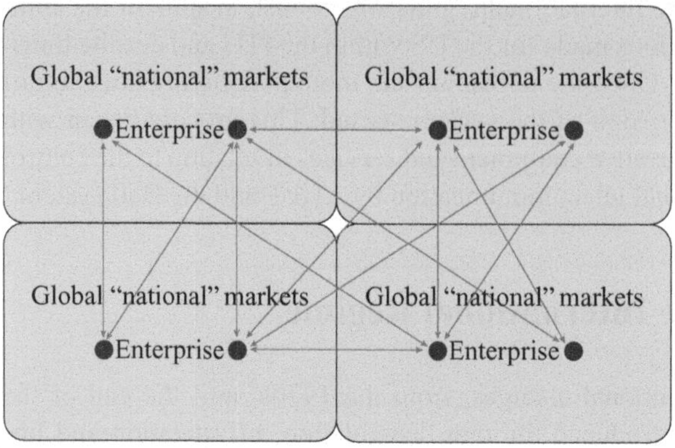

In order to deal with this new complex interdependence between actors in a global issue area, the ITU tried to standardize its way out of the problem. ITU's standard setting processes are anticipatory in type and, in contrast to the Internet Engineering Task Force (IETF) scheme, they can lead to technical closure. Facing private sector outcries[10], it developed the Integrated Services Digital Network (ISDN) throughout the 1970s and 1980s but his politically charged standard did not do the trick[11]. On the other hand, the US strategy of unilaterally offsetting the traditional accounting scheme and of arguing that "joint service" was trade, and thus fell under the General Agreement on Tariffs and Trade/WTO governance scheme with its very different underlying principles, was a major catalyst of the liberalization thrust of international telecommunications markets. In 1997, the WTO ABT signified the generalized acceptance of competition at the global level. This was not enough to severe the old regime's authority-based grip on the telecommunications sector. So much concentration required the loosening up of traditional interpretations of sovereignty over networks. The Butler Draft that mediated the conflicting positions at the World Administrative Telegraph and Telephone Conference of 1998 (WATTC-88) and on which the new International Telecommunications Regulations treaty was based, did not modify the sovereignty principle over networks: states could embrace either open or regulated markets (Drake 2000, pp. 148–150). Seemingly of the opinion that this globalizing outcome was merely the result of

---

10 Drake (2000, p. 138) characterizes the CCITT standardization processes as being slow, consensual (amongst the member-states), and power-based. It can be added that this last characteristic determined the type of standard enacted: sometimes reactive, such that a standard emerged in a "bottom-up" manner, or anticipatory, such that a standard emerged in a "top-down" fashion.

11 ISDN was meant as a convergence platform for leased circuit servicing, but when it was rolled out 20 years later, it was only deployed like a service among many others.

maturing services leaving at last the parental home, the ITU attempted to compensate its loss of authority by enhancing its scope.

When simple interdependence collapsed, the ITU had to adapt to three challenges. First, rapid technological advances were requiring that it produced and supervised a growing set of norms and standards. Second, it had to contend with an increase in the size and diversity of its members, learning to manage new strategic-relational activities such as threats of withdrawal and the enlargement in the number of sharing partners of limited resources. Third, it also had to contend with the increasing importance of private sector participation. This is where regime theory, applied to the ITU—at least its rationalist branch, fails. As soon as complex interdependences kicked in, the regime started to "evolve" in ways that are reminiscent of a slow but steady decline—erosion. It already had some trouble coping with overwhelming shared principles and symmetry of interests among its member-states in the cartel-like regime period and managed to keep its authority intact only at a loss of practical ability to steer course, but when the subject matter of the issue-area complexified, the ITU showed sign of deliquescence. It is now facing a world of global governance.

3. Global Governance and the Internet

The ITU managed the relations between states and, being resistant to technological innovations, engaged in "exceptional" relations with the United States and transnational private actors, until that system was abandoned. The system was international in the sense that it managed the interdependency and interoperability of national systems aimed at providing public services. It could not allow for global private and innovative networks to develop without undermining the regime itself. The decision to allow the opening up of telecommunications markets, media content and the computer sector would, in the long run, have significant impacts on the ITU.

In the 1980s, the United States effectively sought to transform the ITU. Encountering strong resistance, it adopted a strategy of forum shifting (Braithwaite and Drahos 2000), which proved fruitful. The US managed to export changes and induce institutional adjustments of the ITU in implementing a trade agenda, after intensifying the cycle of economic, political and legal reforms. Eventually, this agenda led to the WTO in 1997, through multiple trade agreements, primarily in North America, contradicting the letter and spirit of the ITU regime. Indeed, in the 1980s, the United States had initially tried to influence the ITU, but, facing resistance, it had opted instead for a strategy using trade agreements. They were successful with small-scale agreements such as NAFTA, and then they turned to the WTO, where they gained acceptance of the principle of liberalization of services in the Agreement on Basic Telecommunications in 1997. As suggested by Drake (2004), since multilateral rules would be needed in the new global economy, these rules would be provided by the WTO, other trade-related institutions and a variety of groups representing private actors.

The ITU was forced to recognize there was now a new world in motion—that of competition and trade in telecommunications. Most of its trading partners gradually aligned with US global interests. National control over telecommunications was increasingly difficult as innovations multiplied and competed with "old" services and networks. A new trade diplomacy was gradually established, and its results involved the dropping of the international regime based on the ITU in favour of the global governance of an information-based society characterized by the multiple uncoordinated actions of a wide range of international organizations and forums. Indeed, global networks had to be built and adapted to the realities of integration processes in the era of globalization. It was not enough to regulate national industries and to manage international interdependencies; rather, it was necessary to find rules and forms of regulation adapted to globalization. There was convergence of information, media, and telecommunications, but there was still something was missing, which would spur the process of creative destruction in the economic, socio-political and institutional sense: the Internet. It came with new rules of the game, notably in relation to naming and numbering. Created in the United States, ICANN emerged and started to be the focus of intense rivalry on the part of several players and organizations, notably the ITU, that wanted to maintain or expand their influence[12].

[12] Drezner (2004) made a compelling argument that states were able to find their way in impacting "governance arrangements" more than, say, NGOs, private sector initiatives and new networking forms of governance involving complex alliances. His point is that states' interests were best served by the eventual domination of TCP/IP. Yet, the US and many other governments were fully committed to OSI, and had already directed its agencies to equip with OSI-compliant products. The fact that US DoD (Department of Defense) stuck with TCP/IP on its isolated MILNET can hardly be ascribed an important causal role in TCP/IP's success. The US influence over ICANN might be real but the credibility and legitimacy of ICANN are based on its global and transnational outreach supported by influential global players and a very diverse amalgam of social and community forces. This does not mean that there is no convergence of interests between the US and global economic and social forces, but it does limit the degree of autonomy and authority the US can exert over information and communication networks. The impetus of reform was on the "innovators" (Rasmussen 2007). Drezner was correct in showing that states could get their way more often than so-called "self-regulated" private-led scheme or new form of polycentric governance scheme, but this does not invalidate insights pertaining to evolution of *authority* in globalization studies.

To sum up, the ITU faced three shifts: the shift from politics to economics (monopoly under strong public regulation); the shift from national to global networks; and the shift from an international regime it dominated to a form of global governance slipping out of its control. The literature devoted to these transformations is made up of three branches concerned with: 1) the displacement of authority to the private sector; 2) the impact of globalization on the roles of national and international organizations; and 3) the competition between organizations and diverging institutional trajectories[13]. The world was clearly on a new trajectory.

Table 1 below contrasts two types of institutional trajectories: liberal internationalism and global governance. With regard to global, or transnational governance, this means a plurality of sites of governance and regulation. It thus involves a constellation of institutions, mechanisms, and relationships, both formal and informal, between states, markets, individuals and organizations with differing, often contradictory objectives. Global governance is directly linked to globalization and to its impact on the political role of the private sector. The concept refers to "governance without government" (Rosenau and Czempiel 1992; see also the discussion in Chapter 1 of this volume). The upshot is a new way of thinking about institutional trajectories. In the current situation, some see a competition between two worlds, the end of the Westphalian system and its replacement by a lex mercatoria, a sort of " neo-medievalism " characterized by a plurality of actors, decentralized global networks and voluntary standards. Others see it as a process of transformation of international relations and organizations—including Slaughter (2011), who suggests the emergence of a transgovernmentalism consisting of networking organizations.

[13] A first part of the literature focuses on the shift of authority within the global economy, especially the transfer of authority from the public sphere to the private sphere. Strange (1996) advanced the idea that the telecommunications sector offers an extreme example of the process through which authority has shifted massively from state governments to corporate management. Some authors, in particular Cutler, Haufler and Porter (1999), analyze the "privatization" of governance related to the rise of private enterprises, their ability to exercise market power and the forms of cooperation they adopt between them. The second part, addressing the impacts of these shifts on national and international public authorities, contrasts two ideas: on one hand, the withdrawal of the state and declining relevance of international organizations, and on the other, a redefining of policies and national regulatory frameworks in a context of re-regulation (Levi-Faur 2002). This second idea seems more accurate, because national and international public authorities do not disappear, but rather articulate their policies and actions differently, depending on the needs of globalization for stabilizing interventions. A third part of the literature deals with the competition between organizations. There is now a number of international organizations, including the WTO, which fall within the scope of the ITU and of several new private organizations whose roles overlap with its general mandate. In short, the ITU has not only been forced to change, but must also keep its place in a universe of institutional competition.

Table 3: From the international regime to global governance

International Regime	Global governance
– Centrality of state – Public/politics prevails over private/ economic – Order centred on ITU – Hierarchical decisions and centralization of power – Internationalism, interdependence – Consensus for orderly/organized markets – "Hard" (national) law, binding rules – Search for coherence between institutions and regulation – Multilateralism – Contractual template	– Plurality of actors – Private/economic prevails over public/ politics – Many sites of governance – Decentralization of sources of authority, networks – Transnationalism/globalism; – Consensus for globalized competition – Soft power/soft rules – Competition between institutions and regulations – Mix of multilateralism, regionalism, bilateralism and nationalism – Partnership template

Beyond the binary opposition of the old and new, sites of governance are emerging and developing in the context of three competing trajectories amongst which, in the case of digital capitalism, the Global-Market (G-M) constellation is dominant so far. We introduce a Penrose triangle[14] to build an Impossibility triangle for the analysis of institutional trajectories and their interactions. We distinguish (in Table 2) between three different constellations of regulatory trajectories of instruments: international initiatives (the market-sovereignty constellation); supranational initiatives (the global-sovereignty constellation); and global private initiatives (the market-global constellation). The most favoured trajectories in the 1980s (by most states and private actors) were those preserving market freedoms and the sovereignty of states. This is represented in the first column. In this constellation, we acknowledge the traditionally central role of the "new" ITU. Within the same constellation, the WTO and those trade agreements that incorporate dispute settlement mechanisms provide a way to resolve conflicts and non-compliance. Yet, they provide no direct and effective global rules for enterprises; this is characteristic of the G-M constellation, which, to this day, lacks coherence, legitimacy and effectiveness. In this constellation we situate ICANN. In the G-S (Global Sovereignty) constellation we have the EU, as an ideal type, representing a tentative effort towards the development of a supranational regulator.

[14] A *Penrose* triangle is an impossible object as conceived by Roger *Penrose*.

Table 4:
Constellations of regulatory instruments in global ICT/IS governance

	M-S Constellation (Market-sovereignty)	***G-S Constellation (Global-sovereignty)***	***G-M Constellation (Global-market)***
Instruments Examples	ITU (new), WTO and bilateral, regional trade agreements, WIPO…	ITU (old) EU Telecommunications regulations	ICANN
Objectives	Market autonomy, sovereignty of states *Loss: Difficult to set rules or institutions at the global level above markets or states*	Global rules or institutions above markets or states, sovereignty of states *Loss: Autonomy of markets and liberty of private actors*	Autonomy of markets, Global rules or institutions above markets or states, *Loss: Sovereignty of states*
Enforcement	Based on the hypothesis of efficiency of national laws and international cooperation Surveillance and monitoring of practices and conduct Requires cooperation of private actors	Hierarchical system based on the enforcement of supranational law by supranational institutions	Self-regulation, private systems of rules, Cooperation or negotiation involving private actors and multiple stakeholders
Limits	Alliance of interests of states and firms driving the system towards more market autonomy (M)	States must have a common approach towards market regulation	Variations of codes of conduct, problems of monitoring and enforcement, contestable legitimacy and efficiency

The impossible triangle implies a dynamic interplay that can actually explain institutional shifts. For example, both the ITU and ICANN are pulled towards competing trajectories. The ITU is engaged in a constant discussion of its inclusiveness, in particular regarding civil society organizations, as exemplified by the debate on the Council Working Group on International Internet-related Public Policy Issues (CWG-Internet). ICANN, for its part, has established a joint Board-Governmental Advisory Committee Recommendation Implementation (BGRI) Working Group to implement several recommendations to enhance GAC's position within ICANN (Touré 2012, p. 37). The ITU has embraced multistakeholderism, not only for global Internet and ICT governance, which its Plenipotentiary Conference has explicitly recognized in several resolutions, but also for the organization of the new institutional structures and policy-making techniques it has adopted since the 1990s—including the decision to hold World Telecommunications Policy Forums dating back to the 1994 Plenipotentiary Conference— which allowed it to present itself as a form of multistakeholder organization, even prior to the WSIS.

Both the ITU and ICANN must find ways to deal with the strong competition and dynamic interplay within the dynamics of this triangle. It is reasonable to suggest that the ITU has moved from one side of the triangle (G-S) to another (M-S, Market-Sovereignty) as trade in services at the WTO impacted on the international regime (Figure 4). It would be less reasonable to suggest that ICANN has been successfully pushed to the M-S side of the triangle. Therefore, we can reconstruct the institutional evolution of the ITU as seeking a redefinition of its role in a world of global governance rather than a quest for ways to reassert the kind of authority it once enjoyed. The world might still be fragmented, but it has certainly moved towards transnational and global networks.

Figure 4: The Impossible Triangle

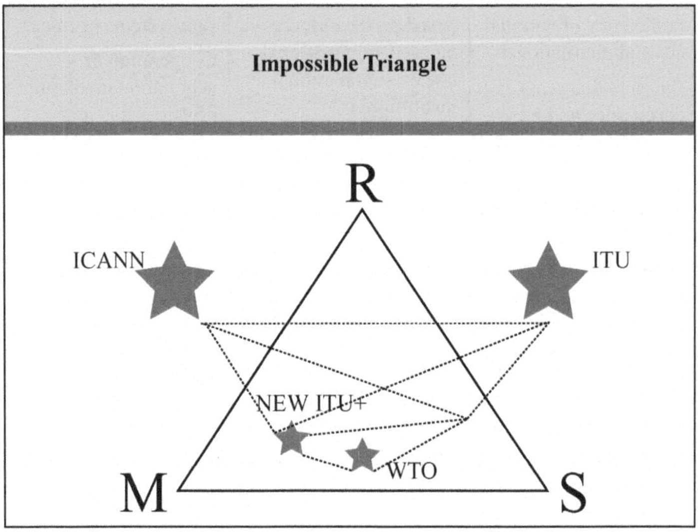

4. Conclusion

Old and new, from actors to institutions, are challenged and reified in a dynamic interplay of institutional and market reordering that involves forms of cooperation as well as new forms of rivalry. The main conclusion of this chapter is that the historical transformation of the sector brings new challenges in understanding the dynamics of global regulation, and that one of the most important issues will be to find new arbitrages and compromises between different institutional trajectories. Internet and ICT governance are likely to remain fragmented. The first step to resolve the main controversies is to unlock their significance, as they point at a more important question today: how to respond to new governance challenges inherent to the structural changes caused by globalization and technological changes? The ITU has shown, throughout history, a very strong capacity to evolve and ICANN is surely there to stay. More important than the rivalry between ICANN and the ITU is to provide answers to the following question: What kind of ICT network regulation can effectively and coherently stand above markets and states? Linkages of rival trajectories might provide interesting solutions for global and coherent collective action. The real challenge is to understand the comparative advantages of the various governing bodies that are taking form and the nature of Internet infrastructures and services that will play a crucial role in shaping the future.

Acknowledgements

This chapter was produced with the funding provided by the Fonds de recherche du Québec société et culture (FQRSC) for the project "Transnational Regulation of the Information Society: Institutional Emergence, Power, Authority". Thanks to Olivier Dagenais and Thomas Scorticuti for research assistance.

Anne-Claire Jamart

Chapter 3
Internet Freedom and the Constitutionalization of Internet Governance

The head of the International Telecommunications Union (ITU), the United Nations agency in charge of making international telecommunications possible, said in Dubai in December last year, in the midst of an international battle between the pro- and the anti-ITR treaty, that such treaty was not against "Internet freedom" (Khalil 2012). By these simple words, Hamadoun Touré has confirmed the existence of the notion of Internet freedom and that Internet freedom was a legitimate concern of international Internet policy-making. If Internet freedom is a legitimate topic of international Internet policy-making, it is of utmost importance to understanding what it is. Some might tell you that Google's monopoly over the search market is a threat to Internet freedom, or that Internet freedom requires that any and all government regulations of the Internet be abandoned, or that intergovernmental control of Internet governance is a violation of Internet freedom. Others will tell you that Internet freedom amounts to online freedom of speech or that trade agreements can serve Internet freedom. What Internet freedom is will depend on who you are asking. So what is really Internet freedom?

In this chapter, I am offering an answer to this question. I am presenting an integrated analysis of recent events in which Internet freedom has been cast a lead role. Internet freedom generally stands for the idea that the Internet should be free. Internet freedom has been evolving from a rather unsubstantiated notion into a global meta-norm of reference in all Internet-related matters. This recent development must be read in conjunction with the 2011 wave of Internet principles. By Internet principles, I mean the various sets of guidelines for the governance of the Internet that were discussed and, but for two, adopted over the course of a few busy months by several governments, sometimes within the framework of an international organization (see chart). Together, the Internet principles and Internet freedom signal the constitutionalization of international Internet governance.

By constitutionalization, I mean the process by which a constitution is being introduced in a legal order, whether domestic, or as in the case at hand, international. Global constitutionalism embraces the idea that a constitution should govern our globalized world, keeping in mind that the form and substance of such a global constitution may have little to do with that of domestic constitutions. There is a continuum of global constitutionalism visions ranging from support for a world government that would resemble domestic governments (Fassbender 1998) to accounts of the emergence of global civil constitutions (Teubner 2004).

Instead of detailing each flavour of global constitutionalism, I rely on Christine Schwöbel's characterization of global constitutionalism as "not a comprehensive concept but rather an amalgamation of ideas (key themes), with some thinkers stressing certain features and some thinkers stressing other features of what they believe would be constitutive of a global constitution" (Schwöbel 2009 p. 51). These five key themes are "the limitation of power, the institutionalization of power, social idealism (meaning an idea for the future that is based on societal values), the standard-setting capacity of constitutions in the sense of a systematization of law, and the recognition of individuals rights" (Schwöbel 2009, p. 4). They provide useful parameters for evaluating the meaning and significance of Internet freedom and the Internet principles.

I will begin with an overview of the concerns that the constitutionalization of Internet governance seems to respond to. I will then describe the two facets of this process, focusing first on the Internet principles before turning to Internet freedom. I will conclude with an analysis of the type of global constitutionalism that the Internet principles and Internet freedom are embracing, underlying the issues that may hamper the flourishing of Internet freedom.

1. A Response to Political and Economic Challenges

The conjunction of the Internet principles and the emergence of Internet freedom at the end of the 2000s were not fortuitous. Since the Declaration of Independence of Cyberspace (Barlow 1996), there have been only a few sporadic attempts at establishing a framework for the conduct of Internet governance. The Tunis Agenda drafted during the second phase of the World Summit on the Information Society (WSIS) in 2005 only offered broad and unsubstantiated goals for the international community to achieve. Two civil society networks drafted their own charter of rights (Association for Progressive Communication 2006 and Internet Rights and Principles Coalition 2009) but such initiatives remained isolated. In such circumstances, a sudden avalanche of principles (7 drafts of which 4 were adopted from April to September 2011) together with high profile speeches on Internet freedom could not go unnoticed. So why the recent hyperactivity? A conjunction of political and economic factors is the likely explanation.

1.1. The Twitter Revolutions and the Arab Spring

The Twitter Revolutions, as have been renamed the popular protests in Moldova in April 2009 (Barry 2009) and in Iran (Cohen 2009), as well as the Arab Spring have certainly contributed to raise the profile of Internet freedom and place it on the political agenda of many governments. Recall the declarations that the Egyptian revolution had started on Facebook (Ghonim 2011) or even the Internet shutdown, which suggested that the Mubarak regime did consider the Internet as a serious nuisance. The failures and successes of these movements, which have been widely reported worldwide, have emphasized that the Internet can be a useful tool in social and political change. Although some have criticized the tendency to overemphasize the role of the Internet, these events were a powerful reminder of what the Internet could achieve.

1.2. The Boom of the Internet Economy in Times of Financial Crisis

In a 2011 report, the consulting firm McKinsey concluded that the Internet economy contributes on average 3.4% of the gross domestic product of the members of the Group of 8 (G8), as well as Brazil, China, and India, South Korea, and Sweden. More significantly, the report showed that the share of GDP contributed by the Internet is increasing quickly, with the Internet "account[ing] for 21 percent of GDP growth over the last five years among the developed countries [McKinsey] studied, a sharp acceleration from the 10 percent contribution over 15 years" (McKinsey 2011). The study also underlined that this economic value goes for the most part to traditional sectors, as opposed to the technology sector, showing that the economy in its entirety is benefiting from the Internet economy. The growing importance of the Internet industry has become clear to many governments, especially in a period of depressed economy. Ensuring the continuing growth of the Internet economy has become an imperative and we have been witnessing a push at the World Trade Organization (Black 2011) towards the recognition of Internet freedom, including the freedom to do business across borders, as a trade issue.

1.3. Mounting Support for a UN Involvement in Internet Governance

The UN takeover claim first appeared in 2005 when the US was fending off the European Union's attempt to shift oversight of ICANN, the entity in charge of the domain name system, from the US government to a UN body. As Milton Mueller explained, the European initiative was described by its opponents as a UN takeover of the Internet (2010, p. 75). The feud finally ended with the US keeping its oversight of ICANN but agreeing to open up discussions on policy to all governments.

The debate was on hold until 2011, when Russia, China, Tajikistan and Uzbekistan (RCTU) on the one hand, and India, Brazil and South Africa (IBSA) on the other hand, started voicing their support for an intergovernmental control of Internet governance. Though both their proposals see intergovernmental oversight as the solution to their concerns, they are significantly different in tone and motives. The IBSA proposal is offered in response to a report prepared by the UN Secretary-General on enhanced cooperation among governments on Internet-related policy issues (UN Secretary-General 2011). Its starting point is that many critical Internet-related issues are not adequately addressed because of a lack of a global policy-making mechanism that would be "open, democratic, inclusive and participatory manner, with the participation of all stakeholders" (India 2011). The creation of a UN Committee for Internet-Related Policies (CIRP) would fill this void (IBSA 2011). Though the proposal does not tell which issues are not adequately addressed, it seems that oversight of ICANN is still one of the chief concerns (see also the discussion in Chapter 2 of this volume). What is apparent is that India, Brazil and South Africa are yearning to play a role in Internet governance. They feel left out and relying on the enhanced cooperation clause in the Tunis Agenda, which provides for the ability of "governments, on an equal footing, to carry out their roles and responsibilities, in international public policy issues pertaining to the Internet" (WSIS 2005), gives them the support they need. CIRP's members would be states only, though other Internet stakeholders would be able to give advice via advisory bodies (IBSA 2011). The negotiation of treaties on Internet policy would be a big part of the CIRP's tasks (IBSA 2011).

On the contrary, the RCTU's main concern is "information security", understood as states' right to protect their "information space and critical information infrastructure" (RCTU 2011) This is an assertion of states' sovereignty over the Internet (for an overview of China's stance on global Internet governance, see Negro in this volume). The RCTU proposal, an International Code of Conduct for Information Security (Code), starts by demanding compliance with the UN Charter as well as "universally recognized norms governing international relations, which enshrine, inter alia, respect for the sovereignty, territorial integrity and political independence of all states" (RCTU 2011). The commitment to fundamental rights and freedoms only comes later. In addition to direct attacks, the possibility of foreign interference in internal affairs is also on RCTU's radar. In particular, the Code provides that no country should use their "resources, critical infrastructures, core technologies and other advantages, to undermine the right of the countries, which accepted this Code of Conduct, to independent control of ICTs, or to threaten other countries' political, economic and social security" (RCTU 2011). This provision would have arguably prevented the US from requesting Twitter to postpone a maintenance shutdown of the website so as to keep it open for anti-Ahmadinejad protesters in Iran just a few days after the Iranian presidential elections in 2009 (Landler and Stelter 2009). The Code also proposes to assist in the creation of a "multilateral, transparent and democratic international management of the Internet" without giving more details as to how such mechanism would look like (RCTU 2011).

Neither the IBSA nor the RCTU proposals rallied enough supporters and both were put aside. But once again the ITU summit in Dubai in December 2012 saw the return of the UN takeover claim. The Dubai Summit was organized by the UN agency in charge of international telecommunications, the old International Telecommunications Union, with a view to update the 1988 International Telecommunication Regulations (ITRs), a treaty that regulates cross-border telecommunications broadly defined. There was disagreement among member states on whether the negotiations, which were intergovernmental in nature, should cover the Internet or not. Some proposals were clearly aimed at the Internet, like ETNO's, the European telecom operators' association, controversial proposal for including a 'sending party network pays' principle in the ITRs, or Russia's bid for an ITU oversight of ICANN (Russia 2011), while other proposals were more ambiguous and resulted in heated debates on interpretation. In the end, the revised ITRs, which were signed by only 89 out of the 144 members, do not mention the word Internet though it is conceivable that some provisions could affect it (see also Chapter 5 in this volume).

These initiatives have been looked at unfavorably, especially by the United States. The concern seems to be that an international organization with a quasi-universal membership like the United Nations will generate agreements ab minima, on the basis of the lowest common denominator. Any oversight of Internet governance by the UN, and more generally by any intergovernmental body, would necessarily result in increased control and decreased freedom of the Internet and Internet users. As Assistant Secretary Posner declared, reacting to the idea of the United Nations getting involved in Internet regulation or management:

> "We have, I think, a range of anxieties about throwing this issue and many others into the United Nations. We believe in the United Nations; it has a lot of important roles to play. But we have great trepidation that if this became a UN-sponsored initiative, all of the most—all of the governments that have the greatest interest in regulating and controlling content and protecting against dissident speech in their own countries would be very loud voices. So I think we're looking for alternatives that provide some form of

governance but in a broader sense, without the race to the bottom" (Posner 2011).

The challenges and issues I have described in this section called for answers, which came in the form of the Internet principles and the emergence of Internet freedom. I shall first turn to the Internet principles.

2. More Than a Hype, Less Than a Success

Wolfgang Kleinwächter coined the phrase "Internet principle hype" to describe those busy months of 2011 when the Internet principles were being negotiated (2011a). The negative connotation of the term "hype", which suggests exaggeration and excessiveness, is not entirely justified. The dramatic increase in the number of such instruments can lead to confusion, especially when governments become signatories of declarations that are not always easily reconcilable with one another. The multitude of principles, with governments often signing several of them, also creates the risk of cherry-picking. This may give the impression that there is no willingness to commit, maybe just a network effect along the superficial lines of "if you do it, I'll do it too".

But more importantly, these principles embody a shared desire in their signatories to establish a framework for Internet governance, some common rules on what can and cannot be done to the Internet and its users. They are meant to be (at least partially) the answer to the concerns I identified in the previous section, usually relying on a mix of substantive and procedural principles. Though the Internet principles are often talked about as a group, they are not homogenous. We can distinguish two waves of Internet principles.

2.1. The First Wave

The first wave consists in the various instruments adopted by a group of Western democracies in 2011, in the framework of international structures like the OECD, the Council of Europe or the European Union. These instruments share a lot of common features. Substantively, the principles usually profess a commitment to fundamental rights and freedoms, in particular freedom of speech. Procedurally, these principles support multistakeholderism as a mode of adopting policies and making decisions. Since the World Summit on the Information Society, multistakeholderism has generally been understood to require the involvement of civil society, the private sector and governments "in their respective role" (WSIS 2005).

However, this definition, which derives from the well-known international relations definition of a regime, fails to specify what the stakeholders' respective roles are and we cannot assume that the traditional pattern centered around states holds any validity, especially in the Internet field. The Internet principles fail to remedy this deficiency, making multistakeholderism hard to implement in practice.

Kleinwächter underlined that the Internet principles constituted soft law, which should not be a reason to discount their importance (Kleinwächter 2011a). As Abbott and Snidal explained, soft law does in some circumstances present advantages over harder forms of law (Abbott and Snidal 2000). For instance, agreements are easier to reach and less costly to negotiate. In the case of the Internet, those advantages are clear. As I mentioned above, the exact role of each of Internet's identified stakeholders is undetermined but multistakeholderism makes it clear that governments shall not be the only participants. Soft law instruments thus make it possible for civil society and the private sector to get involved, though their participation on an equal footing with governments, which civil society seems to be asking for, has not yet been secured. The negotiation of the OECD Principles is a case in point. Despite being involved in the negotiations from the beginning, the Civil Society Information Society Advisory Council to the OECD (CSISAC) ultimately refused to sign the declaration and claimed that governments had imposed their point of view. It is interesting to note at this point that no organization has ever clearly positively articulated how multistakeholderism should be implemented (as Doria explains in Chapter 6). ICANN or IETF may represent the "ideal" scenario of exemplary collaboration between stakeholders but civil society's expectations for instance are not clearly set out.

2.2. The Second Wave

The second wave (which had not yet happened when Kleinwächter introduced the "Internet principle hype" phrase) consists of two widely different proposals, the IBSA and RCTU initiatives I mentioned in the section 1.

The RCTU's International Code of Conduct for Information Security did not come out of the blue but has a long history. It all began when Russia first put the topic of information security on the agenda of the UN in 1999 (UN General Assembly 1999). Russia has since raised the issue of cyber disarmament every year at the UN, without much result so far. Russia's ideas were far more successful within the Shanghai Cooperation Organization, an organization founded in 2001 and counting Russia, China, Kazakhstan, Kyrgyztan, Tajikistan and Uzbekistan as members. In 2009, they adopted a Cooperation Agreement in the field of international information security based on Russia's ideas (Shanghai Cooperation

Organization 2009). Threats to security are defined very broadly and encompass direct and indirect acts of aggression to a country's political, economic, social, spiritual and cultural integrity. Included in the list of threats are abuses of a dominant position, defined as more developed states willfully maintaining or even increasing the digital divide, preventing participation in international information technology cooperation, or controlling the market for information technologies. They also cover the "dissemination of information harmful to the socio-political and socio-economic systems, spiritual, moral and cultural environment of other states", even if it merely "distorts the perception of the political system, social order, domestic and foreign policy, important political and social processes in the state, spiritual, moral and cultural values of its population" (Shanghaï Cooperation Organization 2009).

The Code has the same goals and conveys the same ideas as the Cooperation Agreement, albeit slightly less explicitly. The dissemination of information that "undermines other countries' political, economic and social stability, as well as their spiritual and cultural environment" must be curbed and states are prohibited from "using their resources, critical infrastructures, core technologies and other advantages to undermine the right of the countries to independent control of ICTs" (RCTU 2011). Interestingly, India, along with Pakistan and Iran, is about to join the Shanghai Cooperation Organization, and these countries might very well sign on to the 2009 Agreement, with India moving from a moderate to a more radical approach to Internet governance.

The IBSA proposal to the UN focuses on a single issue, namely the unequal state participation in Internet governance. The CIRP is IBSA's answer to the issue. CIRP would have 50 members that equally represent all regions in the world (IBSA 2011). In CIRP, multistakeholderism is minimalistic, with civil society and the private sector only allowed to give advice via advisory bodies (IBSA 2011). The tasks of CIRP are wide-ranging. They include oversight of the technical and operational management of the Internet, the negotiation of treaties and policies on the Internet and even dispute-settlement, as well as the protection of human rights (IBSA 2011). This would basically make CIRP the one and only place to discuss and decide on Internet issues, with governments in sole control.

2.3. A Failure

Up until now, the principles, whether from the first or second wave, have not had much success or impact. They have not been mentioned much in the media or by the parties themselves. They were generally forgotten the moment they were signed. Of course, it might be too early to tell whether the principles will ever have an impact. The RCTU Code suffers from too many defects to ever have a chance of adoption. As for the IBSA proposal, the creation of an intergovernmental Internet governance body is an impossible hurdle to overcome. The US and its allies, as demonstrated during the Dubai Summit, are set against any intergovernmental control of Internet governance. Those initiatives would also not fare well with other stakeholders, who want to be involved in decision-making.

As for the first wave of principles, if their content is generally less controversial, they suffer from flaws that might prove to be fatal, in terms of content, for instance. The balance struck by the OECD Principles between the protection of intellectual property rights and freedom of speech was in part the reason why CSISAC did not sign on to those principles. Civil society organizations often favour free speech over protection of intellectual property, while governments generally tend to be more circumspect.

There are also legitimacy issues. When multistakeholderism is professed as a norm, it is difficult to go ahead without one of the stakeholders. For this reason, the OECD Principles will have a lesser impact because CSISAC refused to sign. A similar problem was seen at the eG8, the Group of 8 Summit on the Internet in 2011, which came under fire for not opening up to civil society. Without the support of civil society organizations, it is harder for the instrument to be diffused broadly.

The Council of Europe seems to have understood the lesson and is working on a new project that is significantly different from the Internet principles. The Council of Europe has brought together Internet stakeholders and academics in an effort to create a Compendium of Existing Rights for Internet Users (Council of Europe 2013). Although this may seem less ambitious than creating principles from scratch, it might turn out to be more successful. It relies on rights that already exist, in the European Convention on Human Rights and other international instruments, so that no further governmental action is required. It also relies on citizens to enforce the Compendium, in a move that is in tune with the individual empowerment ethos of many of the principles. This Compendium mostly deals with substance rather than procedure, though one can argue that it encourages civil society participation in Internet governance, by helping individuals enforce their rights and standing up to governments and the private sector. The current draft lists 10 rights that come with detailed information on what they mean in the context of the Internet. However the drafters' views might not translate into automatic victories in national courts. For instance, the drafters agree with UN Special Rapporteur on Freedom of Expression Frank La Rue that the protection of intellectual property rights can never justify a restriction on freedom of speech as grave as Internet disconnection (UN Special Rapporteur on Freedom of Expression 2011).

In that respect, they clearly disagree with the French Constitutional Council in its decision on the three-strike law, which provides that third-time online copyright infringers may see their Internet connection suspended for a period of time (Constitutional Council 2009). Although the French Council did recognize the right to access the Internet, it did not hold that disconnection was unconstitutional, as long as a judge, as opposed to an administrative agency, made the decision. It stated that disconnection was both necessary and proportionate to the purpose it sought to achieve, i.e. protection of intellectual property. The Court logically extended the legal regime applicable to freedom of speech, which allows for necessary and proportionate restrictions, to this new freedom to access Internet services. The Compendium therefore encourages plaintiffs to take their case to the regional level, where the Court might be more sympathetic to their cause.

The two waves of principles reflect a divide between Western democracies and the rest of the world that is negatively impacting the conduct of Internet governance matters. The first wave mostly involved Western democracies, with the US leading the charge, though a few non-Western countries, like Egypt, signed on to the OECD principles as observers. In those instruments, governance issues are toned down, in favor of more substantive issues, like freedoms, rights, net neutrality and due process; however, the very existence of this web of informal principles tells us something about the concern of the West for governance—an international treaty is not the way forward. The second wave involved the main emerging economies, the so-called BRICS—Brazil, Russia, India, China and South Africa—who are clearly unhappy with the current division of power in Internet governance and are trying to struck a very different balance, whether under the cover of cyber security or outside of it.

If the principles hype seems to have stalled since 2011, a record year for Internet principles, the search for a framework for Internet governance has since then taken a new turn, which does not involve the same actors.

3. The Rise of Internet Freedom

Internet freedom as a concept dates back to the turn of the 21st century. In addition to becoming a mainstream term widely used in the media, the term has been used in several laws in the US, such as the Internet Freedom and Family Empowerment Act, albeit without being defined. In parallel, Secretary of State Condoleezza Rice already had set up in 2006 a Global Internet Freedom Task Force in the State Department with a view to "maximize freedom of expression and the free flow of information and ideas, to minimize the success of repressive regimes in censoring and silencing legitimate debate, and to promote access to information and ideas over the Internet" (US Department of State 2006). This vision of freedom of expression on the Internet constituted, for the then-Administration, Internet freedom. The approach of the current Administration to Internet freedom goes further.

3.1. Clinton's Remarks as Internet Freedom's Founding Moment

Secretary of State Clinton's first Remarks on Internet freedom in 2010 must be understood as the founding moment of Internet freedom. It is the first attempt at institutionalizing Internet freedom, which up until then, had been a rather elusive concept.

According to Secretary Clinton, Internet freedom is the translation of the commitment of the United States to Franklin Roosevelt's four freedoms in the digital age. Freedom of expression, freedom of worship, freedom from want, and freedom from fear are as relevant to the Internet as they were in 1941, when Roosevelt first laid them out. The Internet should not be a forgotten place where these freedoms are neglected, especially since "the Internet is a network that magnifies the power and potential of all others." Although freedom of expression obviously has a central role to play on the Internet, so do the other three freedoms. Freedom from fear finds its translation in the concept of cybersecurity, freedom from want relates to the potential of the Internet (in particular on mobile phones) to help people out of poverty by giving them access to education and markets while freedom of worship is there to protect Internet users from persecution on religious grounds. Turning these four freedoms into reality however also requires, according to Secretary Clinton, that a fifth freedom be protected. Freedom to connect, that is "the idea that governments should not prevent people from connecting to the Internet, to websites, or to each other" (Clinton 2010), is a necessary complement to the four freedoms in the digital age.

As promoted by the State Department, Internet freedom is a conglomerate of various freedoms that are, with the exception of the freedom to connect, non-Internet specific. The overarching goal of Internet freedom goes beyond what is occurring on the Internet strictly speaking. In Clinton's words, "[i]t's about whether we live on a planet with one Internet, one global community, and a common body of knowledge that benefits and unites us all, or a fragmented planet in which access to information and opportunity is dependent on where you live and the whims of censors" (Clinton 2010).

Internet freedom 1.0 has a rather classical human rights core, just like the Internet principles. Obviously, there is such a consensus—though not absolute—around human rights that it can safely be relied on when introducing a new concept like Internet freedom. It is fairly easy to believe the legitimacy of an idea anchored in human rights and comparably hard to reject it. The human rights discourse, which is otherwise abundant in Internet matters, provides Internet freedom with undisputable legitimacy. The UN Human Rights Council declared in July 2012 that human rights apply online as they do offline (UN Human Rights Council 2012). UN Special rapporteur to the UN Frank La Rue campaigned for human rights on the Internet in his famous report (UN Special Rapporteur on Freedom of Expression 2011). Together with the OSCE Representative on Freedom of the Media, the Special Rapporteurs of the Organization of American States and the African Commission on Human and Peoples' Rights, he also issued a declaration to this effect (UN Special Rapporteur on Freedom of Expression et al. 2011). Internet's own institutions are also embracing the human rights movement. ICANN is playing a role in the implementation of human rights online with its policy on the introduction of new generic top level domain names (gTLDs). Objections to applications for new gTLDs must comply with international law, in particular article 19 of the UDHR on freedom of speech (ICANN 2012). The human rights discourse also helps keeping the Internet Pandora box closed for a little longer. The human rights framework, with the treaties, the courts, already exist so there is no need to discuss sovereignty issues and the implementation of multistakeholderism as would be the case if a treaty had to be drafted.

But the State Department's approach to Internet freedom leaves Internet freedom unsubstantiated. In particular, it does not provide guidelines on the limits to such freedoms, which Clinton asserts do exist. "Now, all societies recognize that free expression has its limits. We do not tolerate those who incite others to violence, such as the agents of al-Qaida who are, at this moment, using the Internet to promote the mass murder of innocent people across the world. And hate speech that targets individuals on the basis of their race, religion, ethnicity, gender, or sexual orientation is reprehensible" (Clinton 2010). The challenge obviously is to determine where in practice to set the limits to Internet freedom. How to strike a balance between the protection of intellectual property rights and Internet freedom? Between law enforcement and Internet freedom? These are just a few of the many questions that proclaiming Internet freedom will not answer.

State Secretary Clinton's second speech on Internet freedom a year later dealt more specifically with this issue and how to achieve the oftentimes contrary goals of liberty and security, transparency and confidentiality, free speech and tolerance and civility. The speech took place shortly after the Cablegate, i.e. the release by the whistleblower website WikiLeaks of US diplomatic cables that the US administration condemned as not just "an attack on America—it's an attack on the international community." (Clinton 2011) Vice-President Biden even said that he "would argue that [Assange] is closer to being a high-tech terrorist than the Pentagon Papers." (McAskills 2010a). Some alleged that Senator Joe Lieberman, Chair of the Senate Homeland Security Committee, even pressured Amazon and MasterCard, VISA and AmEx to stop hosting and processing donations for WikiLeaks, a controversial move that sparked criticism all around the world.

The content of the State Secretary's speech was thus driven in large part by these events and by the necessity to reconcile, in the eyes of the public, her severe condemnation of WikiLeaks (MacAskills 2010) with her Internet policy, at the heart of which lies Internet freedom. She took this opportunity to declare that "WikiLeaks does not challenge [the United States'] commitment to Internet freedom." (Clinton 2011) She isolated the WikiLeaks debate from the general one on transparency and openness by reducing WikiLeaks and the Cablegate to a theft of government documents. She emphasized that those documents could be misused by terrorists and criminals or used against human rights activists whose identity would be revealed in the stolen documents. She voluntarily touched sensitive cords and chose extreme examples to try and win over support. Though Clinton did generally address limits to Internet freedom, she did not get into details and the guessing game as to how Internet freedom would ultimately fare when faced with national security concerns or intellectual property claims could continue.

It should also be noticed that in Clinton's two speeches, Internet freedom was originally conceived by the American administration as a foreign policy notion. The scene for the fight for Internet freedom was circumscribed to those countries like China or Iran that have established a high level of control of the Internet. In those countries, it was hoped that online freedom would help promote offline freedom.

In line with this view, Internet freedom seemed to concern only the most egregious censorship and surveillance techniques used by authoritarian states. Certainly one could argue that the repertoire of Internet freedom violations goes beyond and that democratic states have not been immune to criticism. But in this first conceptualization of Internet freedom, that is not the case. The threshold for finding a violation of Internet freedom is high.

Whatever the shortcomings of Clinton's approach to Internet freedom, it cannot be denied that Clinton's speeches have given it unprecedented publicity that certainly contributed to its further development. Translated into 7 languages (Arabic, Chinese, French, Persian, Urdu, Spanish and Russian), Clinton's speech was widely publicized by the State Department and received widespread coverage in the media both in the United States and abroad. We can observe a 5-fold increase in the number of times the term "Internet freedom" was used in major English-language newspapers from 2009 to 2010, when Clinton gave her first speech on Internet freedom. Internet freedom has become a topic of concern outside of the US State Department, which brings me to another quality of Internet freedom: its plasticity.

Internet freedom offers a new frame for thinking about freedom and the Internet, one that can be stretched in new unforeseen directions.

3.2. A Bright Future? The Plasticity of Internet Freedom

Unlike what happened with the Internet principles, Internet freedom is being internalized. Internet freedom is becoming more than what was initially contemplated by its "creator," the American administration. It is expanding, both in terms of who is getting involved in its development and in terms of its substantive scope.

3.2.1. Civil Society Gets Involved—Declarations of Internet Freedom

The mobilization against the passing of Preventing Real Online Threats to Economic Creativity and Theft of Intellectual Property Act (PIPA) and Stop Online Piracy Act (SOPA) during the 2011–2012 fall-winter season marked a new stage in the development of Internet freedom. PIPA and SOPA would have created more avenues for copyright holders to terminate infringements by imposing content policing duties on intermediaries that go well beyond what is currently required under the 1998 Digital Millennium Copyright Act. Some argued that PIPA and SOPA violated the first amendment and due process clause of the US Constitution and challenged the efficiency of the measures introduced by SOPA and PIPA, in particular of mandating DNS-blocking (Tribe 2011). With PIPA and SOPA, it was no longer events abroad that were driving the Internet freedom agenda in the US but events at home. The strong and somewhat surprising mobilization—in particular the Internet blackout on January 18, 2012—against the passing of PIPA and SOPA has inspired some to build on this popular success by creating an Internet freedom day and by asserting an alternative vision of Internet freedom. Two declarations of Internet freedom were announced by two distinct groups of civil society organizations, mostly based in the US, on July 4, 2012. The first declaration was adopted by a large number of organizations and individuals, including the American Civil Liberties Union, the Electronic Frontier Foundation (EFF) or Amnesty International (ACLU et al. 2012). The second one was supported by a smaller group of organizations and individuals, including John Perry Barlow, the author of the cyberlibertarian Declaration of Independence of Cyberspace (Tech Freedom et al. 2012).

Both declarations of Internet freedom are short documents that spell out rights and freedoms for Internet users that governments should promote and protect. Free speech, protection of privacy, freedom to innovate, access are the main, and fairly standard, tenets of the declarations. Both declarations are engaged in a dialogue with one another, since the second declaration was precisely intended as an alternative to the one posted by ACLU and its numerous allies. These declarations are also meant to start a dialogue with the public at large since both are open for comments (they are posted on collaborative sites like Reddit). If they cover the same topics, the declarations are adopting different approaches.

The first declaration of Internet freedom carefully avoids any reference to any existing legal instrument and does not even mention the word "rights". This is necessary for the declaration to be used all around the world in all circumstances. Indeed, the first declaration envisions itself as part of an "international movement to defend our freedoms" and is addressed to all Internet stakeholders. Stripped of a legal vocabulary and relying on a layman lexicon, this declaration is meant to be used by anybody anywhere. Of course, this lack of specificity makes it hard to predict the impact that these principles may have. In particular, they do not solve any of the hard questions, those that arise when you need to strike a balance between freedom of speech and copyright for instance. That is an advantage and a disadvantage at the same time. An advantage in that it is easy to adhere to such a declaration packed with good intentions and without saying much that could be controversial, except in dictatorship. A disadvantage in that it does not take a stance on any tough questions.

By contrast, the second declaration refers to specific legal provisions in US law, for instance the First and Fourth Amendments. The addressee of this declaration is primarily the American government, who should play only a minimal role in Internet governance. It fits in the "how much government?" debate that underlies American political life. The drafters of the second declaration explained that they were worried that the first declaration would give too big a role to the government and thus felt compelled to offer an alternative as to what the appropriate role of governments should be. For instance, while the first declaration encourages governments to promote universal access to fast and affordable networks, the second one holds that governments are the "greatest obstacle" to the emergence of fast and affordable networks. In the view of the second declaration drafters, the government's intervention should be limited to ensuring free competition. By mentioning American legal texts, the second declaration is limiting its audience to the United States. Unlike the first declaration, which aspires to universality, the second declaration sees the nation as the appropriate level of discussion.

3.2.2. Beyond Human Rights—the Control of International Internet Governance

There is one important issue that the declarations of Internet freedom and Clinton's speeches do not address: international Internet governance. As I mentioned above, intergovernmental control of Internet governance was the main topic of contention at the ITU Summit in Dubai. We know it is a recurring issue that gets raised on a regular basis. Thus the novelty at the Dubai Summit did not reside in the issue but in its framing. The argumentation was no longer focused on whether a "UN takeover of the Internet" was about to happen and instead consisted in saying that the UN takeover of Internet governance violated Internet freedom.

The media, especially in the US, relayed the Internet freedom message that came from various sources (Aljazeera 2012; Dugdale 2012; Mello 2012; O'Neil 2012). US Federal Communications Commissioner (FCC) Commissioner McDowell has been a particularly vocal promoter of Internet freedom and opponent to the ITU Summit (McDowell 2012). He started as early as December 2011 warning against the potential UN takeover (Devaney 2011). His declarations were quoted in many articles and his piece in the Wall Street Journal, titled "The UN threat to Internet freedom" received a lot of attention and was relayed in many newspapers. Google has also been very active, publishing a blogpost in November 2012 noting that "there is a growing backlash on Internet freedom" and that "not all governments support a free and open Internet," before concluding that "the ITU is the wrong place to make decisions about the future of the Internet" (Google 2012). Vint Cerf, Google's iconic chief Internet evangelist, also participated in the campaign (Cerf 2012a; Cerf 2012b). More unexpectedly, the Internet freedom discourse has also been adopted by Hamadoun Touré, the head of the ITU, himself. His declaration that the ITU Treaty is not against Internet freedom showed that the Internet freedom discourse has penetrated even those who would not necessarily agree with the US position. By adopting this discourse, Touré is acknowledging the existence and legitimacy of Internet freedom as a notion. Obviously Internet freedom sounds so good that it would be hard to come out against it without appearing as a monster. But it would be possible to simply ignore it and what it stands for. The head of the ITU chose to attack the position that the ITU Treaty would have violated Internet freedom, instead of challenging the underlying position that intergovernmental control of Internet governance is against Internet freedom.

This new dimension of Internet governance is clearly controversial. We have seen that the BRICS countries would disagree with the proposition that intergovernmental control of Internet governance violates Internet freedom. Note that what is being rejected here is not so much the idea that Internet governance could be dealt with by treaty (though the legitimacy of such treaty, which would make no room for civil society and the private sector would likely be disputed as not complying with multistakeholderism). The issue is the content of the treaty, and in particular the provisions that could possibly be construed as granting more control to governments.

The Internet freedom campaign against intergovernmental control of Internet governance did not decrease in the wake of the summit. In February 2013, the House of Representatives' Energy and Commerce Committee held a hearing with a very explicit title: "Fighting for Internet Freedom: Dubai and Beyond" (US House of Representatives 2013). Among the witnesses was FCC Commissioner McDowell. In his testimony, he mentioned only China, Russia, Saudi Arabia and Iran as countries favouring intergovernmental control, though more open and democratic states, like Brazil and South Africa, sided against the US on the ITU treaty. McDowell generally paints a very dire picture of Internet governance, conveying that the Internet is under serious and imminent threats and that the US is fairly lonely in its fight for Internet freedom. The House went on to approve an "Internet freedom bill" in May 2013 (US House of Representatives 2013), despite concerns regarding the language of the bill, which could be construed as rejecting any and all governmental intervention in Internet governance, thereby threatening existing legislation on consumer protection, privacy, or net neutrality (Open Tech 2013). The bill would make it the official policy of the US to support a multistakeholder control of Internet governance. It is currently before the Senate.

The Dubai summit was the occasion to see how powerful and malleable Internet freedom is. The notion is expanding and being more and more accepted as the norm of reference when deciding Internet-related issues. Where does this leave us?

4. Conclusion: What Kind of Constitution for Internet Governance?

The development of Internet principles and Internet freedom fits in well with global constitutionalism generally. Most of the key themes of global constitutionalism can be found in the developments that I have described above. The recognition of individual rights is obviously present. The Internet principles and Internet freedom are focused on the promotion and protection of human rights, in particular freedom of speech, but also extend beyond human rights and for instance, support the recognition of the freedom to innovate. The focus on human rights also serves to place limits on the exercise of power at the local and international level, another key theme of global constitutionalism. So does the rejection of intergovernmental control, which deprives states of their traditional role at the international level. The Internet principles and Internet freedom work to create a vision of a better future in which individuals enjoy freedom and have more opportunities to connect, learn and do business. It is hoped that the Internet will help achieve the United Nations Millennium Development Goals.

Taking the analysis one step further, we can see that the brand of constitutionalism represented by the development of Internet principles and Internet freedom is not aiming at mimicking domestic constitutional orders that revolve around states. Internet principles and Internet freedom do not embrace state-centered constitutionalism. Internet freedom, in its latest iteration, rejects the intergovernmental control of Internet governance. By denying governments what is their traditional predominant role on the international scene, Internet freedom declares that states are not the only players. This fits in well with multistakeholderism, a principle that is present in the Internet principles and that has been an integral part of the rhetoric against the intergovernmental control of Internet governance at the recent ITU Summit. Rejecting intergovernmental control is making room for civil society and private sector participation, though the modalities and level of that participation are not defined. We can only infer that the current arrangements in Internet governance are implicitly approved.

Questions of legitimacy necessarily arise as we step away from traditional structures, such as intergovernmental organizations that rely on state consent. Legitimacy may come from several sources. In terms of content, the human rights core of Internet freedom can be seen as a great—though not absolute as the debate over relativism evidences—source of legitimacy. However, as we have seen, the same does not hold for the proposition that intergovernmental control of Internet governance violates Internet freedom. An argument can be made that prohibiting intergovernmental control of Internet governance is in line with the Internet's decentralized architecture, which, according to Lawrence Lessig (1999a), may be compared to the Internet's constitution (in the British understanding of the term). But in the case of Internet freedom, it is exclusively the intergovernmental control of Internet governance that is being rejected, and not all governmental intervention. If the decentralization argument targets intergovernmental control, it should also target governmental control as a form of centralization of power. In any case, it is doubtful that this very theoretical line of argumentation would convince the BRICS countries and their allies.

Legitimacy can also derive from the method by which the content is defined, as discussed by Weber in Chapter 5. As I have shown, the constitutionalization process seems driven to a large extent from the US. The government's involvement has been major, from participating in the negotiation of the Internet principles, placing Internet freedom on the agenda of international politics thanks to Hillary

Clinton's speeches to promoting the idea that it prohibits intergovernmental control of Internet governance. American NGOs, as well as US-based companies, among which Google, have been taking part in the promotion of Internet freedom abroad, and importantly, at home. By adopting the Internet freedom discourse though he disagreed with the positions of the American delegation to the Dubai Summit, Hamadoun Touré has invited others to contribute to the process. But a lot remains to be done and given the importance of Internet freedom, the question of how best to invite broader participation in its development becomes pressing.

One key theme of global constitutionalism that has not yet been really touched upon is that of the institutionalization of power, which is concerned with the accountability of decision-makers. For Internet freedom to continue gaining substance and result in increased freedom, we need some form of a control mechanism. To the extent that Internet freedom is partly entrenched in law, specifically human rights law, Internet freedom may benefit from the general compliance mechanisms already in place, mostly at the domestic or regional level. For instance, a few courts have recognized freedom to connect as a constitutional right. But it may not always be easy to vindicate such rights, in particular in cross border cases. And what about those rights that are not considered as human rights, like the freedom to innovate or right to participate in decision-making on an equal footing? Conceiving of a compliance mechanism in a decentralized bottom-up context, where power is distributed among a great number and a wide variety of actors, is quite a challenge. The role of civil society would no doubt be important. Civil society has already achieved success on several important matters, like the anti-PIPA/SOPA campaign in the US. The ITU Summit has also shown that organizations from all over the world were mobilized on Internet freedom topics. The Council of Europe is betting on this mobilization to make its Compendium on the existing rights of Internet users a success. But we should not overestimate the power of civil society. For instance, the PIPA/SOPA victory in the US should be contrasted with the Cablegate debacle. How to explain these widely different outcomes? First of all, NGOs may not have presented a united front regarding the Cablegate. For instance, while some, like the Electronic Frontier Foundation or Reporters Without Borders, were being openly critical, others, like the Center for Democracy and Technology, only commented on a side technical issue, namely the legality of subpoenas served on Twitter as part of the investigation of the Cablegate by the authorities. In addition, the private companies that were not directly involved in the matter did not voice any concerns, possibly because they felt that the debate did not affect them directly. Finally, and perhaps more importantly, from the government standpoint, the Cablegate represents a threat to its sovereignty and it was not willing to compromise, no matter how much it would get criticized. Understanding what turns civil society mobilization into a success is of paramount importance: is it the support of Internet powerhouses, like Google or Wikipedia? Is it the type of interests at stake, for instance the private interests of copyright owners in the PIPA/SOPA case or the governmental interest in controlling what the public knows of governmental affairs in the Cablegate? If the latter, how to obtain that governments, in particular the US government which has a prominent position in Internet governance, compromise when Internet freedom demands it? Could the answer lie in the resilience of WikiLeaks, which is still operating despite the "multi-system attack" it has suffered and which is making the most of what the Internet has to offer?

Acknowledging that recent evolutions in Internet governance, namely the adoption of Internet principles and the emergence of Internet freedom, actually amount to a constitutionalization of Internet governance might be the first step toward addressing these weaknesses. It certainly exposes the stakes in a very clear manner. Internet freedom is not just a nice-sounding idea that looks good but does not mean much and the Internet principles are more than just a hype. Individually, it is easy to underestimate the impact of these events but taken together, they draw a picture of Internet governance that deserves our attention.

ACKNOWLEDGEMENTS

I would like to thank my husband, my parents and my grand-mother as well as my many friends at Cornell Law School for their constant and immensely precious support.

Part 2.
Multistakeholderism and its Limits

Richard Hill

Chapter 4
Internet Governance: The Last Gasp of Colonialism, or Imperialism by Other Means?

It is undeniable that the Internet has transformed telecommunications in recent years, and it has also had very beneficial effects on national economies and on international trade. However, the benefits have not been distributed evenly around the world: developed countries have benefited relatively more, as have some of their major private companies. Historically, empires have always striven to improve communications: early well-known examples are Roman roads and the message system of the Mongol empire. With the advent of telegraphy, empires started to use telecommunications, and actively pursued international telecommunication policies that were in their interest (for example Hills 2007).

During the twentieth century, there has been a long-term shift in geopolitical power first from Europe towards the United States and the former Soviet Union, more recently towards the so-called BRICS (Brazil, Russian Federation, India, China, and South Africa). That shift resulted in the demise of the former European colonial empires and a rise in the competing ideological and economic empires comprised respectively by the United States and its allies and the Soviet Union and its allies. Following the demise of the Soviet Union, the United States was left as the most powerful military and economic force in the world. Not surprisingly, US dominance is also reflected in today's dominant telecommunications technology, the Internet (we use here the broad definition of Internet found in Hill (2014, section 3.2).

This chapter reviews briefly the history of the Internet and its governance, points out that the US government still exercises some (at least nominal) control over some aspects of the Internet, and links that to the well-known historical phenomena of colonialism and imperialism. The chapter argues that a new form of imperialism, techno-imperialism, is conflated with traditional political imperialism for what concerns Internet governance. It concludes that new governance models should be envisaged so as to achieve true democratic and multilateral Internet governance.

1. A Short History of the Internet

It is worth recalling that the invention and early deployment of the Internet were funded by the US Defence Department Advanced Projects Agency (DARPA), in competition with the parallel developments of comparable technologies under the Open Systems Interface (OSI) umbrella; the OSI work was carried out by private companies (former telecommunications monopolies and their captive manufacturers, together with computer companies, in particular those competing against the dominant company of the time, International Business Machines (IBM) (Abbate 1999).

Subsequently, deployment of the Internet was funded in the US by the National Science Foundation (NSF) and in Europe by various academic funds. That is, the invention and the early deployment were primarily funded by governments.

An important component of the Internet, the world-wide-web, was invented in Geneva, Switzerland, by an English national working for an inter-governmental organization Commercial use of the Internet was allowed starting in 1995. Not coincidentally, this is when public discussions started regarding Internet governance (Mueller 2002a).

2. A Short History of Internet Governance

It is important to note that the early discussions regarding Internet governance were focused on reducing the historical role of the US government and on finding multilateral solutions, and these discussions were carried out in a manner that would subsequently be referred to as multistakeholder. However, the US government did not accept the results of that multistakeholder consultation—precisely because that consultation envisaged a multilateral approach to Internet governance—and so the US government unilaterally imposed an alternative approach, based on US entities which were bound by contracts or agreements with the US government, in particular the Internet Corporation for Assigned Names and Numbers (Mueller, 2002a).

It should be noted that, when ICANN was first envisaged, it was not intended to be multistakeholder. The US statement of policy that resulted in the creation of ICANN states that the transition from management by contractors of the US government to what became ICANN should "allow the private sector to take leadership for DNS management" and "national governments now have, and will continue to have, authority to manage or establish policy for their own ccTLDs" (NTIA 1998).

Despite the promise made in 1998, the US government has never relinquished its role as the ultimate authority for the management of critical Internet resources (Kruger 2013; NTIA 2012). Indeed, the existence of this role has been openly acknowledged in an analysis prepared for the US Congress, which raises as a point to consider: "Should the U.S. government maintain its current legacy authority over ICANN and the DNS [Domain Name System], and if so, how can the U.S National Telecommunications and Information Administration (NTIA), an agency under the US Department of Commerce, best use this authority judiciously in order to advance U.S. government interests, while at the same time minimizing the perception by other nations (as well as the international community of Internet stakeholders) that the United States has an inappropriate level of control or influence over the Internet and the DNS?" (Kruger 2013, p. 20).

3. Perceptions of the US Role

Not surprisingly, not all countries are comfortable with the role played by the United States with respect to Internet governance (see also Chapter 2, 3 and 7 in this volume). As a former senior US official put the matter (Verveer 2013):

> "Defence of status quo is perceived as saying the US created the Internet, the US controls the Internet, US corporations profit disproportionately from the Internet, US security services have privileged access to everything that traverses the Internet. […] Internet has become a mechanism of overarching importance for every country in the world, both in terms of economic activity, but also for social, political and cultural considerations. Yet for many countries there is no reliable modality that permits them to influence, let alone to control, what happens … The content conveyed over the Internet largely reflects US legal and cultural sensibilities, which sensibilities are not universally shared. […] Cybersecurity is a large and growing problem, and there is very substantial uncertainty on the part of many countries regarding how to address these cybersecurity issues".
>
> "Western countries prefer the status quo. … There are countries such as Brazil and India and India that have a whole set of concerns about the Internet. They need it, they want it to work for them, they also feel rather acutely that they don't have nearly as much influence about how the Internet may evolve as their position in the world entitles them to. These are

> countries that have a strong preference for bringing issues to the UN and having them resolved in that framework".

Note the mention of a perception that US security services have privileged access to everything that traverses the Internet; this is apparently a reality, not just a perception (National Security Agency 2013; Savage et al. 2013). A well-known Internet technologist expressed thoughts broadly similar to those expressed above (Huston 2012):

> "It's true that a number of critical elements of the Internet's infrastructure, including the IANA function of oversight over the Internet's names and addresses remains a contracted activity with direct oversight by an agency of the US government. It's also reasonable to observe that over the past 14 years or so the US Government's hold over this function has tightened rather than relaxed, and what might have been a vague intention to pass this function over to an industry-based self-regulatory private sector body at some indefinite time in the future has transformed to a grim determination never to relinquish reserve control of these functions. On the other hand, many nations see the role of a single nation state in this global communications system as anomalous and threatening, and would prefer to see control be placed in the hands of an international treaty body that specializes in international telecommunications, namely the ITU. They see the US as exerting an undue and improper level of influence and control and would like to see this function be more accessible to other nation states on a peer basis".

But the criticism is not limited to ICANN and the management of critical resources (names and addresses). It is also related to the general dominance by US companies of many key sectors of information and communication technologies (ICTs). As the same technologist put the matter (Huston 2012):

> "They [developing countries and Brazil, Russian Federation, India, China, and South Africa (BRICS)] evidently see the dramatic explosion of online content as services as a form of colonial exploitation, where a small number of enterprises, located predominantly in the United States, were engaged in global enterprises with little or no constraint or balance, and the result was once more a form of technological exploitation where the benefits of this global network were flowing into a single national economy and everyone else was paying. Individual national interests were effectively powerless to stand up to this new international cartel, and it would only be through collective action undertaken by many nation states would some form of balance be restored".

A similar thought has been expressed by the former senior US official cited earlier (Verveer 2013):

> "The foundation for international cooperation continues to be the nation-state. We have adhered to the agreements that were reached in Westphalia in 1648, and we continue to do that. It is not something that is going to go away any time soon. [...]For many countries, the United Nations and its organizations are the central place where they want to go to resolve issues and the one-nation one-vote aspect of those organizations is important."

A well-respected academic summarized the situation as follows (Mueller, 2013a):

> "Calls for US leadership, however, must take into account the fallout from the NSA surveillance revelations [Prism], the continuing irritant of US control of the IANA contract, and the broader perception among some countries that multistakeholderism is merely a cover for U.S. dominance of the whole domain."

4. The Real Issue

But for most developing countries the real issue is not whether or not the US is exercising an asymmetric role, but whether the results of the current Internet governance model are consistent with the aspirations of developing countries. As the cited former senior US official put the matter (Verveer, 2013):

> "There are many countries for which the big issue is development. Whether or not there are ways to approach Internet governance to expand broadband networks, to improve the cybersecurity environment, and a range of development issues that they would like to see improved."

Indeed, there has been considerable criticism of the current model with respect to development issues (Hill, 2014, section 6). In particular, the cost of international Internet connectivity is too high, in relative terms, for developing countries[1].

At present, it is disputed whether the current financial arrangements for the Internet will result in sufficient return on investments to finance the rollout of sufficient new infrastructure (AT Kearney (2010) and conversely Weller and Woodcock (2013)).

1 What follows is partly taken from section 6.2 of Hill (2014).

The Internet is based on a "receiver pays" model. This model applies at two levels: at the level of the end-user, and at the level of the international interconnection.

There is general agreement that it is logical for an end-user to pay for something that he or she asked for, for example a video; but there is some question regarding whether the provider of the content should also pay, for example if it wishes to ensure the speed of transmission of its content (this is the "net neutrality debate").

But "receiver pays" also applies to international interconnections at the wholesale level, and developing countries have long taken the view that it penalizes them, because these countries produce little content and access much content, so they use proportionately more international bandwidth (see for example ITU-T 2013).

Fundamentally, it is obvious that, in a "receiver pays" system, a relatively poor country will obtain less information than a relatively rich country, simply because the relatively poor country has less money to spend.

One might take the view that there is nothing wrong with this: after all, nobody thinks that everybody should drive luxury cars. On the other hand, one might take the view that access to what is undoubtedly the world's fundamental communication and information system (the "free and open Internet") should be made available to all at prices they can afford.

So the question becomes how to address the fact that (1) for people in developing countries Internet access is relatively less affordable than it is for people in developed countries; and (2) people in developing countries have relatively less access to Internet than they do to mobile telephones, again when compare to people in developed countries[2]. That is, how can we make Internet as available as voice services provided by mobile phones?

Some take the view that liberalization will achieve this goal (Weller and Woodcock, 2013). Others point out that liberalization has not had the desired effects in some countries (Crawford, 2013). It is not disputed that developing countries have questions and legitimate concerns (Wentworth, 2013). And it cannot be disputed that discussions on the topics outlined above should continue. Thus the question is: in which forums should the discussions take place?

2 Broadband and Internet penetration rates are markedly higher in developed countries than they are in developing countries, while the differences with respect to mobile cellular penetration are smaller. In most of the developing world, 2.5G and 3G mobile has grown far faster than fixed Internet. See ITU-SG (2013, sect. 2.3.1 (k)).

5. The Multistakeholder Approach

Because the Internet is different from other networks, its governance is not the same as that of other networks[3]. In particular, certain aspects of the Internet are not regulated by governments and they are governed by a variety of private sector organizations which are open to a broad range of participants, including in some cases governments (for a discussion see Sylvan in this volume). This situation is often referred to as "the multistakeholder model", which has been defined as engaging "technologists, the private sector and civil society in a bottom-up, consensus driven approach to standards setting, Internet development, and management" (Wentworth, 2013). It has been said that Internet governance matters call for open multistakeholder participation in an open dialogue that directly reflect the diversity of the interests and activities that collectively form the Internet itself (Huston, 2013b). That is, it is argued that no particular Internet governance matter should be decided except by multistakeholder bodies[4] (see also Chapter 6 for a more detailed description of the implementation of multistakeholder processes in Internet governance institutions).

Taken literally, this means that the World Intellectual Property Organization (WIPO) should not decide online copyright or patent matters, unless one takes the view that those matters are not related to Internet governance. But this is rarely argued. Indeed, the US explicitly argues the contrary, namely that the WIPO treaties should be applied to the Internet (Saez 2013) and the US, the European Union, and Australia argue that the World Trade Organization (WTO) is competent to make certain decisions regarding the Internet (WTO Council for Trade in Services 2011; 2012). And nobody has (at least yet) argued that the US Department of Commerce, the US Congress, the European Commission, the Council of Europe, or the European Parliament should not discuss Internet governance matters because those institutions are not multistakeholder institutions.

Rather, what is really being argued is that certain particular Internet governance matters should be decided by multistakeholder bodies. Perhaps not coincidentally, the matters in question are those that are handled by the existing prominent Internet bodies such as ICANN, IETF, W3C, and the Regional Internet Registries (RIRs). Also perhaps not coincidentally, the bulk of the organized political support for this view comes from countries whose companies and citizens participate intensively in the work of those bodies (Bucak 2012; Geist 2012; Gurstein 2012; Nothias 2012 and 2012a; Schiller 2013; Singh 2012; Westby 2012). There is noth-

---

3 What follows is partly taken from section 5 of Hill (2014).

4 What follows is partly taken from section 7 of Hill (2014).

ing new in this: opposition to inter-governmental agreements was explicitly stated as early as 1949 by the US operator AT&T (Hills 2007, p. 51).

Indeed, in a multistakeholder model private companies are able to intervene at multiple levels: within some components of the multistakeholder model (including governments) and directly as private companies. Thus it is not surprising that most private companies favour the multistakeholder model (Hill 2014, section 5).

And of course the most important private companies active in providing Internet products and services are located in developed countries.

6. Is this Colonialism?

Colonialism can be defined as a policy by which a nation maintains or extends its control over foreign dependencies. One of the motivations for colonialism is the economic exploitation of the dependencies[5]. It should be noted, however, that the wealth extracted from the dependencies is not necessarily evenly distributed amongst the citizens of the colonizing nation, see for example (Muller 2002, p. 71), who cites Adam Smith[6].

In this sense, an insistence on US (or developed country) control of Internet governance is indeed an example of colonialism (including at times the denigration of ability of developing country representatives to understand the issues and to take appropriate decisions on their own). Thus it is not surprising that the most vocal advocates of changes to the current approach are the most powerful developing countries: Brazil, China, India, Russian Federation, and South Africa.

Imperialism can be defined as the policy of extending a nation's authority by territorial acquisition or by the establishment of economic and policy authority over other nations. The current Internet governance model fits well into this definition: it allows the US to enforce rather easily its domestic policies, at times with extraterritorial effects. For example, the US could easily seize domain names used for well-known poker sites, because those domain names are provided by US entities (Bennett 2011). The seizure prevented people outside the US from using those sites (the sites were later restored with the stipulation that they could not be accessed from within the US). Another example is provided by the Prism surveillance program, whose implementation was facilitated by the fact that key In-

[5] There is a vast literature on colonialism and its effects. A pithy and cogent account is given in Morris (2011, pp. 515–521).

[6] For the Internet, it can be noted that one well-known company had, in 2012, some US$ 48 billion in cash and short-term investments and the amount was increasing (Google 2013).

ternet companies are US entities (National Security Agency 2013; Savage et al. 2013), and by the fact that the Internet security community is predominantly from the US (see Schmidt in this volume). Requests for surveillance of US citizens are subject to approval by an independent judge, whereas such approval is not required for surveillance of non-US citizens. Thus the Prism surveillance program is an example of the well-known tendency of empires to accord special rights to their own citizens[7].

Apparent agreements between the US and Europe to share information on Prism (Keating 2013; Le Monde 2013)[8], and between the US and the Russian Federation to cooperate to improve ICT security (US White House Press Office 2013), are not likely to alleviate perceptions of continuing colonialism and imperialism, especially given the US refusal to agree to any language regarding cooperation on security matters during the World Conference on International Telecommunications (WCIT) (Hill 2013)[9]. And an apparent US intent to conduct offensive cyberwarfare activities (Schneier 2013) is also not likely to alleviate perceptions of imperialism. Nor are calls for increased US-European Union (EU) cooperation and coordination in matters such as standards-making[10]. Further, the current Internet governance model allows US entities to influence the economic and policy authority of other nations (and indeed even, to some extent, of the US itself[11]). Indeed, the flow of funds of Internet traffic is less favourable to developing countries than was the flow of funds of traditional voice traffic prior to liberalization. The ITU estimates that, in the period 1993–98, the net flows of settlement payments from developed countries to developing ones amounted to some US$40 billion (ITU and Telegeography 1999). Due to the shift away from the traditional accounting rate system, and reductions in rates, the net flows of settlement payments from developed to developing countries decreased significantly, and may even have turned in the other direction (Walden 2009, pp. 741 and 743). In particular, various unilateral actions by the United States were viewed as resulting in a net flow of rev-

---

7 But also to assert jurisdiction over its own citizens even at the expense of the sovereignty of other nations (Payne, 2013).

8 For a different view, see Whittaker (2013).

9 See also the statements of Brazilian Foreign Affairs Minister Antonio Patriota in Bosco (2013).

10 Such calls are explicitly found, for example, in the initial EU position paper on technical barriers to trade prepared for discussion relating to the EU-US trade and investment partnership (European Commission 2013).

11 For example, the US government approved the implementation of the gTLD ".xxx", despite some domestic opposition, because the decision was formally taken by ICANN and the US government did not wish to be seen to override an ICANN decision. On the other hand, the US government imposed a price cap, in November 2012, on the price charged by Versign for registration under the domain name ".com" (McCarthy 2012; US Department of Commerce 2012).

enues from developing countries to developed countries, in particular to the US (that is, taking from the poor to give to the rich) (Hills 2007, p. 207; Walden 2009, p. 744). As one author puts the matter (Fernández González 2011): "The existing economic mechanisms in international communications networks establish the financial flows in favour of the developed countries."

In this light, it is not surprising that, as the cited Internet technologist (Huston 2012) puts the matter:

> "The US government sees this [control of IANA] as a necessary part of their stewardship of the multistakeholder model of a free and open Internet. Their stated concern is that were they to pass control over to an international organization then it's a distinct risk that this organization would be captured by hostile national interests and the consequent risk, as they state it, is that the open nature of the Internet would be destroyed. The US is not alone in this view and many other countries perceive the potential of a similar form of threat and see the US role as either a positive force or, at worst, they see this as the lesser of many potential evils."

It is worth noting at this point that there is little transparency regarding the financial flows for Internet traffic, because the bulk of the traffic is carried under "peering agreements" that are zero-cost arrangements between the concerned operators (Weller and Woodcock, 2013). Thus, today's prevalent telecommunications technology is largely run as a barter economy, unlike any other important infrastructure. One can wonder whether this contributes to the relatively unfavourable situation of developing countries with respect to Internet access. As stated in Supplement 2 to Recommendation ITU-T D.50 (ITU-T 2013a):

> "Some take the view that the mechanisms to be established [to implement D.50] must take into account the costs engendered by the activities of the various players in the value chain, in particular regarding investment costs. From this point of view, the full set of users of the international Internet interconnection (IIC) infrastructure should each bear a portion of the cost, according to its use of the infrastructure. (ITU-T 2013a, sect. 1.7)
>
> "In this way, each player will contribute to financing the cost of the infrastructure in an objective matter, and will contribution to the development and deployment of the IIC infrastructure, and will thus contribution to reducing the digital divide between the North and the South" (ITU-T 2013a, sect. 1.7).
>
> "[…] There are a number of reasons for the cost of Internet connection. The first and most important is still the cost of international Internet bandwidth. The tariffs for connection between Africa and Europe bear no comparison with the much lower charges applied between Europe and North

> America or even between Asia and Europe. These high tariffs are the result of an absence of competition in the international Internet connection market and of the current Internet interconnection model" (ITU-T 2013a, sect. 2).
>
> "In particular, the cost of international Internet connection is too high in sub-Saharan Africa compared to the rest of the world. The market is in the hands of a limited number of commercial groups, which include the major operators, former incumbent operators and various financial consortia. This market is somewhat non-transparent and monopolistic" (ITU-T 2013a, sect. 2).

In addition to the economic domination, there is also a tendency for the developed countries to impose certain policy choices on developed countries. For example, at the 2012 World Conference on International Telecommunications (WCIT-12), developed countries strongly objected to a proposal to include the following in the International Telecommunications Regulations (ITRs):

> "Member States may seek information on the international route of their traffic, where [technically, financially and legally] feasible. Member States shall cooperate—consistent with their national laws [and respective international obligations]—to provide this information to the Member State concerned." As a result of those objections, no such text was included in the ITRs (WCIT 2012a).

Objections to the inclusion of such a provision included statements to the effect that it could lead to violations of freedom of speech. Further, at WCIT developed countries strongly opposed proposals from developing countries to include provisions in the ITRs regarding cooperation on improving on security and combating spam, again, on the grounds that such provisions could threaten freedom of speech.

But in fact the provisions in question could not threaten freedom of speech; on the contrary, cooperation on such matters is more likely to preserve freedom of speech (Hill 2013). Indeed, as noted above, the US has acknowledged that it unilaterally monitors certain foreign Internet traffic (National Security Agency 2013; Savage et al. 2013). Thus one might wonder whether the strong US resistance to inclusion in the ITRs of an article regarding cooperation on security matters was motivated by a desire to be able to carry out unilateral monitoring without any constraints, which is something that some proponents of the Internet consider to be undesirable (Barabas and Bankston 2013; Internet Society 2013). In the absence of cooperation, countries have greater freedom to implement domestic restrictions and surveillance (Musil 2013).

Indeed, some commentators have suggested that the revelations of such unilateral US actions might increase calls for changes in the current Internet governance structures (Hruska 2013; Nothias 2013)[12]. As one journalist put the matter (Kampfner 2013):

> "The fact that the Americans and the British are apparently employing surveillance techniques not dissimilar to the Russians and Chinese makes a laughing stock of their otherwise admirable policy of promoting free expression and an open Internet around the world. One can already hear the chortles of President Putin. One can only imagine the schadenfreude of the Chinese president, Xi Jinping, as he met Barack Obama in California last weekend".
>
> "What is needed is a determined effort to bring international human rights law up to date to meet the many, and changing, opportunities and dangers posed by the Internet..."

7. Is there Also Techno-Imperialism?

In addition to the economic and policy domination noted above, there is also a certain imposition by developed countries of technical norms on developed countries. This imposition arises because the entities that produce the technical norms used for the Internet are developed in organizations (such as IETF and ICANN) that are open to direct participation by individuals[13]; however, there are barriers to participation in those organizations, including the ability to speak English, to travel, and having sufficient technical knowledge, and indeed some of those organizations have been criticized as lacking the consensus of a sufficiently broad community (Kruger 2013, pp. 7–14; Weber 2009, pp. 612–614; Weber 2013; Weber and Heinrich 2011).

Further, certain key norms are developed by private companies and imposed de facto without formal input from users (apart of course from the input that arises when users refuse to use a particular product or service). In competitive markets, this is normal: consumers vote with their feet and no other form of input is required. But not all Internet markets are competitive, and norms developed by in-

---

12 The matter was discussed at a Brookings workshop, see Brookings (2013).

13 The President and Chief Executive Officer of the American Registry for Internet Addresses (ARIN) put it this way: "One of the consequences of self-governance for critical Internet resources is that it is the majority of those *who actually participate* which counts most heavily in these processes." (Curran 2013).

dividual companies appear to be growing in importance[14]. Indeed, the European Commission is investigating whether the leading search service provider has a dominant position and promotes its specialized search services in a way that unduly diverts traffic away from its competitors, thus abusing its dominance (European Newspaper Publishing Association 2013).

As a well respected technologist puts the matter (in the context of a discussion regarding the slow rate of the transition to IPv6) (Huston 2013):

> "We are witnessing an industry that is no longer using technical innovation, openness and diversification as its primary means of propulsion. ... Today's Internet is serviced by a far smaller number of very large players, each of whom appear to be assuming a very strong position within their respective markets. The drivers for such larger players tend towards risk aversion, conservatism and increased levels of control across their scope of operation. The same trends of market aggregation are now appearing in content provision, where a small number of content providers are exerting a dominant position across the entire Internet."

Since the individual companies concerned are developed country companies, and since developed country companies still largely influence the discussions in the various norm-setting bodies, one can use the term "techo-imperialism" (Adas 2006) to refer to a policy by which a group of private companies maintains or extends its control over economic and policy matters by controlling the development and use of certain technologies. Reliance on intellectual property rights such as copyrights, patents, and trade secrets are some of the means used to exercise such control (for the importance of trade secrets regarding search engines, see Kohl (2013).

Such techno-imperialism is not motivated just by the economic interests of private companies, it is also motivated by the sincere belief of some technologists that they know best what should be done (see the extensive discussion in (Hill 2014, section 2). Unfortunately, the record shows that the choices made by the technologists are not always the ones best suited to real-world applications[15].

---

14 For private company restrictions on the market for smartphone applications, see Mac Síthigh (2013); for the situation regarding search engines, see Kohl (2013).

15 We cite here two well-known examples. The decision to use the Domain Name System (DNS) to implement hyperlinks when the DNS was explicitly not designed to cater to real-world objects, as stated in RFCs 920 and 1034. And the decision to rely on an extended IP address protocol (IPv6) that is not backwards-compatible with IPv4 (WTPF 2013a); the choice of the IPv6 protocol was not made casually, it was the result of extensive discussions, see DeNardis (2009) But also to assert jurisdiction over its own citizens even at the expense of the sovereignty of other nations. It remains to be seen whether the current expansion of generic top-level domains (gTLDs) will result in additional mismatches with respect to the

Indeed, in general, technologies such as printing, railroads, steam-powered ships, gasoline-powered automobiles, airplanes, etc. have affected the real world, but they have in turn been influenced and constrained by the real world (for example, restrictions are imposed to ensure safety, to reduce pollution, to facilitate law enforcement, etc.). Thus it would seem reasonable to expect that non-technologists might wish to impose restrictions on the Internet technologies.

It is not surprising that technologists resist calls for such restrictions; what is less obvious is why developed countries tend also to resist such calls. A possible explanation is that the interests of the technologists are conflated with the economic and policy interests of the developed countries, so that traditional colonialism is conflated with techno-imperialism.

8. The Way Forward?

If indeed we are in a situation akin to colonialism, and if we accept that this situation is not desirable (because it is obviously not consistent with the democratic ideal that is widely accepted worldwide at present), then we should seek ways to change the situation.

Various steps can be envisaged to encourage discussion of changes:

1. Accept the discussion, rather than refuse it (WCIT and WTPF both provide good examples of refusal to discuss the situation, as do numerous other meetings), see for example Weber in this volume.
2. Accept discussion of the fundamental issues, rather than peripheral issues on which there isn't much disagreement (for example, at WTPF there was much discussion of the role of Internet Exchange Points (IXPs) but no discussion of the Internet financial flow issues summarized above, and no discussion of the fundamental issue: how to subsidize access for people who live in low-income, low-density geographical areas such as much of Africa and the Pacific Islands, see Fernández González (2011, p. 7), citing Kunigami and Navas-Sabater (2010).
3. Accept comparison with other infrastructures, in particular the mobile telephone infrastructure (Hill 2014, section 7). As noted above, usage of this in-

real world, for example regarding whether the gTLD "amazon" should be created and, if so, whether it should be assigned to the private company that is so named or to the geographic feature that is no named.

frastructure has grown more rapidly than has usage of the Internet[16]. Perhaps this difference in growth is at least partly related to the fact that the governance of the GSM infrastructure is rather more traditional than the governance of the Internet infrastructure (or perhaps not, but the matter should be discussed seriously, and not dismissed out of hand).

4. Seek an agreement that gives equal rights to all countries, that is, address the current asymmetric role of the US government.

Regarding point 4 above, one solution could be that the US relinquishes its current privileged role, with the existing structures remaining as they are. That is, there would be no new formal agreements involving governments, and the current contracts and agreements with the US government would be discontinued.

Another solution could be "back to the future": developing a multistakeholder multilateral memorandum of understanding similar to the one originally proposed in 1997 (IAHC 1997) Another historical proposal was presented by Syria to the 3–4 May 2005 meeting of the ITU Council Working Group on WSIS. After describing issues very similar to the ones described above, Syria proposed to replace the current role of the US Department of Commerce with the ITU, and in particular that there should be a Memorandum of Understanding between ITU and ICANN (Kisrawi 2006).

More recently, it has been proposed to consider discussing proposals to (Cuba 2013)[17]:

a) Establish a mechanism to internationalize the monitoring responsibilities in respect of the Internet Corporation for Assigned Names and Numbers (ICANN), which is currently the responsibility of a single country.
b) Take steps towards transforming the Internet Corporation for Assigned Names and Numbers (ICANN) into an international organization, subject to international law, and for that purpose, sign an agreement with the host country.
c) Establish an intergovernmental mechanism enabling governments, on an equal footing, to carry out their role and responsibilities in international public policy issues pertaining to the Internet.

One can also consider a federated model, with much greater diversity than the present model, that it, separate networks that interconnect in specific ways[18]. At

---

16 See for example the description of the use of mobile payments systems in developing countries (ITU-T 2013b).

17 I thank Juan Alonso Fernández González for having brought to my attention this proposal presented by Cuba at the Fifth Meeting of National Coordinators of the CELAC that was held in Havana on 9–10 May 2013; no consensus was reached regarding the proposal.

18 Such an approach was outlined by Eli Noam (2013).

some point, the various options presented above should be discussed seriously, with the understanding that the status quo is not considered satisfactory by all (for an overview of the criticism of the current situation, see Hill (2014, sections 5 and 6). As suggested elsewhere (Hill 2014, section 7), the ITU would appear to be a proper forum in which to conduct some of those discussions.

Rolf H. Weber

Chapter 5
Visions of Political Power: Treaty Making and Multistakeholder Understanding

Political theory is regularly analysing some basic questions in assessing possible political systems, for example: How should the international system be structured? Do states need to be nation-states? To what extent, and in which form, are supra-state institutions necessary to supplement a system of states? Depending on the structure, the question of the political power allocation becomes relevant.

Traditionally, two visions of political power exist, namely (i) the dominance of state power and (ii) the power distribution (Klimburg 2013, p. 1). State power is founded on the sovereignty concept; power distribution relies on a variety of stakeholders. The divergent visions of political power were apparent in recent debates about Internet regulations; therefore, strengths and weaknesses of the different power allocation models need to be analysed.

1. Visions of Political Power

1.1 Sovereignty Approach

During centuries international treaty making was a domain of state power, however, the globalization by way of the Internet has led to a loss of sovereignty of nation-states. The concept of sovereignty goes back to the Westphalian Peace Treaty of 1648 (Weber 2010, p. 13) and remained the basis for the constitution of the United Nations, still being based on nation-states after World War II. However, in its traditional form, sovereignty lost importance for several reasons.

First, more and more private and professional activities are of a cross-border nature. Already at the end of the last century, the then UN Secretary General Kofi Annan expressed the opinion that a global era would require global engagement and that necessary actions in favor of humanity could not embark on the basis of the traditional sovereignty approach (Jackson 2003, p. 787). In particular, sovereign borders are becoming less significant in the light of global communications possibilities that lower barriers to social and commercial intercourse, meaning that the logic of geographically defined and confined legal rules and systems, based on the principle of territoriality, loses importance (Weber 2010, p. 12; Chick 2010, pp. 7, 10).

Secondly, sovereignty is deeply interwoven into the fabric of international law, and to abandon the concept of sovereignty requires very serious thoughts about the substitute that could efficiently fill the gaps left by its absence (Weber 2010, p. 12; Jackson 2003, p. 790). For example, intermediaries in the Internet have assumed a strong power in shaping norms, even legal norms, giving such kind of customary norms sufficient legitimacy (Wu 1997, p. 666).

In this context, as an alternative, the bottom-up-processes in form of different multistakeholder approaches gained importance in the management of the Internet: to a large extent, academics, specialized technical bodies, and civil society have assumed the responsibility for the programming and protocols designing the global communication systems. At the origin, the US Department of Defence has been involved in the development of the ARPA/DARPA (see Hill in this volume), but as soon as the network of the networks was exceeding the stage of a "pure" communications' exchange system, universities and technical experts assumed the role of improving the Internet's functionalities, as illustrated by the work of Berners Lee (CERN) to establish the WWW or by the search engine companies.

1.2 Multistakeholder Approach

As experience has shown, governance, in particular Internet governance, needs to involve more actors, traditionally not granted with sovereign power, such as business entities implementing self-regulation, non-governmental organizations, and members of civil society (Waters 2009, p. 33). During the last years, the inclusion of all stakeholders in governance and legislation processes (multistakeholderism) has become a hotly debated topic. Some have argued that the joint involvement of all stakeholders having the necessary know-how is desirable (Weber 2013a, p. 367) to strengthen the public's confidence in decision-making processes (Weber 2008, p. 7). Additionally, public participation increases the transparency and accountability of the governing bodies (Weber 2009a, p. 326).

The most prominent approach has been developed by the Working Group of Internet Governance (WGIG) prior to the second summit of the World Summit on the Information Society (WSIS), identifying a number of roles and responsibilities of the various stakeholders such as governments, the commercial world, civil society and the academic/technical community (WGIG 2005). Thereby, the interests of the parties involved should not be defined by any specific group, but through (procedural) participatory mechanisms that reflect the views of the whole society (Weber 2012a, p. 8).

The design of multistakeholder participation[1] depends on the given factual situation. However, it should not be overlooked that apart from the field of Internet governance many other markets and areas have known the inclusion of a variety of stakeholders for (quite) some time now[2]. The most commonly used evaluation criteria for the assessment of standards are the following (van Huijstee 2012, p. 45):

- *Level of the standards:* The level element can concern for example high technical security standards or limitsto living wages;
- *Completenessof the standards:* The completeness aspect depends on the question whether the standards refer to multiple issues or are limited to a single issue only;
- *Market coverage:* The broader the market coverage, the more likely is a widespread functionality of the multistakeholder involvement;
- *Accountability:* It is important to see to it that the standards contain regulations regarding the monitoring, reporting or verification of actions taken by an entity as well as potentially some sanctions;
- *Economic model:* A decentralization of economic decisions and an easy market access lead to a higher chance of having several stakeholders involved;
- *Extent of the involvement of stakeholders:* Entry barriers for stakeholders should be lowered and participation possibilities facilitated;
- *Impact of the existing standards on the decision making of an entity:* Corporate governance as well as corporate social responsibility concepts support the involvement of multistakeholders in participating in the entity's decision-making processes.

Even though multistakeholderism is no longer a new phenomenon, a debatable and critical aspect of this approach still consists in the concretization of multistakeholders' inclusion and participation (see Doria in this volume). Therefore, not surprisingly, the Internet Society (ISOC) announced in early August 2013 the launch of a survey to gain greater insights into multistakeholder governance perceptions and processes at all levels (Internet Society 2013a).

[1] To the definitional background, see Fransen (2012, p. 166).
[2] See the overview given by Mena and Palazzo (2012, pp. 534–535).

2. Infancy of a New Cybersecurity Approach?

2.1 Tendency Back from Multistakeholderism to Cyber-Sovereignty?

Political forces have always intended to get involved in the organization and administration of the Internet. During the last few years, this interest was intensified: Many countries claim that the current mainly private order of the Internet would impair their national security, as illustrated by the position of Russia, China, Tajikistan and Uzbekistan (see Jamart in this volume). For quite some time now, and particularly at the occasion of the World Conference on International Telecommunications (WCIT) in Dubai (December 2012), advocates of a "cyber-sovereignty" approach have raised their voices louder. They are of the opinion that for public interest and security reasons control over the Internet should remain in the competence of national governments including the right to regulate the activities occurring in the Internet as far as accessible by the domestic population.

With the objective of renewing the existing International Telecommunication Regulations (ITR) developed in 1988, member states of the International Telecommunication Union (ITU), the independent United Nations specialized agency for information and communication technologies, recently assembled at the World Conference on International Telecommunications (WCIT). Prior to this event, several motions of the Non-Commercial Users Constituency (NCUC) were published, discussing the promotion of cyber-security, human rights on the Internet, multistakeholderism, as well as the role of governments. Advocates of a liberal approach of Internet regulation identified freedom of expression and privacy as key policy issues[3], beyond the discussions surrounding the creation of new top-level domains.

These debates became possible, since, for the first time in its history, the ITU made a good part of the negotiation documents available to the public and also invited some civil society representatives to attend the conference. During the second half of 2012 many voices raised concerns that the free environment of the Internet could be endangered by the WCIT (also discussed by Jamart in Chapter 3). As a result, thousands of delegates went to Dubai in order to participate in the WCIT-discussions.

3 Intellectual property questions mainly concentrated on the objections against the ratification of the Anti-Counterfeiting Trade Agreement (ACTA) which must be considered to have failed in the meantime.

2.2 Diverging Concepts

The negotiations in Dubai have shown two different visions of political power: Whereas "cyber-sovereignty"-oriented countries advocated for an extension of the mandate of the ITU to include Internet governance issues, proponents of a liberal regime voted for a retention of the *status quo*. Besides, a third camp existed, following neither of the two visions completely.

a) National Control Advocates

As indicated, the participants' interests and expectations regarding the content of the new ITR diverged to a great extent. The negotiations in Dubai have shown that some countries such as Russia, China or Saudi Arabia are attempting to subordinate the management of the Internet to governmental control, mainly by referring to issues such as security and public order. National control is not only a political, but also a technical issue. Such kind of development would namely lead to a (national) fragmentation of the Internet. Certain signs can already be seen: some years ago about 12 million web domains under the Chinese domain ".cn" were registered, now only about 4 million domains have "survived", i.e. China has closed 8 million domains on the way to nationalize the Internet (for a detailed discussion of China's Internet governance policies, see Negro in this volume).

In this context, the so-called "Iranian Internet Resolution" also needs to be taken into account having formerly been submitted to the plenary session at the WCIT by some Arab Countries (Arab States 2012). After nearly two weeks of fruitless discussions, the Iranian representative called for a vote on the inclusion of the "right of access of Member States to international telecommunications services" into the ITR Preamble. Having been adopted by majority decision[4] and included in the preamble of the ITR (WCIT 2012), Western media have presented this amendment as an attempt to open the ITR up to governance and content regulation; they additionally argued, that such a right could be used to force Internet application, content and service providers to provide services to particular organizations (Lynch and Burstein 2012).

b) Preservation of Status Quo Advocates

In contrast, the United States and some allied countries envisaged to only implement minor modifications of the existing regulations. Being of the opinion that the

4 By a vote of 77 for the ITR, 33 against them, and 8 abstentions.

multistakeholder approach represents the best opportunity to regulate the Internet, the US aimed at including general principles without widening the ITR's scope towards the whole Internet framework, as required by Russia for instance. Bearing in mind that the majority of the Internet institutions such as ICANN, IETF etc. have their headquarters on the territory of the United States, the fear of losing influence existed.

Two years ago, *The Economist* expressed the opinion that something so central to the modern world, namely the Internet, would be "shambolically governed" (by a "hotch-potch of organizations with three-to five-letter acronyms") and continued then: "It is in short a bit chaotic. But sometimes chaos, even one that adherents like to claim somewhat disingenuously is a 'multistakeholder' approach, is not disastrous: the Internet mostly works. And the shambles is a lot better than the alternative—which nearly always in this case means governments bringing the Internet under their control" (The Economist 2011). This statement, not coming from government officials, but media deserves further thinking: Is it advisable to change a smoothly running system?

Furthermore, freedom of expression and freedom of information are guaranteed by most international human rights instruments as well as national constitutions. Clear commitments can particularly be seen in the US constitution. Among the big Internet enterprises are many US companies that—based on the guaranteed fundamental rights—strongly disapprove censorship of the Internet also for ideological and economic reasons. After the WCIT, a similar approach was taken by Canada, Australia, Germany and other EU members, although their interest was more centred on avoiding the Internet's fragmentation.

c) Chances of a Moderate Approach

Apart from the two "extreme" positions, a good number of ITU member states such as India, Brazil, South Africa or Egypt fall in between the two camps (Klimburg 2013, p. 2). Following neither of the above mentioned positions regarding the governance of the Internet, they reject Internet censorship and closed networks, but fear that the United States could use Internet governance as a diplomatic tactic. They are also critical of role of the United States and of the big Internet companies on the Internet (Kleinwächter 2013).

The problem of the moderate approach's advocates consists in the fact that flexibility in the decision-making processes has been limited because of the political situation. Quantitatively, the promoters of cyber-sovereignty seem to have a slight majority amongst the ITU members as the unfortunate vote at the end of the WCIT has shown. However, the minority is still controlling the major part of the global infrastructure allowing these countries to also play a "power card". Therefore, in the long run, both sides need to move and try to find a compromise.

3. Lessons from the WCIT

At first, the differentiation between (i) the proponents of a liberal structuring of the Internet, having confidence in a private-economic fulfilment of tasks with as little state interventions as possible and (ii) the representatives of a concept featuring national control interests, may appear rather insignificant. However, this distinction, points into the direction of different regulatory approaches: one in which the political power is increasingly distributed and includes none-state actors, and one in which state power is dominant (Klimburg 2013, p. 1). This analysis is independent from the assessment of whether the WCIT is considered to be a success or a failure.

3.1 WCIT Findings

During the negotiations, the potential implementation of multistakeholderism by the WCIT has been partly perverted since the most important motions (such as the initiative of the United Arab Emirates and some other countries at the end of the first week) were discussed in closed rooms. Beyond that, civil society representatives were hardly heard in the plenary sessions. Furthermore, the Chairman of the WCIT has not complied with the principle observed traditionally in the ITU that consensus should be achieved: he submitted the International Telecommunication Regulations (ITR) and the late presented ("Iranian") Internet Resolution to a majority vote instead of trying to come to the unanimous adoption of the documents.

Politically it might be of interest to realize that the most liberal countries (such as the United States, members of the European Union, Canada, Australia) are in a minority; from a legal point of view, however, the ambiguity of having an international instrument which is only applied in a part of the world is less than ideal since it resulted in a split amongst ITU Members. After the WCIT, a binary global scene seems to have emerged, most of the developing world (with the exception of India) had sided with the cyber-sovereignty advocates. The WCIT had morphed into a "battle", partly (and problematically) even called a "digital cold war" (for a detailed discussion, see Mueller 2013), of the liberal West against the rest of the world. Obviously it can be argued that the new provisions of the ITU should be interpreted in the sense of the human rights-driven ITU charter, but reality (in particular in the context of the WCIT debates) shows that national control approaches seem to have prevailed.

Some authors defend the way how the WCIT in Dubai has been conducted and describe the conference as a success, mainly arguing that the key issues were identified and discussed and therewith some progress has been achieved with the revision of the International Telecommunication Regulations (ITR) (Hill 2013, p. 3). This assessment from an insider of the ITU reflects the enormous efforts taken during the last few years and months to come to an adaptation of the outdated ITR. In fact, a couple of questions could be resolved and those countries not ratifying the ITR do not let their population benefit from the respective advantages (for example on roaming prices). Nevertheless, from a more theoretical point of view, it cannot be overlooked that the "divide" between the cyber-sovereignty promoters and the multistakeholder advocates was widened in Dubai (see Kuehn in this volume).

3.2 Consequences for Multistakeholderism

a) New Situation after the WCIT

The outcome of the WCIT in Dubai must be seen as a set-back for the multistakeholder approach. Not only have the civil society's voices been hardly heard at the WCIT, but also the vague wording of certain provisions, particularly of the (not legally binding) Internet Resolution leads to a wide discretion of national legislators in implementing the global rules. As a result, the risk exists that a fundamental re-interpretation of the multistakeholder governance concept as formulated in the WSIS 2005 could occur in the future. In other words, the broadening of political debates as introduced by the WSIS is confronted with the challenge of being re-narrowed to negotiations between nation-states.

Not only has the ambivalent Internet Resolution the potential to be (mis-)used in order to re-state the previous Internet governance principles in a fundamental way by limiting the scope of Internet freedom, but also substantive norms are not ideally designed: (i) The provision on freedom of access to international telecommunications services is granting the right to ITU Members and not to individuals (paragraph 3 of the preamble) and (ii) the broad understanding of the term "security" in article 5A of the ITR invites to be referred to for any policy reasons by ITU Members. These provisions appear to be a drawback for the proponents of multistakeholderism. Finally, some issues such as data protection/privacy and cyber-security have been completely left out from the WCIT debates.

b) Foundation of Multistakeholderism

Based on the experiences of the last months, multistakeholder advocates need to identify and describe the objectives of this approach afresh: For a better understanding it is important "to analyse (i) what the organizations do (ii) how they do it (iii) what characteristics, values, and best practices are widely shared among these organizations" (Waz and Weiser 2012, p. 341). In this context, an assessment of the "success" (including guidelines on how to measure "success") would be worthwhile to conduct, encompassing the stated and executed functions of multistakeholder organizations, the scope and scale of existing problems, the diversity of participation and the incentives to participate, as well as the role of, or relation to, sovereign government entities.

In this context, the substantive issues of multistakeholder initiatives need to be elaborated in more detail. To this end, the following factors are to be taken into account (see also Waz and Weiser 2012, pp. 242–243):

- *Openness:* Access to discussions, negotiations and decisions must be open for interested and concerned persons;
- *Transparency:* Procedures have to be transparent in formal and substantive respects allowing to make an appropriate picture of the situation;
- *Accessibility:* Information sources need to be accessible for interested and concerned persons;
- *Accountability:* Decision-makers must be accountable to those being exposed to the respective decisions, i.e. responsibility is an important element in corporate structures;
- *Credibility:* Decision-makers should seek to achieve an acknowledgment of their credibility by the concerned persons;
- *Adequately resourced:* Multistakeholder involvement and participation requires sufficient human and financial resources in order to enable the respective processes;
- *Consensus-based:* Acceptability for decisions taken will increase if they are reached by consensus of all concerned persons and not by (sharp) majority votes;
- *Opportunity for appeal/challenge:* An entity of any nature should provide for a possibility to file a complaint against a given decision to an independent panel of "judges".
- *Ability to resist capture:* Decision-making bodies must avoid to be captured by lobbying groups.

The new modes of governance as introduced by the multistakeholder approach must also gain democratic accountability by constituting a link between the public sphere and civil society. Such link should include the media-based critical public debate of their operation and outcomes, which may function as a (diffuse) corrective (Héritier and Lehmkuhl 2011, p. 138). Thereby, the public debate must allow to define the potential accountability of the involved actors. Accountability is the acknowledgement and assumption of responsibility for actions, decisions, and policies within the scope of the designated role. Accountability embraces the obligation of the accountable to the accountee, according to which the former must give account of, explain and justify his functions' exercise against criteria of the same kind (Weber 2009, p. 133).

Improved accountability in the Internet regulations' environment requires an extended consultation and inclusion of civil society. Public accountability can take place through institutional checks and balances based on transparent information. In addition, supervisory authorities must have the capacity to oversee the proper execution of the respective duties (Weber 2009, pp. 140–142; Grant and Keohane 2005, pp. 29–33). In order to enhance accountability, it is helpful to build upon this principle by addressing the following three elements (Weber 2011, p. 147). First, standards need to be introduced which hold governing bodies accountable, at least on the organizational level. Such standards help to improve accountability. Second, information should be made more easily available to accountability-holders, enabling them to apply the standards in question to the performance of those who are held to account; in order to make information flow active rather than passive (seen from a recipient's point of view) consultation procedures are to be established. Third, accountability-holders must be able to impose some sort of sanction in order to attach costs to the failure to meet the standards; such kind of "sanctioning" is only possible if adequate participation schemes are realized through direct voting channels and indirect representation schemes. Appropriate accountability must also go hand in hand with procedural fairness allowing the concerned and interested parties to be heard in discussions and negotiations as well as to be in a position to challenge a decision[5].

c) Ongoing Initiatives

Multistakeholder advocates must speak up on several occasions (Kleinwächter 2013), among others—as already shown—at the World Telecommunication/ICT Policy Forum (WTPF) in May 2013 in Geneva or particularly in the context of the newly established UNCSTD Working Group on Enhanced Cooperation (CSTD

5 See below 4.3.

2013a) in order to (re)claim some lost power and to contribute to a multistakeholder regime of Internet governance, which is based on several pillars (international organizations, national governments, civil society, technical and academic community).

Contrary to the WCIT, the conclusion of an international agreement cannot be expected in the context of these meetings. Aiming at being a "high-level international event to exchange views on the key policy issues arising from today's fast changing information and communication technology (ICT) environment" (ITU 2013), the WTPF is (just) geared to adopt recommendations. The multistakeholder-based UNCSTD Working Group on Enhanced Cooperation will probably start its work in late 2013; the final report should be available by 2014 and will be discussed during the 69th UN General Assembly (Kleinwächter 2013). Notwithstanding the informal nature of these initiatives and the non-binding character of the Internet Governance Forum (IGF) strong multistakeholder voices could help to push the decision-making procedures towards a power distribution model.

4. Way Forward

Obviously, there is no easy way forward to overcome the emerging tensions between the cyber-sovereignty and the multistakeholder approaches. Moreover, different routes exist and the choice of the way forward depends on the specific environment. Nevertheless, a few general thoughts may be expressed in order to lay further ground for an appropriate framework governing global Internet relations.

4.1. Operation of Global Politics and Adjustment of Sovereignty Concept

a) Concept of Cosmopolitanism

According to an acknowledged understanding of global politics, different levels at which political theory may operate can be distinguished (Caney 2006, pp. 2–3): (i) A global political theory needs to be liaised with domestic political theory, i.e. it must be assessed to what extent notions of domestic importance (such as "nation" or "state") are to be adapted at the global level, and if so, how it should be done. (ii) A global political theory must be able to provide guidance as to what principles should be adopted and which institutions should be put into practice.

(iii) Finally, the question is to be tackled how general principles should be applied to specific issues.

In view of the globalization of (inter-)governmental relations and governance (see Weber 2012a, p. 7), political theory refers to the notion of "cosmopolitanism", embracing three elements defined by Pogge (1994, pp. 89–90):

- *Individualism:* The ultimate units of concern are human beings or persons, rather than ethnic, cultural, or religious communities, nations, or states, being units of concern only indirectly, in virtue of their individual members or citizens.
- *Universality:* The status of ultimate unit of concern attaches to every person being equal, not merely to some subsets of persons, such as men, whites, etc.
- *Generality:* Persons are ultimate units of concern for everyone, not only for some, such as compatriots or fellow religionists.

From this philosophical understanding the conclusion can be drawn that guiding principles for humanity do have a global nature, even if influenced by smaller entities. In particular, the values that motivate democratic and effective governance at a domestic level can also motivate some form of democratic and effective global governance[6].

Consequently, the traditional understanding of political structures as command by an understanding which allocates to the law- or rule-makers the incentive of inducing people to execute certain actions in the sense that people think about what to choose and what to do should be replaced by a more decentralized approach (see Weber 2012a, p. 6; Raz 1994, p. 214; Reed 2012, pp. 248 *et seq.*). In order words, the absence of hierarchical structures and the fact that new issues are complex must be acknowledged. Flat structures on different appropriate levels facilitate decision-making by including the relevant persons and organizations at the actual point of their concern (Weber 2012a, p. 8).

b) Flat Structures in a Complex Environment

The current problems in the context of Internet regulation require by nature a broader and more collective decision-making than in a traditional state. Insofar, the movement towards global governance is unavoidable. Global governance refers to a new "order, characterized in part by porous borders and power sharing amongst the states, non-state-actors, and new geographic and/or functional entities" (Winchester 2009, p. 22). Consequently, global governance encompasses

6 See also Caney (2006, p. 266); for a general overview to structural visions of post-national law, see Krisch (2010).

collective efforts enabling the concerned persons to identify, understand, and address worldwide problems going beyond the capacity of individual states to solve (Weber 2010, p. 15).

Global interactions encompass a variety of exchanges between a large number of communications' participants. Therefore, hierarchical structures will become less important and new issues will become more complex. Flat structures on different appropriate levels facilitate the decision-making by including the relevant persons and organizations at the actual point of their respective concern. These ongoing developments necessarily lead to an altered notion of state sovereignty and at least partly to a reduction of its importance in favour of a flourishing of sources, actors, and authorities; in certain circumstances, sovereignty could even be enhanced by leveraging it through joint action (Weber 2010, p. 15).

Since regulatory regimes evolve in view of the societal and political context, private autonomous regimes are part of the multi-layered governance if developed with the objective to increase institutionalization, based on initiation and wide building support (Weber 2012b, p. 7; Bernstein and Cashore 2007, pp. 349–351). Other elements are the significance of institutional environments, the dynamics of relationships, and how non-sovereign bodies respond to multiple legitimacy claims in complex and dynamic structures (Black 2008, pp. 137–164). Not concentrating on normative validity allows to put more emphasis on efficiciency and public value maximization (Senn 2011, p. 228).

Therefore, the power allocation analysis tackling the "core sovereignty" concepts must also shed light on legitimacy questions. The following elements must be considered (Weber 2010, p. 16; Jackson 2003, pp. 796–800):

- Recognition of certain non-governmental international institutions as the legitimate entities for regulation of some of the relevant parameters;
- Development of a general theory of sources of international law based on what is often called *"acquis communautaire"*; and
- Elaboration of a more sophisticated concept of "interdependence" as a consequence of the cooperative sovereignty approach.

Cultural relativism also needs to be taken into account. Based on the assumption that all cultural views and perceptions are equally valid and no culture is superior to any other culture when comparing systems of morality, law or politics, the concept of cultural relativism describes the principle of evaluating the beliefs, values, and practices of a culture from the viewpoint of that culture itself (Howson 2009). All cultural norms and values derive their meaning within a specific social context. Considering the respective culture individually helps avoiding judging other cultures by the standards of one's own culture which may result in a more neutral assessment of the respective country's values, practices and regulations.

4.2. Extension of Multistakeholder Foundations and Inclusion of Human Rights

a) Network Structures

In "A New World Order", Anne-Marie Slaughter developed already nine years ago a model offering a solution for the "governance dilemma" by referring to "governmental networks" (Slaughter 2004, p. 12/13). These networks should be set out as "relatively loose, cooperative arrangements across borders between and among like agencies that seek to respond to global issues" (Anderson 2005, p. 1257; Slaughter 2004, p. 14). In order to close gaps through coordination among government from different states (Weber 2010, p. 13) they are "creating a new sort of power, authority and legitimacy" (Anderson 2005, p. 1257; see also Slaughter and Zaring 2006, p. 215).

Presupposing disaggregated states, this proposed concept sees governments as a decomposed collection of disparate institutions, each with its own powers, mandates, incentives and motivations and is therefore contrary to the perception of unitary states according to traditional international law (Slaughter 2004, pp. 12–13). Since national governments cannot effectively address every problem in a networked world they, in Slaughter's view, should delegate their responsibilities and "actual sovereign power to a limited number of supranational government officials" (Slaughter 2004, p. 263). These competent bodies would have to engage in intensive interactions and in the elaboration and adoption of codes of best practice and agreements on coordinated solutions to common problems (Slaughter 2004, p. 263).

Subsequent to Slaughter's concept, further concepts were introduced within the last decade, gradually extending the initial concept. Most theoretical approaches are based on the understanding that informal law-making must play a more important role. Thereby, the challenge of "informal" international law-making consists in maintaining the law's neutrality and protective force and in balancing informality, which may be needed to enable effective cooperation or to avoid traditional structures (Weber 2012b, p. 5). According to Pauwelyn (2011, pp. 137–139), such an approach requires a shift in international law from being a value-free instrument enabling state-to-state cooperation to a genuine regulatory order, as well as a process balancing effectiveness with democratic accountability. This approach's advantage consists in the fact that it reduces formal requirements and increases dynamic adaption potential. Additionally, being a center-piece of any stable order, "informal" law-making can be controlled by law for making it more accountable (Weber 2012b, p. 5).

A similar approach was developed by Chick who analyzed the disjuncture between the law and practices in cyberspace caused by the information technologies' developments (Chick 2010), thereby emphasizing the suitability of customary international rules as a template for formulating Internet law-making rules by adapting customary rules for developing a set of determinants for Internet law (Chick 2010, pp. 185 *et seq.*). Lately, Kulesza has shown the development from international governance to "International Internet Law" being a customary legal framework based on international cooperation of all stakeholders and the incorporation of the idea of "civic virtue" (Kulesza 2012, pp. 125 *et seq.*).

In the context of these theoretical approaches, the more practice-oriented approach of multistakeholderism must be assessed. Developing policies in a transparent and open step-by-step process from below, the multistakeholder approach led to remarkable innovations and new forms of international rule-making within the past 20 years. Replacing the multistakeholder approach by an intergovernmental system following a "policy from the top" would hamper growth and restrict human rights (Kleinwächter 2013). According to these new theoretical approaches, the concept of multistakeholderism calls for different forms of "co-governance" in a multilayer and multiplayer mechanism of coordination and collaboration (Weber 2012a, p. 8).

b) Human Rights Inclusion

In addition, thereby avoiding to be squeezed into the technical field of the ITR, multistakeholder advocates should now also broaden their perspectives and better include the on-going human rights debates following the Resolution on the promotion, protection and enjoyment of human rights in the Internet (UN Human Rights Council 2012) that could add to the multistakeholder approach's credibility.

This approach is all the more justified (i) as human rights have been included into the preamble of the ITR by the delegates at the WCIT and (ii) as human rights gain importance in the context of the ongoing discussions about the concept of an improved corporate social responsibility understanding (Weber 2012). Thereby, the risk of a digital "Iron-Curtain" fragmenting the Internet and discrediting the international system providing for robust connections (as expression of security) could be mitigated.

In making fundamental rights fruitful for the design of a co-operation framework between states, reference can be made to existing standards as expressed in international human rights instruments, but private initiatives should also not be disregarded. For example, the Global Network Initiative (GNI) has developed soft law principles (guidelines) for adoption by major Internet companies (Global Internet Initiative 2013). The GNI is a privately organized lobby group of information and communications technology companies, civil society organizations, investors and academics, founded with the goal to protect and advance the Internet users' fundamental rights.

Such fundamental principles should lead to internal mechanisms which are designed to achieve their purposes through the respective behavioural processes (Weber 2013):

- *Values:* Procedures should not only delineate rules, but also basic sets of ethics.
- *Reputation:* Negative externalities could cause serious problems making it advisable to promote greater citizenship.
- *Respect:* Efforts to foster mutual respect with communities and stakeholders need to be realized.
- *Integrity:* Positive and negative impacts of a certain behavior on the society in general and the human, health, and social environment in particular should be evaluated.
- *Excellence:* The encouragement to achieve excellence in actions and decisions is of importance.

The increased tendency of having businesses complying with human rights and ethical standards is helping to establishing common interest positions of individuals and corporate entities in Internet governance debates. Therefore, cybersovereignty advocates could be encouraged to adequately take into account the respective interests and objectives of the civil and the economic society.

4.3. Accountability and Legitimacy

a) Strengthening Accountability

As already mentioned, global accountability is well suited for augmenting the scope and range of public international law. The establishment of standards in terms of specific values that lay the foundation of accountability could provide for a viable way forward (Weber 2009, p. 147). The more towards accountability goes along with the present trend in international law to dynamically protect humanity rather than states by international norms, for example by strengthening the set of rules about human rights. Thus, a government may acknowledge certain groups as legitimate representatives of public interest, although the persons in power refer to the rule of non-intervention (Lane 2013, p. 17).

Generally looking, multistakeholder organizations and processes have the potential to play an important role in governance issues if the stakeholders can (i) build trust, knowledge and expertise among a diverse set of interests, (ii) bring the characteristics and values represented by them to the relevant governance processes and (iii) bring greater flexibility, adaptability, speed, or efficiency to the governance processes than is possible in case of use of traditional tools of governments, thereby fostering innovation in policy-making (Waz and Weiser 2012, pp. 343/44).

A further important element concerns the procedural fairness: The legitimacy of a democratic decision-making process depends on how the included stakeholders are able to influence this process (Mena and Palazzo 2012, p. 539). Procedural fairness includes for example the right to be heard in proceedings and the right to file a complaint if a decision has a negative impact on the concerned individual or entity.

b) Legitimacy and Inclusion

Inclusion of concerned individuals and corporate entities means (i) accessibility through the creation of mechanisms for the potentially affected stakeholders to have meaningful substantive engagements (Mena and Palazzo 2012, p. 539) and (ii) involvement in the activities, structures, and processes having an influence on the way how certain matters are governed. In view of the difficulty to operationalize this approach, Jürgen Habermas (1992, p. 161) tried to link the procedural aspects with the "discourse principle", assuming that just those norms can claim validity which receive the approval of potentially affected people, insofar as they participate in a free rational discourse. In this context, openness facilitates direct participation and appropriate representation of all interested and impacted persons. Insofar, when assessing the WCIT negotiations in Dubai, it cannot be overlooked that the multistakeholder representatives have been partly marginalized in the decision-making process. Therefore, to be fair, deliberations must be structured in a way that power relations between stakeholders are neutralized (Waz and Weiser 2012, p. 342).

The criteria to be applied in assessing the democratic legitimacy of multistakeholder initiatives should thereby encompass input and output factors as follows (Mena and Palazzo 2012, p. 537):

Table 5: Criteria and definitions for democratic legitimacy

Dimension	Criterion	Definition
Input	*Inclusion*	Involvement of stakeholders affected by the issue in the structures and processes of the MSI
	Procedural fairness	Neutralization of power differences in decision-making structures
	Consensual orientation	Culture of cooperation and reasonable disagreement
	Transparency	Transparency of structures, processes and results
Output	*Coverage*	Number of rule-targets, following the rules
	Efficacy	Fit of the rules to the issues
	Enforcement	Practical implementation of the rules and their verification procedures

Consequently, strategies for strengthening the multistakeholder approach could embrace many elements of choice and exploration (Waz and Weiser 2012, pp. 345–346), such as:

- "Nudging" stakeholders to engage in relevant multistakeholder initiatives or to help create new ones (for example through the bully pulpit or informal pressure);
- Providing recognition or encouragement for multistakeholder initiatives or developing approaches;
- Providing "a seat at the table" in policy development (for example by helping to shape the policy);
- Procurement policy;
- Post-hoc enforcement (providing a "regulatory backstop" in the event of non-compliance by a party with the objectives of the multistakeholder initiative;
- Standard-setting or rulemaking (formally embracing the norms and standards developed by the relevant multistakeholder organization).

In sum, the multistakeholder community should be integrated into stable and predictable decision-making processes designed to develop democratic structures and compliance with fundamental rights, leading to the mentioned "cosmopolitanism" in decision-making procedures. Such kind of cosmopolitanism should be much broader than the old cosmopolitanism that can be found in the Kantian framework (Lane 2013, p. 22) highlighting global distributive justice besides launching civil and political rights.

In order to overcome the obviously still existing gap, it will be necessary to strengthen the efforts to establish appropriate structures and organizational elements for multistakeholder processes. Concretely, representatives of nation-states and international organizations should increasingly recognize that decentralized decision-making procedures involving a variety of stakeholders are usually modern and dynamic; it also allows the implementation of adequate fora for debates and discussions. Furthermore, sufficient coverage with reasonable reputational and retaliatory tools can generate a sufficient degree of compliance (Weber 2012b, p. 9).

Avri Doria

Chapter 6
Use [and Abuse] of Multistakeholderism in the Internet[1]

Multistakeholderism has become the Internet governance regime choice of many. While it is certain that everyone does not have the same modalities in mind when they utter the term, it is apparent that for many the multistakeholder model shows the way forward. Though popular as the idea is, it is worth pointing out at the beginning of this chapter that this is not universally shared, "the model is actively being challenged on a routine basis" (Alexander 2011).

Thus, the term multistakeholderism is being used in many contexts in Internet Governance. It has been used, and perhaps abused, to explain why one organization has greater legitimacy than another. It has been used in cases where most of the participants believe the term is being used properly. And it has been used by single stakeholder groups who exclude other stakeholders in an attempt to mask the organization's single stakeholder nature. A first step in exploring the use, and possible abuse, of the term, and to find a way forward for Internet governance, is to briefly review the term itself, its origins, its related practices and its current state of development. In order to move forward, it helps to know how the model has developed and is developing.

---

1 With apologies to Friedrich Nietzsche. In looking at the history of the term *multistakeholderism,* while looking forward I am aware that: "life is in need of the services of history, however, must be grasped as firmly as must the proposition … that an excess of history is harmful" (Nietzsche 2013). The words [and Abuse] are placed in brackets in the style of the diplomatic negotiation in the realization that anything this chapter calls an abuse would not be regarded as such by those making the utterance.

1. The Setting

1.1. Definition

Multistakeholderism in Internet governance refers most directly to the words found in Paragraph 34 of the Tunis Agenda for the Information Society (WSIS 2005):

> "A working definition of Internet governance is the development and application by governments, the private sector and civil society, in their respective roles, of shared principles, norms, rules, decision-making procedures, and programmes that shape the evolution and use of the Internet."

It is a definition that allows for many interpretations; it does not propose a "central Internet authority" or a "one-stakeholder leadership model" as some governments suggested during WSIS I. Instead, it proposes a decentralized but inclusive and participatory concept which gives all stakeholders a place by referring to their "respective roles". It links them together in a network of shared rights, duties and responsibilities and encourages everybody to participate in transparent, open and bottom-up policy development and decision-making processes (Kleinwächter 2011b, p. 7).

As more and more organizations claim to be multistakeholders, though, it is becoming obvious that there may be other definitions for this word. While some may be using the word cynically and just trying to jump on a popular bandwagon, most are using the word genuinely. It has become clear that there are at least two basic categories of definition: (1) those that uphold the belief in a structure with equivalent stakeholders who participate on an equal footing; and (2) those that uphold the belief that one stakeholder is more equal than the other stakeholders and that the primary stakeholder discharges their duty by consulting the other stakeholders before making decisions. The first definition lends itself toward a notion of multistakeholder effort to create full democratic participation. The second sense lends itself toward continuation of a hierarchical model where decisions are determined by a single dominant stakeholder group. In this chapter, the primary frame of reference will be the first interpretation that reads the working definition of Internet governance as a call for participatory democracy in Internet governance.

The community has termed institutional processes that meet, or attempt to meet the requirements of the working definition, as multistakeholderism. Other terms that refer to governance models that implement paragraph 34 are multistakeholder models or multistakeholder governance. The primary requirement of multistakeholder models is the inclusion of all stakeholders in decision making processes.

1.2. Is Multistakeholderism the Right Term?

What is an -ism? We often speak of -isms, for example, absolutism, bullionism, capitalism, deism and many other -isms. The Phrontistery (2013) lists 2343 -isms representing "philosophical, political or moral doctrine or a belief system(s)"[2].

The Oxford English Dictionary (OED 2002) defines -ism as: "a form of doctrine, theory or practice having, or claiming to have a distinctive character or relation", whereas the Merriam-Webster dictionary (2013) defines -ism as: "1. a distinctive doctrine, cause, or theory; 2. an oppressive and especially discriminatory attitude or belief". The suffix -ism has had the following uses (Thorne 2013) that pertain to Internet governance: "the practice of", "the condition of", "the belief in". At some point in time, the suffix became a term in itself. I first encountered the term -ism as a concept in "Today's ISMS: Socialism, Capitalism, Fascism, Communism and Liberalism" (Ebenstein et al. 2000)[3]. In all of the -isms discussed in "Today's ISMS", there is both a theoretical framework and an active political component. Calling something an -ism is a way to categorize a concept and to criticize it and, sometimes, to condemn it. Any reader looking at the global political dialogue will notice that if an author wishes to condemn an idea, it is called Socialism or Liberalism, depending on the speaker's political alignment. According to Anriette Esterhuysen, some of us "use of the term 'multistakeholderism' as if it is an established philosophical approach, based on commonly understood principles" (2011, p. 58).

Is multistakeholderism an -ism? Markus Kummer (2013) speaks of the concept of multistakeholder cooperation having been "elevated to an -ism by some". In the literature, one finds references to multistakeholder models, multistakeholder processes, multistakeholder structures and a multistakeholder architecture. Additionally, the question remains as to whether there are theoretical frameworks and political movements for multistakeholderism. It seems that the theoretical frameworks are just being created; and that it may be fair to consider the multiple coordinated and uncoordinated actions meant to further the multistakeholder model in Internet governance, as a nascent political movement.

I personally have long resisted the impulse to use the term multistakeholderism. In speech and in writing, I refer mostly to the multistakeholder model or to multistakeholder structures. Not only do I believe that political -isms have a bad reputation, I believe that -isms are concepts that have become fixed in their definitions. As the multistakeholder framework is still evolving, I find it difficult to accept the

2 Multistakeholderism is not on the list.

3 Liberalism was added to the title in the Eleventh Edition in 1985. This was not in the version of the book I read in 1967.

term multistakeholderism. Others have also written of their discomfort with the term: "I do not believe multistakeholder participation, as outlined in the WSIS principles, has reached that stage. Nor do I think we should strive for such a stage" (Esterhuysen 2011, p. 58).

Briefly, but for completeness sake, looking at the prefix of the word, "multi", one may also have questions about a working definition that only includes "by governments, the private sector and civil society". Previous work on global public goods as early as 1999 had defined another term—tripartism.

> "Since effective solutions to pressing global problems are unlikely to emerge from forums that exclude these important actors, a new tripartism is recommended, involving government, business and civil society" (Kaul et al. 1999, p. XXX)

Some of the current tussles in the area of multistakeholderism concern this part of the definition. Are there only three stakeholder groups? Various groups, e.g. the academic and technical community have long been advocating for their role as stakeholders. The Tunis Agenda, and subsequent diplomatic based documents, excludes this community:

> "36. We recognize the valuable contribution by the academic and technical communities within those stakeholder groups mentioned in paragraph 35 to the evolution, functioning and development of the Internet" (WSIS 2005).

That which some see as a stakeholder group is relegated by the dominant stakeholder, governments, as being a sub-group within other stakeholder groups.

So far, only the suffix and the prefix of the term have been described, leaving the core of the term "stakeholder" for last. The UN system defines three stakeholder groups, with one above all the others. Other models define the breakdown differently, e.g. ICANN defines many types of stakeholder split: governments and users, technologists and policy wonks, commercial users and non-commercial users, policy makers and implementers, and contracted parties and non-contracted parties; each of which is considered equal, at least for some definition of equality. The Internet Engineering Task Force (IETF) does not divide its participants into stakeholder groups at all, yet I include it among the multistakeholder organizations. In the IETF's case, all participants are welcome to participate as equals regardless of their stakeholder group.

There are many issues around the use of the term multistakeholderism. Nonetheless, it is the term that is commonly used and thus must be discussed and understood. In this chapter, multistakeholderism will be used in addition to "multistakeholder model" and "multistakeholder framework"—in the sense of "the belief in, and the practice of, and the condition of". An attempt will also be made to distinguish between the uses and the abuses of the term.

1.3. Multistakeholder Models

Internet governance was not the first field to explore multistakeholder models of governance. The earliest work on various models of participatory democracy that lead the way for multistakeholderism can be found in the work of Elinor Ostrom (Ostrom 1990) of economic governance models. Some of this century's references were in the field of sustainable development (Weiner 2000). This paper focuses on the use of multistakeholder terminology in the field of Internet governance.

> "While there is no one single multistakeholder model, it is a form of participatory democracy that allows all of those who have a stake in a policy to take part in crafting that policy. There are many variants of the model and the theoretical underpinnings of the model are still an active discussion topic. While the composition of the stakeholder groups may vary, when used in reference to Internet governance, the stakeholders generally include governments acting in behalf of their citizens, civil society and non-governmental organizations that are self-selected advocates of the interests of the global public good[4] as they understand it, the private sector commercial organizations that reflect the businesses that affect and are affected by the Internet, the Internet technical community that is responsible for the development and maintenance of the network itself, and academics" (Liddicoat and Doria 2012).

4 While discussion of Global Public Goods is beyond the scope of this chapter, the reference to the Internet as a Global Public Good recognizes that: "defining a public good is no easy task. Nor is identifying one: areas treated as public goods in some contexts may elsewhere be treated as private; public goods may be converted back into privately delivered services; and even the clearest examples of public goods can also be conceived of as bundles containing both public and private attributes. Yet even within this ambiguity, the Internet undeniably has the makings of a public good" (Spar 1999, p. 348).
14 years later, the discussion on whether the Internet is or is not a Global Public Good is still being discussed. At the risk of being called an Internet exceptionalist, I believe that it might be in a class of its own and hence difficult to pigeon hole.

2. Multistakeholderism in Internet Governance

Multistakeholderism in Internet governance finds its origin in the work of the Working Group on Internet Governance (WGIG). During the first part of the World Summit on the Information Society (WSIS), governments came to an impasse over the issue of "who should govern the Internet".

The origin of the term's usage in Internet governance is described as:

"It was WGIG that consolidated the use of the term multi-stakeholder. The WGIG Report itself uses the term 11 times and, among other things, identifies the need for a 'global multi-stakeholder forum to address Internet-related public policy issues'. Also the WGIG Background Report uses the term 11 times. Finally, it was via WGIG that the term found its way into the Tunis Agenda. The Tunis Agenda has 18 references to 'multi-stakeholder', four of them related to the Internet Governance Forum" (Kummer 2013).

2.1. The Question of Bottom-up Processes

While sometimes used as a synonym or a requirement for the multistakeholder model, bottom-up processes, also known as grassroots processes, are neither necessary nor sufficient to define a multistakeholder process. Bottom-up processes are defined as processes where all decisions come from cooperation of the communities affected by the decisions. In Internet governance, the bottom-up process means that no decision can be made that does not find its origins in the affected stakeholder group(s). It should be noted that the true degree to which a processes adhere to a bottom-up model depends on the degree to which all relevant interests are represented among the stakeholders and the degree to which the organizations respect their own bottom-up processes.

Bottom-up participation of all stakeholders is not the same as full participation of all stakeholders. In this chapter it is not assumed that a bottom-up process is necessary in order to implement a multistakeholder process. In the examples given later in this paper, one can argue that none of them adequately meets the strict definition of bottom-up processes. And even ICANN, which has the most well-formed model of bottom-up processes, may follow it more in the breech than in practice.

2.2. Relation to Democracy

To misquote Winston Churchill on democracy (Drake 2011)[5], "multistakeholderism is the worst form of governance, except all the others that have been tried". This is not as disrespectful as it sounds; the essence of the multistakeholder framework is a form of democratic governance. More specifically, it is a form of participatory democracy that attempts to go beyond the limitations of representative democracy while building on, and including, representative democracy.

> "Democracy is defined in different ways in a multilateral context and by different stakeholders according to their particular perspectives. Governments generally hold to a view based on national sovereignty with equal say for all countries and decisions reached through consensus. Each citizen is held to be represented and to be able to influence decisions through national consultation and decision-making mechanisms. Some are of the view that most governments include members of their civil society in their delegations to the extent practical and in any case they take into account the interests of their civil societies when establishing agreements at multilateral bodies. Civil society advocates on the other hand would argue that the term goes beyond this, requiring direct full participation in decision making by many nongovernmental groups from the private sector and civil society. Furthermore, they have expressed the view that governments are not actively or consistently consulting with other sectors of society prior to establishing agreements within multilateral bodies" (WGIG 2005, p. 239).

Often an underlying issue is the degree of representativeness of a participant in the Internet governance process. Governments assume they are the representatives of the people, even when they come from states that have a limited democratic practice or tradition. And given the assumption of their own status as representatives, they often deprecate other stakeholders by asking questions of "who do you represent and how did they select you?". The presumption of this question is always that the Westphalian government is the only representative that the people need, and that the other stakeholders are, at best, self-selected pretenders to representativeness. The question "who do you represent" is one that misunderstands the multistakeholder process, where it is the interests of the people, and not the people themselves, that are represented[6].

---

5 "It has been said that democracy is the worst form of government except all the others that have been tried."

6 Some have argued that the stakeholder model is flawed in that it does not allow for the direct representation of the people in its workings. Pivotal to this discussion is the perceived inability to scale such a process of direct democracy, instead relying on democratic processes within each stakeholder group to reach the grassroots.

Beyond that, most government representatives are not close to the people represented in the country, as they are often bureaucratic appointees that are not subject to the vagaries of the democratic process. It is not unusual for the same national representative to hold the job for a lifetime, allowing them to become very experienced at diplomatic processes, but also leaving them quite distant from the population they purport to represent.

Granting, however, that to some degree, these diplomatic representatives do represent a country with a democratic tradition and that there is a link to the population whose interests they represent, the question is often asked: why is this not enough? The answer comes from understanding that to represent the complex interests of any individual, it takes more than a government representative. A government only represents an individual as a citizen situated geographically within the confines of a single state. In a world with transnational culture, global relationships and an Internet that transcends geographical borders, the representation of an individual as citizen, while necessary, is not sufficient. Each individual is situated in a complex world of affinities, capabilities and needs. Each individual belongs to many stakeholder groups, and needs the voices of all of these groups to cover his or her myriad of interests. I am a citizen, a researcher, a consumer, a parent, an Internet user, an employee of several companies and have interests that need to be recognized and served in all of these aspects of my person and life. No single type of stakeholder group can serve all of the aspects of the world's population. Additionally, there are many interests that are cross-border in nature, that cannot be served by a single country's representatives. It is often non-governmental organizations (NGOs) that serve these cross-border interests without discrimination based on geography, nationality or other circumstance.

Non-governmental organizations and epistemic (or expert) communities provide various kinds of information that are relevant to the pursuit of collective goals. NGOs also have important effects on agenda setting and the evolution of public attention to global goals (Martin 1999).For humanity's interests to be truly represented, we must have a multistakeholder form of framework. Whether it is NGOs that represent the needs and interests of the people they serve, the technical community in their role as the creators and maintainers of the technology, or the academics who attempt to understand the dynamics of the social systems within which we live in this highly interconnected world, all of the stakeholder groups have a place at the table where they can discuss the issues and decide on solutions for Internet governance on an equal footing. Anything else leaves some interests without representation, and thus leaves the populations who feel and express these interests unrepresented, at least in that respect. Full representation requires multistakeholder representation.

2.3. Equal Footing

Equal footing does not mean that in all cases all stakeholders have the same role; capacities and needs vary from circumstance to circumstance. What it does mean is that stakeholders have equivalent status and an equal access to the deliberations and to the decision-making processes. This can be challenging given the inequality in power experienced in the world.

The world, of which the internet is a part, is not an equal place. There are vast differences in access to resources and power, between countries, and within countries. Governance bodies and processes need to recognise these differences, and try to redress them to achieve legitimacy over time (Esterhuysen 2011, p. 56)

One of the great challenges for those who advocate the multistakeholder model is how to not only be inclusive, but in finding ways to overcome the structural differences in the status of the various stakeholders so that they can all participate on an equal footing. Whether the disparity is based on the Global North-South split or the wealth differential between Industrial actors and NGO advocates, this is a challenge for all of the Internet governance institutions. It is a challenge that has not yet been met adequately by any organization as of this writing.

The notion of equal footing is closely allied to the notion of "respective roles".

2.4. Respective Roles

This subject is often referred to as "respective roles and responsibilities" in current discussions, though in the earliest discussions, as in the working definition of Internet governance, the reference was to respective roles[7].

> "...the wording <in their respective roles> was a perfect example of what diplomats usually describe as constructive ambiguity: agreements on terms that conceal a disagreement of substance" (de La Chapelle 2011, p. 15)

This constructive ambiguity has become one of the great impediments to the success of the multistakeholder model. The definitions of roles and responsibilities first put forward by the Governments in the Geneva Plan of Action, were included unchanged in the WGIG work and ultimately were preserved in the Tunis Agenda.

7 It was in the Geneva Plan of Action in the definition of the WGIG charter that "roles and responsibilities" was referenced.

From the Geneva Declaration of Principles (2003, paragraph 49):

> "The management of the Internet encompasses both technical and public policy issues and should involve all stakeholders and relevant intergovernmental and international organizations. In this respect, it is recognized that:
>
> a) Policy authority for Internet-related public policy issues is the sovereign right of States. They have rights[8] and responsibilities for international Internet related public policy issues.
>
> b) The private sector has had, and should continue to have, an important role in the development of the Internet, both in the technical and economic fields.
>
> c) Civil society has also played an important role on Internet matters, especially at the community level, and should continue to play such a role.
>
> d) Intergovernmental organizations have had, and should continue to have, a facilitating role in the coordination of Internet-related public policy issues.
>
> e) International organizations have also had, and should continue to have, an important role in the development of Internet-related technical standards and relevant policies."

In the Geneva Declaration, governments, while attempting to find their own role in the administration of Internet policy, a field that most of them had not been involved in, nor been interested in up until that time, presumed to involve themselves by putting themselves in charge. They did not consult the other stakeholders when they made this decision. They did not include the other stakeholders in the discussions when they developed this list of roles and responsibilities. Rather they unilaterally relegated all other stakeholders to subordinate roles.

While a multistakeholder model was eventually recognized in the WSIS, it did not emerge from a multistakeholder process.

> "When the WSIS started, civil society was not allowed in the conference room, except for five minutes before start and five minutes before the end of the session to give comments. How were they supposed to be able to comment without having been present in the room? Although the importance of multistakeholder participation was emphasized, UN rule had to apply (something that many developing countries were keen to underline). (Dufborg 2005, p. 17)

8 This paragraph also introduces a concept of States as having Rights. This is a novel concept that needs further discussion.

Ironically, it was not until the Tunis Agenda that the role of the Technical and Academic community, the very people that created the Internet, was specifically recognized in:

> "36. We recognize the valuable contribution by the academic and technical communities within those stakeholder groups mentioned in paragraph 35 to the evolution, functioning and development of the Internet" (WSIS 2005).

The Tunis Agenda did not, however, recognize them as stakeholders among the other stakeholders, but rather identified 'academic and technical' as attributes belonging to the stakeholders from the tripartite model. This has changed somewhat in practice today, but has still not been recognized formally by governments.

The WGIG was chartered with refining these roles and responsibilities in the Geneva Plan of Action:

> "13 b) We ask the Secretary-General of the United Nations to set up a working group on Internet governance, in an open and inclusive process that ensures a mechanism for the full and active participation of governments, the private sector and civil society from both developing and developed countries, involving relevant intergovernmental and international organizations and forums, to investigate and make proposals for action, as appropriate, on the governance of Internet by 2005. The group should, inter alia:
>
> iii. develop a common understanding of the respective roles and responsibilities of governments, existing intergovernmental and international organizations and other forums as well as the private sector and civil society from both developing and developed countries" (WSIS 2003a, para. 13)

The WGIG, however, never reworked the definitions of respective roles and responsibilities, despite civil society's insistence that we needed to, and despite discussion in the Background Report.

> "The decentralized and collaborative process of underlying technological development and core resource management: the technological development and administration of the Internet, allowing participation by all interested parties and rejecting centralized advance validation of content, services and technologies, helps ensure that the network is interoperable, functional, stable, secure, efficient as well as scalable in the long run" (WGIG 2005, p. 24).

Instead, the respective roles and responsibilities from the Geneva Declaration of Principles were carried forward as agreed language[9] and discussion in the WGIG of respective roles and responsibilities was discouraged. The definition of respective roles and responsibilities provided by the Governments in the Geneva Plan have been a great impediment to furthering the multistakeholder model. Whenever a serious discussion begins on respective roles, there is likely to be at least one country that quotes the governments' ideal view of respective roles as agreed language and argues that, thus, it is not a topic to be reopened.

To this day, including at the ITU World Telecommunications Policy Forum (WTPF) in May 2013, some governments were still attempting to force the stakeholders into roles that are inappropriate given their actual roles in Internet governance and in society in general. By using a definition of the "respective roles and responsibilities" as outlined in Tunis Agenda paragraph 35, Governments and Inter-Governmental Organizations (IGO), such as the ITU, deprecate the participation of their necessary partners in a dialogue that must be a dialogue among equals. "This is counterproductive and will not lead to the enhanced cooperation that is one of the ultimate goals of the Tunis Agenda. The definitions of "Roles and Responsibilities in Tunis Agenda paragraph 35 will instead, lead to a continuing impasse and prevent progress in multistakeholder Internet governance" (CS-IEG 2013).

While it may be agreed language among governments, it was never agreed upon by the other stakeholders. One of the great myths perpetrated in current Internet governance discussion is that the Roles and Responsibilities as defined in the Tunis Agenda were the work of experts in the WGIG. As the document history shows, this is not the case—these are definitions put forward by governments at the beginning of the process, before they were even able to define the Internet or Internet governance. These definitions were decided on at a time when non-governmental actors were being excluded from the discussion except for five minutes at the beginning and end of each meeting as described above.

Defining respective roles is a complex task. A helpful set of definitions would take into account the various capabilities and needs of the stakeholders. A reasonable set of definitions would also recognize that the respective roles differ at different times in the process of governance. Bertrand de La Chappelle has produced an analysis (de La Chapelle 2013) that breaks the process of Internet governance into a set of stages: Framing, Drafting, Validation, Implementation and Disputes. In each of these stages, the roles and responsibilities of the various stakeholders will vary depending on their respective capacities and needs. This form of analy-

[9] "Agreed language" is a phenomenon in diplomacy, where once a set of countries agree to a linguistic formulation, of as part of a compromise, that language is used unchanged in future documents in order to avoid reopening the discussion.

sis is at the very early stages, but is a necessary next step in defining an appropriate meaning for respective roles.

This remains one of the unfinished tasks of Internet governance; it remains to be seen when, if ever these definitions get revised to match the realities of stakeholders real roles and responsibilities. For so long as governments insist on operating as if these descriptions were correct, true multistakeholder cooperation, a necessity for enhanced cooperation, will remain difficult. Respective roles cannot be defined by one stakeholder for the other stakeholders, rather the understanding must evolve during the multistakeholder cooperative processes. Having the wrong definitions of respective roles and responsibilities interferes with the development of a well-formed multistakeholder process.

The WGIG recognized that "full involvement of all stakeholders" would not necessarily mean that every stakeholder group should have the same role in the development of policies, the preparation of decisions, the actual decisions and then the implementation of decisions (WGIG 2005, p. 20). It recognized "that any of the three societal sectors may play a role, depending on the particular case at hand" (WGIG 2005, p. 45). That Background Report went on to note that:

> What is less clear, and subject to discussion, is the precise nature of the balance that will be most beneficial to all stakeholders (WGIG 2005, p. 178).

And recommended:

> participatory governance processes that enable all stakeholders to fulfil their roles and responsibilities effectively and in a coordinated manner should result in better outcomes. (WGIG 2005, p. 221).

It is one of the failures of the WSIS, WGIG, and the IGF process that the discussion of respective roles has never been engaged in as a serious multistakeholder topic. It is to be hoped that the CSTD Working Group on Enhanced Cooperation (WGEC) will allow for a proper multistakeholder discussion on this topic. Two of the questions in the questionnaire the WGEC sent out include the option for that subject to be discussed:

> "5. What are the roles and responsibilities of the different stakeholders, including governments, in implementation of the various aspects of enhanced cooperation?
>
> 6. How should enhanced cooperation be implemented to enable governments, on an equal footing, to carry out their roles and responsibilities in international public policy issues pertaining to the Internet?" (WGEC 2013)

As of this writing, those answers have not yet been analysed.

3. The Models and the Crucibles

The multistakeholder model in Internet governance is more than just theory, if still less than reality. While the spread of the model is still very fragmentary, there are several organizations that describe themselves as multistakeholder organization. There are several varieties of organization that describe themselves as multistakeholder, though not every organization that self-identifies as being multistakeholder will be identified as such by others. The organizations that are serious about implementing multistakeholder processes have become crucibles for a framework that is still rather young and for which there is not much supporting organizational theory yet.

I define crucible as environments that take the multistakeholder model seriously and put energy in developing processes that allow all stakeholders to participate according to their capacities and needs. While this is in contrast to the substantive actual work of an organization, the process issues are tied to the substantive issues, for the various stakeholder views on any issue, define the substantive framing of an issue. While it is our habit to try to divide the process from the substance of Internet governance, they are too firmly linked to ever be strictly dirempted.

This section will briefly describe 3 variants of the multistakeholder model in Internet governance: (1) ICANN—the Internet Corporation for Assigned Names and Numbers; (2) IETF—The Internet Engineering Task Force; (3) IGF—The Internet Governance Forum. These three organizations have different but critical functions within the Internet. ICANN is in charge of the policies for the technical and operational management on assigned named and numbers, i.e., IP addresses, Autonomous System Numbers and Domain names. IETF is involved in the development of technical standards for a stable, secure and interoperable Internet. IGF represents a forum where all stakeholders can discuss the complex policy issues involved the broader Internet issues and possibly contribute inputs to other organizations involved in managing and governing the Internet.

The ITU is not discussed as an example of the multistakeholder model, even though it is currently claiming to be a multistakeholder organization. The reason it is not considered a multistakeholder organization in this chapter is because there is only one group, governments, entitled to participate in making decisions. It is difficult not to see ITU usage of the term multistakeholder as aspirational at best, and abuse at worst. There was a moment of hope after the World Telecommunication Policy Forum (WTPF) meeting in Geneva in 2013, that there would be a genuine attempt to open ITU substantive discussion to the non-governmental stakeholders. An appeal by stakeholders endorsed by Poland and the United States was made to the ITU Council requesting that it opened participation in the

Council Working Group on International Internet-Related Public Policy Issues (CWG-Internet) to non-governmental stakeholders. At its June 2013 session, the ITU Council rejected the proposals for open participation in CWG-Internet. In other words it decided to remain a single stakeholder organization that had no intention of transforming into a genuinely multistakeholder organization. While the nations of the ITU may on occasion permit non-governmental actors to offer comments and may even let them sit at the same table from time to time, there is no manner in which non-governmental actors are allowed to participate on anything resembling equal footing.

Sometimes the members and secretariat of the ITU argue that they are multistakeholder because governments appoint the representatives and governments serve all the stakeholders of their respective countries. Even if this were the case, and it so rarely is, this is not the same as allowing all stakeholders to come to the table. While it is advisable that all stakeholder groups consider allowing all the sub groups within the stakeholder group to participate on an equal footing, this does not make a group, e.g. the ITU, that is composed of just one stakeholder group, the governments, an example of the multistakeholder model. The discussion is, however, purely academic, as very few ITU delegations are multistakeholder—at the World Conference in Information Technology (WCIT 2012), very few national delegations included non-governmental actors. In fact if multistakeholder is defined as having an equivalent role in decision-making process, there are almost no multistakeholder government delegations, despite there being some that included non-governmental advisers.

There are issues, however, with the degrees of representation even in the three examples picked for further discussion:

> First, the scope of stakeholder participation remains too narrow. While there has been much debate in recent years about the "democratic deficit" in multilateral institutions, multistakeholderism unquestionably faces its own challenges with respect to participation and accountability. Many of us make jokes about the "traveling circus" of "usual suspects" flying around the world to meetings, or some similar formulation, but the awkward humour reflects an awareness of the implications. The on-site presence of only those who have the financial support, expertise, and interest required raises normative and operational issues that cannot be offset fully by even the excellent remote participation facilitation in the IGF and ICANN. It goes without saying that the overwhelming majority of the world's two billion users remain uninvolved, as do the many more non-users who may be affected by patterns of Internet usage in the political, economic, and social spheres. But participation is also very limited among those who one might have expected and hoped to engage, e. g. technology entrepreneurs, small

> and medium sized businesses, civil society advocacy or service provision organizations, and so on. While these problems are common to most global governance arrangements, and the IGF and ICANN have worked to promote outreach within their respective constraints, inadequate participation does impact on both the character of debate and the external acceptance of the processes (Drake 2011, p. 69).

To fully understand, any of the three organizations that are being described as crucibles for multistakeholder models, would take a chapter each, if not an entire book each. In this chapter, each will be discussed very briefly, with reference to some of its relevant multistakeholder structural aspects. No attempt will be made to provide an exhaustive description of the organizations or of their internal structures. It is also freely admitted that there are many more examples of multistakeholder based organization in Internet governance than could as reasonably have been discussed in this chapter, for example each of the five Regional Internet Registries (AFRINIC, ARIN, APNIC, LACNIC and RIPE) has a multistakeholder process tuned to its region and its stakeholder groups.

3.1. ICANN—Internet Corporation for Assigned Names and Numbers

ICANN is responsible for coordinating the following critical Internet resources including Top Level Domain names (TLD), the assignment of IP addresses, Autonomous System (AS) numbers and Protocol numbers. It has, since the end of WSIS, claimed that is a bottom-up multistakeholder organization. Before WSIS, ICANN called itself a private sector-led technical coordination body.

ICANN has a matrix organizational architecture (Doria 2013) with two types of groups: (1) Supporting Organizations that are responsible for recommending policies in a specific subject area, that are reviewed and then approved, or not, by the Board after extensive community review and discussions; and (2) Advisory Groups that give advice to the Board on any issue that concerns ICANN, including the policy recommendations made by the Supporting Organizations.

As one of its activities, ICANN provides a regulatory function for generic Top Level domains (gTLD), though it is loathe admitting this. This regulatory function is provided through the use of contracts. One of the elements that is special about ICANN contracts with Registries and Registrars[10] is that certain contractual clauses can be changed while the contract is in force, by use of a consensus pro-

[10] Registries and Registrars are two of the main contracted parties in ICANN. Using the model of a supply chain, Registries are loosely equivalent to manufacturers, while Registrars would

cess that allows the entire community, in a bottom-up manner, to discuss and decide on necessary changes. Any changes approved by the community following this process become enforceable under these contracts. Until recently this community process was the only way to alter the contracts other than at renewal time. Recently ICANN has begun to add provisions to contracts allowing it to unilaterally change various aspects of the contracts without any intervening community process. This has received a mixed reception among the ICANN community organizations. Among the contracted parties this is seen as a betrayal of the ICANN compact with its community, whereas with others, it is seen as ICANN finally taking its role as a regulator seriously. Whichever perception one takes, this is a major change in the fabric of ICANN and it will take several years to understand the full effects on the organization's multistakeholder processes. According to the process model, however, there is a multistakeholder process that must be followed in order for new contract-based regulatory conditions to be instituted.

Soft Oversight at ICANN

One of the more important evolving structures in multistakeholder legitimacy has been instituted at ICANN. This mechanism provides a form of soft bottom-up oversight. In addition to its identity as a multistakeholder organization, ICANN has a unique relationship to the US Department of Commerce (DOC) and specifically to the National Telecommunications Information Agency (NTIA). Since its creation with a combination of contracts and memoranda of understanding, the US DOC has maintained oversight over ICANN. In 2009, due to many forces, including pressure from other governments, DOC and ICANN took action to lessen the direct oversight by the US government. The vehicle for doing this was the creation of a joint Affirmation of Commitments between the DOC and ICANN, consisting of a set of cyclical community reviews. The reviews are done by teams composed of people picked by the bottom-up processes of the ICANN constituent organizations appointed by a combination of the leaders of ICANN and of GAC. These review teams come from all ICANN stakeholder groups and are responsible for reviewing different aspects of ICANN including: transparency and accountability; stability and security of the Internet; information on domain name registrants (WHOIS); the new GTLD program[11].

ICANN has finished the first cycle of these reviews and has begun the second cycle. It remains to be seen whether this method works. Although it is a bold experiment, a lot of its success will rest on ICANN's willingness to be transpar-

be loosely equivalent wholesalers and retailers. Other entities in the supply chain are the Resellers who are roughly equivalent to retailers, and Registrants who are the consumers.

[11] This was not done as part of the first review cycle as the new gTLD had not been released yet.

ent and accountable and to accept the recommendations of the review panels. The first review of the second cycle, which includes a review of how well the process worked in the first cycle, is planned for release at the end of 2013.

3.2. IETF—Internet Engineering Task Force

Of the three multistakeholder organizations being discussed in this chapter, the IETF is the oldest. While it currently has a defined existence as part of the Internet Society, for many years it was just a collection of engineers who self-organized so as to cooperate on building and maintaining the interoperable Internet. While some would describe it as collection of individuals and not of stakeholders, I believe that it is indeed composed of stakeholders. In one way of looking at the organization, the participants come from all stakeholder groups and participate without any recognition of the fact, participating as technical contributors without conscious regard to their original stakeholder group, though the self-selected affinity to those external stakeholder groups can never be completely avoided. In another sense they are members of a single stakeholder group, the technical community. Beyond that, for scalability and process issues, it divides participation according to the layer of the protocol stack one works on: Applications, Internet, Operations and Management, Real-time Applications and Infrastructure, Routing, Security and Transport. While participants may participate in more than one of the areas, generally each participant focuses their efforts in just one of these stakeholder groups by a different name[12]. In a sense, the technical area one works in is the definition of one's stakeholder groups within the IETF.

One important point about the IETF is the elaborate organizational structure that has been created in response to participant capacities and needs, and that continues to evolve to give all of the participants fair access to its processes. It has developed a well-formed process for picking leadership from a very fluid population base: those who have participated recently. It has a selected leadership that has decision making abilities that have been granted by the community and has a multilayer appeals mechanism. As one of the crucibles of multistakeholder activity, it has created a stable but evolving structure. While being fully stakeholder driven, as there is no other way for work to get done, the organization has invested its leadership with great power, even giving a virtual veto to its Steering Group members, which they can use when necessary to protect the architectural and protocol stability of the Internet.

[12] This other form of stakeholder definition, in fact the entire subject of how stakeholder groups can be defined, involves a longer discussion and it not included in this chapter. It is included here just as an example of this added complexity.

For most of its history, the IETF considered itself a purely technical organization with no policy responsibilities. While that is still largely the case, members of the community have begun to realize that while policy should not be instantiated in protocols, the protocols must enable various policy options and that policy issues might provide requirements for protocol design. A major effort, for example, has recently been completed in creating a set of guidelines for protocol designers on privacy considerations in their protocols (Cooper et al. 2013).

Another policy aspect of the IETF in its recent development has been its activity in promoting its protocols such as IPv6 and DNSSEC. Originally, the IETF had focused on creating protocols and leaving it to the market to decide which ones would be used and which would get left behind. With the advent of IPv6, the IETF decided that it was such an important effort that it needed to become active in promoting the technology. It still remains to be seen whether this is an effective strategy for the Internet's future and how making such policy decisions (i.e. the importance of deploying a particular solution), affects its technical mission.

Another aspect of the future of the IETF relates to the community that participates in the IETF. It is a community consisting of the elite of the technical world. Recently the IETF has begun working on international diversity and on attracting a younger population.

3.3. IGF—Internet Governance Forum

In the Tunis Agenda, in paragraphs 67–72, the Internet Governance Forum is defined as the place where all stakeholders can consult with each other on an equal footing with regards to Internet policy. This was the formula given for achieving enhanced cooperation, the Holy Grail of the Tunis Agenda.

Unfortunately, the General Assembly undid the original assumption about the IGF being the location for Enhanced Cooperation (UNGA 2011). This produced two mandates in apparent opposition to each other: the Tunis agenda indicating that the IGF should work on a wide notion of Enhanced Cooperation among all stakeholders, and a General Assembly resolution indicating that another process was needed to work on Enhanced Cooperation among governments only. This produced a tension in the IGF on whether it was a place to work on Enhanced Cooperation solutions or was just a talking shop not allowed to discuss enhanced cooperation. This is a bind that is only passing now with the latest General Assembly (UNGA 2012) decision to have the UN Commission on Science Technology for Development (CSTD) review the issue of Enhanced Cooperation. There is a nascent awareness that one can work toward both enhanced cooperation among all stakeholders while also working on greater enhanced cooperation among governments. One form of enhanced cooperation does not obviate another form of enhanced cooperation. And together they would produce the Enhanced Cooperation that is currently still an aspiration among those engaged in Internet governance.

Organizationally, the IGF is quite simple. There is a Multistakeholder Advisory Group (MAG), appointed by the United Nations Secretary General (UNSG) or his deputies. The MAG is basically composed half from the 5 UN geographical regions, and half from the non-governmental stakeholder groups. While half government and half non-government is not the best example of equal footing, it represents the current extent of UN comfort with equal footing (at least the non-governmental MAG members are equal as a group to the governmental MAG members). The MAG is responsible for advising the UNSG on the programme and other aspects of the IGF; though the extent to which it is able and/or empowered to do anything beyond the programme is open to question. The IGF has a tiny secretariat that varies between one and four individuals. As a United Nations unfunded mandate, it relies on charity to function and is kept on a very short leash by the UN, requiring a renewal of its mandate every five years.

Despite these limitations, the IGF has become a very influential body. While not quite endowed with the power of a bully pulpit, its musings affect the organizations responsible for Internet management and governance.

Over the last few years, the IGF has been teetering on the verge of change. On 19 July 2010, the Economic and Social Council (ECOSOC) adopted by consensus resolution 2010/2 on the "Assessment of the progress made in the implementation of and follow-up to the outcomes of the World Summit on the Information Society". By this resolution, ECOSOC "invites the Chair of the Commission on Science and Technology for Development (CSTD) to establish, in an open and inclusive manner, a working group which would seek, compile and review inputs from all Member States and all other stakeholders on improvements to the Internet Governance Forum (IGF), in line with the mandate set out in the Tunis Agenda" (CSTDWG 2011).

The group met and to its credit adopted many of the working techniques of the multistakeholder model for its own process, a significant achievement for the UN CSTD. In its final recommendations (WGIGF 2011) they recommended some of the goals for a more active IGF, specifically: (a) to develop more tangible outputs; (b) to focus discussions, the preparation process of each IGF should formulate a set of policy questions to be considered at the IGF, as part of the overall discussion. The results of the debates on these questions, with special focus on public policy perspectives and aimed at capacity building, should be stated in the outcome documentation; and (c) the outcome documentation should include messages that map out converging and diverging opinions on given questions. Nearly two years after the report, few if any of the changes have been implemented. The IGF in 2013 may be the first to test some of the proposed changes.

4. Ways Forward for the Multistakeholderism

Several recommendations emerge from the discussion in this chapter. The first and most important is that all stakeholders need to recognize the dynamic nature of respective roles of the stakeholders in Internet governance. Whether it is in the WGEC or in the IGF or a combination of arenas, the stakeholders in cooperation need to discuss the notion of respective roles in terms of capabilities, responsibilities and needs. There is a need to remove the contradiction created by Tunis Agenda's paragraph 35 "Roles and Responsibilities" that subordinates other stakeholders to government control. All stakeholders need to accept that Internet governance only works when it is a situation where equivalent stakeholders all contribute on an equal footing based on their capabilities.

Outreach must become a greater focus in order to increase inclusion. The multistakeholder model relies on ever increasing participation by those with interests, capacities and needs. Continued progression from simple representative democracy to participatory democracy that includes not only the representatives of representative democracy, but also the stakeholder groups that represent the multiplicity of interests and affinities on the global population.

Groups must cease being afraid of the multistakeholder model. Every group, at times, realizes that in a fully multistakeholder model, things will be different and the circumstances under which groups operate within the governance environment will need to change. For example:

- Governments will need to learn to sit at the table with other stakeholders on an equal footing. Some have already begun to learn this. Others have yet to begin.
- Businesses will need to learn to be more transparent. Businesses will need to do less of their persuasion by lobbying legislators and more of it by presenting arguments in multistakeholder fora.
- Civil society will need to become more flexible and to compromise on some of its ideological purity. It also needs to give up the victim mantra and needs to realize that its power to affect change lies in maintaining both an inside and outside strategy. Much is to be achieved by working inside the system with those who have power, whether it is financial power or political power, yet sometimes, civil society must be ready to go outside the system to make sure it is not ignored.

- Technologists need to give up the comfort of believing that science and technology are free of financial and political aspects. The mythology that finances and politics are layers 8 and 9 in the protocol stack and are irrelevant and irritating, hold technologists back in their participation as stakeholders on an equal footing. Technologists need to learn to communicate and cooperate with policy concerns. Technologists also need to learn to balance an inside strategy with an outside strategy.
- Policy wonks have to learn to understand and cope with technological realities.

All need to figure out how to enhance the cooperation among all the stakeholder groups.

More groups need to commit themselves to the process of multistakeholder cooperation.

> "… belief in the multistakeholder model is however not universally shared. In fact, the model is actively being challenged on a routine basis. In the last year, there have been more and more instances of restrictions on the free flow of information online, disputes between various standards bodies and even appeals from incumbent carriers in Europe for government intervention on the terms and conditions for exchanging Internet traffic. There have also been statements by international organizations and even some governments calling for more direct Internet regulation" (Alexander 2011, p. 28).

Capacity building that explains the value of the multistakeholder models is just beginning. There needs to be more research, more education and more writing on the many crucial issues within multistakeholderism.

The ITU could live up to the promises made at the WTPF, and on many previous occasions. From the Secretary General's closing of the May 2013 meeting of the WTPF:

> "The dialogue will continue in ITU council group and other fora such as IGF and CSTD, not limited to those three. It could be any other. Depending on which of the membership and all the stakeholders" (WTPF 2013).

But I would like to say to you as for the framework is concerned in the ITU, the ITU council Working Group that will be discussing this, I will propose to that council group to be open to all stakeholders in the same format and I will bring that proposal to the ITU council.

4.1. Further Development within the Stakeholder Groups Themselves

The multistakeholder model is at a crossroads. It is a new movement and it is under attack from all sides. It is under attack from some governments that have opposed it from its beginnings in the WGIG. It is under attack from those who feel it has not met its promise quickly enough. It is under attack from those who did not manage to get appointed to the various leadership groups in the multistakeholder organizations. It is even, sometimes, under attack by those who champion the method, but get frustrated by the slow progress being made.

Each stakeholder group should also apply the multistakeholder model to the extent that their subgroups constitute separate stakeholder sub-groups within the stakeholder group. The multistakeholder model is fractal in that each of the stakeholder groups, and in turn each of its sub-groups, faces the same challenge of inclusivity and participation that is broad enough to be worthy of the group's diversity. This is subject to each group's subsidiarity, and its ability to identify the sub-groups within the stakeholder group.

Until the stakeholder groups are identified and are allowed to develop themselves according to their own subdivisions and resulting unities, multistakeholderism cannot really occur. Or at least it will always be stunted. The future is uncertain. Multistakeholderism has become a buzzword, with every organization claiming itself to be multistakeholder. Continued theoretical, research and political work is needed on developing the multistakeholder framework.

5. Conclusion

I have apprehension for the future of the word "Multistakeholderism", everyone uses it and everyone defines it differently, especially those who use it as a cloak for practices that bear little or no resemblance to forms of participatory democracy. I have high expectations, however, for evolution in multistakeholder models that enhance participatory democracy.

In a presentation given by Bertrand de La Chapelle at Meissen in 2013 on the multistakeholder model in Internet governance, he concluded one part of his talk with the following:

> "A Bold Bet: The right for anyone to participate in an appropriate manner in the governance processes dealing with their issues of concern" (de La Chapelle 2013).

I believe that this is a worthy multistakeholder goal that we should all work towards, no matter which stakeholder group(s) we might participate in. Getting back to definitions, however, the word "appropriate" is one of those special words in diplomacy that can mean everything or nothing.

Part 3.
Internet Security between Competition and Cooperation

Gianluigi Negro

Chapter 7
Chinese Internet Governance—Some Domestic and Foreign Issues

The management of the Domain Name System (DNS) remains a crucial issue for Internet governance. The aim of this chapter is to provide a historical overview of the relationship between the Chinese government and the DNS implementation decision-making process. Since the end of the 1990s the DNS has become a sort of database of the Internet (Klensin 2003, p. 2) and its main task is to translate domain names into the numerical Internet Protocol (IP) addresses needed to locate computer services and devices worldwide. The introduction of this system replaced the host table approach which was used in the first decade of the Internet and which required frequent updates of the list of host names and their mapping to and from addresses; however, it was unable to scale properly and did not support new services.

The DNS was created to "identify network resources" and to accommodate "new data types and structures, both through the addition to the initial <Internet> class of new record types and, potentially, through the introduction of new classes" (Klensin 2003, p. 4). From a historical point of view, it can be argued that DNS names were limited to a subset of the American Standard Code for Information Interchange (ASCII), an approach basically derived from human and political limitations, in an attempt to avoid possible ambiguities in an international context. It is worth highlighting that at the time of the DNS design some experts warned that these shortcomings aimed at reducing ambiguities would cause problems in the future.

These fears proved to be justified, as illustrated by the ongoing debate since the early 2000s on the involvement of countries that are not pursuing the ASCII. One of the most hotly debated issues was the unsuitability of the DNS for fully internationalized domain names (IDNs) which are visible, accessible, and predictable for users. China was involved in this controversy and it originally proposed a match of Traditional and Simplified Chinese characters that represent the same words. However, this decision would have had major consequences for other languages, increasing the general complexity of the process; indeed, matching Traditional and Simplified characters would have impacted Japanese and Korean uses of the same 'traditional' characters and, for example, it would have not made it be possible to map Kanji into Simplified Chinese.

China's role in the IDN dispute must be assessed against the following background: over the last two decades, China and the Chinese have increased their presence on the Internet and, according to the most recent statistics provided by the China Internet Network Information Center (CIIC) in January 2013, the People's Republic of China (PRC) is still the leading country in terms of the number of Internet users (CNNIC 2013; Tan, Muller and Foster 1997; Wu 1996; Zhu & Wang 2005, Lai 2012). Chinese Internet users surpassed the American online population in July 2008 (CNNIC 2008) to become the country with the highest number of users in the world. The extraordinary growth in the number of Chinese internet users means that it now has more users than the entire population of Western Europe and accounts for over 51% of Asia's Internet Users.

In this chapter I will provide a historical overview of Chinese Internet development and China's role in Internet governance from a geopolitical perspective, taking as an example the case of the DNS. The second part will discuss three issues that have characterized and still influence Chinese policy-making in the field, analyzing the role of the Chinese language, the economic relevance of the DNS and the most important policies adopted by the Chinese government inside its borders and in ICANN. The last part of the chapter discusses three issues including the implementation of the International Name System.

1. A Historical Overview of the Chinese Internet

Even though the first attempts to implement the Internet in China were made in the most prestigious academic circles during the mid-1980s, it could be argued that the construction of a network that offered access to the general public did not begin until the mid-1990s.

1.1 From External Support to Internal Management

China's access to the Internet was supported by both Europe and the US. The first official step was taken in September 20, 1987, when Professor Qian Tianbai, at that time in charge of the Internet project of the Chinese Academy Network (CANET), sent China's first email outside the Chinese borders. The email was entitled "Crossing the Great Wall to join the world" and was the outcome of a project developed by Karlsruhe University in the former West Germany (Negro 2011, p. 2).

Another crucial role was played by the Advanced Research Projects Agency Network (ARPANET) under the supervision of the US Department of Defense, which supported the Chinese government in registering the first domain name ".cn" in October 1990. Then, in early 1994, the US National Science Fund (NSF) issued an official authorization to link China to the Internet. The official recognition of China on the Internet dates back to 20 April 1994, when Sprint Co. from the United States set up a fully functioning link. This was the start of an exponential growth both in terms of Internet infrastructure and number of users. The record number of Chinese Internet users is even more impressive if we look at the first report published by the China Internet Network Information Centre in 1997, which indicated that there were only 620,000 registered users.

Most Chinese officials at the time were aware of the economic benefits and social transformations that the Internet would bring to the country. The academic literature shows how the development of Internet in China brought about major economic (Qiu 2003; Shirk 2010) and social (Yang 2003,

2007; Rosen 2010) changes which should be framed within a juridical diachronic process; such a process could be divided into three main pillars, that the official Chinese management tried to find a good balance for:

- government issues—mainly aiming at social stability;
- netizen issues—concerning those who use Internet without a coherent legal framework and sometimes with limited awareness of their rights;
- market issues—related to the activities of private actors such as Internet Service Providers (ISPs), Portals, web companies, etc., that have to take into consideration both government issues and the increasing demand of the Chinese population for a freer and better defined legal environment;

The above-mentioned pillars are described clearly in one of the most detailed and important studies published by Tan (1999), which provides an overview of the history of the Chinese Internet regulatory regime. From its beginning to the present day, the Chinese Internet has moved from significant external support for the creation of its Internet infrastructure to a more coherent and complete management of its networks.

The study identified three generations of regulatory regimes, starting off with the old experimental regime (before 1994) with a fragmented structure. This was followed by the transitional regulatory regime (1994–1998) characterized by a single regulatory coordinator, the State Council's Steering Committee of the National Information Infrastructure (NII). This stage envisioned the "transitional" convergence of regulatory authorities with different rival government agencies. During this time, the Steering Committee was unable to fully manage all the regulatory responsibilities because of it did not have a permanent status, and possessed only limited financial means and administrative power. The final stage is characterized by the drafting of a set of converged regulations implemented following the creation of the Ministry of Information Industry (MII) in March 1998.

The setup of the MII was crucial in the history of Chinese Internet regulation because it was tasked—among other things—with defining strategic plans, industrial policies, regulations and laws for the information industry; maintaining the central planning functions for China's backbone telecom networks and administrating the entire information industry; deciding rational resource allocation; preventing overlapping projects from being developed; and ensuring information security (Tan 1999, p. 9).

1.2 From Internal Management to Internet Governance

Another trend emerging during the definition of the institutional framework needs was the distinction between "global cyberspace" and "domestic cyberspace". Some scholars also pointed to the potential isolation of China's Intranet from the global Internet (Sherman & Westland 2009; Tan 1999; Taubam 2007; Zittrain 2003) due to the creation of the biggest firewall in the world, whose main purpose is to filter and censor users' activities by blocking specific IP addresses. *The Golden Shield Project* (jindun gongcheng 金盾工程) was funded by the Ministry of Public Security; its first operations began in 1998, yet it became fully operative in 2003. It is not possible to have detailed information about the costs that the Chinese government bore to set up this project but, according to the CCTV, the preparatory costs amounted to 6.4 billion Yuan ($1.05 billion). As regards its maintenance, at least 30,000 policeman are involved in its daily operations (Negro 2011, p. 4). Both scholars and journalists paid and continue to pay attention to this phenomenon also known as "The Great Firewall of China" (Brame &Ye 1997).

The control of the Internet networks is crucial for both political and economic reasons. Indeed, as confirmed by Zhao (2000), the growth of the Chinese Internet falls within a broader process characteristic of the entire telecommunication reform. At the beginning, the telecommunication system was basically a tool of elite political communication or, in the case of the Internet, a tool mainly used in academic circles. The priority to develop an infrastructure which would have guaranteed an economic development was started only in a second stage. The new telecommunication system was particularly important also because it contributed to support a more profit-making state enterprise approach (Zhao 2000). A special role was played in this by the "four modernization sectors" policies targeting agriculture, industry, national defence, and science and technology. Nevertheless the importance of the Internet was highlighted by the party General Secretary Jiang Zemin who said that "none of the four modernizations would be possible without informatization" (ibid). Another landmark event was the approval of the "National Informatization Plan of the Ninth Five Year Plan and Long-term Goals of 2000" in which the central government officially recognized the economic importance of Internet development and made network development a priority in national economic policy (Loo 2004). Following the marked growth in the number of users as well as the huge investments made, web penetration in China now reaches 42.1% of the Chinese population of 1.3 billion people (CNNIC 2013). This trend will probably be confirmed in the near future, also reinforcing the importance of China in Internet Governance.

In the mid-2000s, China was already aware that Internet governance evolved through the multi-stakeholder process in which states have to collaborate with non-state actors in order to solve technical and operational issues such as standardizing communication protocols and managing names and numerical addresses on the Internet. Indeed, China was one of the most active countries in criticizing the US supremacy in internet-related issues. In particular, the People's Republic of China (PRC), with the support of 77 developing countries, proposed the creation of an international Internet organization and the drafting of an Internet treaty (see Jamart in this volume). This proposal was submitted in December 2003 during the first phase of the World Summit on the Information Society (WSIS). At that time, China was very critical of the Internet Corporation for Assigned Names and Numbers (ICANN) and pushed for radical changes in Internet governance. As a result, the US made some concessions. On June 30, 2005, the US government published a document on "US Principles on the Internet's Domain Name and Addressing System". One principle states in this document pointed out the recognition from the US government of the right of each country to manage its country-code top-level domain (ccTLD) in a sovereign manner. The last principle mentioned in the document was the need for a forum of dialogue on Internet governance issues. As a consequence, the Chinese government, which acted as the leader of the sovereignist movement, stopped its attacks on the existing system during the WSIS (Kleinwächter 2008).

After a long debate involving the US and European governments—which were more oriented towards supporting the private sector and limiting state involvement—a compromise was reached with the creation of a Working Group on Internet Governance (WGIG), whose goal was to identify the primary roles and responsibilities of the main stakeholder groups. The success of this compromise is confirmed in the WSIS Plan of Action in which the group identifies itself "in an open and inclusive process that ensures a mechanism for the full and active participation of governments, the private sector and civil society from both developing and developed countries, involving relevant intergovernmental and international organizations and forums" (WSIS 2003a).

2. When China Speaks Out—the Role of the DNS and IDN System

In this part, three of the most important components of the Chinese Internet governance policy-making process will be analysed in order to explain the shift in China's Domain Name Registration system administration policies. First, the role of the Chinese language in the Internet will be discussed; a second part will look at the importance of DNS management from an economic point of view; finally, the third part will describe the most important policies implemented by the Chinese government in order to take part in policy-making which should promote the Internationalized Domain Name (IDN) and a more influential position for China in Internet governance.

The history of the Chinese government with the international DNS has always been an important issue. Indeed, one of the most striking episodes dates back to 2010, when the Internet Governance Forum was hosted by Lithuania. On that occasion, a Chinese official stated that China has "problems of domain names [...]. China uses one fifth of the Internet but the domain names in China represent only one twentieth of all those used throughout the world, so the management of Internet resources is of crucial importance for China and, if we talk about the actual management of the critical Internet resources, so is China's cooperation with many countries around the world. We have the same common position. We are prepared to communicate with other countries to resolve problems that arise in relation to the Internet all over the world" (IGF 2010).

2.1. The Role of the Chinese Language on the Internet

At the Pacific Telecommunication Conference in January 2002, the question of the presence of the Chinese language on the Internet was raised, when the PCR Minister for Information Industry at that time, Wu Jichuan, stated that:

> "For historical and technical reasons, 90% of the information available on the Internet is in English and the overwhelming majority of it is generated by developed countries, whereas developing countries are mostly information receivers. As information flows across borders and developing coun-

> tries are absorbing advanced technological and cultural information, their cultural traditions, moral standards and values have been severely challenged" (Rollnick 2002, p. 206).

After more than a decade the situation has changed greatly and the scenario forecast by Wu Jichuan appears very different. From 2000 to 2011, the presence of English content on the Internet decreased from 39% in 2000 to 27% at the end of 2011 (Smartling 2011). It is interesting to note that even though 56% of online content is in English only, the percentage of English speakers dropped from 26% in 2000 to 3% in 2011. According to UNESCO, in 2008, just 12 languages accounted for 98% of Internet web pages and at that time English was the dominant online language with 72% of all web pages. Something began to change in 2010, with other languages gaining popularity; one interesting example was the modest 20% of English pages on Wikipedia in 2010 (ISCO OECD & UNESCO 2011). At the same time, the Chinese online content increased its presence on the Internet: in 2000, only 9% of online content was in Chinese, in 2005 it reached 13%, and by the end of 2011 it reached 24%. Moreover, in 3 years, China added more Internet users than the US and became the most populated country in the world in terms of Internet users by 2008. According to the latest official figures, at the end of December 2012, China had more than 564 million Internet users, 42.1% of the entire Chinese population (CNNIC 2013).

In the mid-1990s, when the Chinese Internet began to be more economically-oriented, the first complaints regarding the difficulties encountered in spelling and properly memorizing Latin-script names (for domains, web addresses and email addresses) were received. In this respect, the WGIG Plan of Action dedicated part of paragraph C8.23 to cultural and linguistic diversity; moreover, one of the goals expressed is "through public/private partnerships, to foster the creation of varied local and national content, including that available in the language of the users, and to give recognition and support to ICT-based work in all the artistic fields" (WSIS 2003a, § C8.23.g)[1].

2.2.1. The Economic Factor

The Chinese government was (and still is) aware of the importance of the Internet; this awareness is confirmed in a study conducted by the Boston Consulting Group in 2012, which states that, even if much of the world may still be in recession, the Internet keeps growing and so does its economic weight. According to the report, in the 20 countries investigated, online economy will grow by more than 10% an-

[1] Other important references about the role of cultural diversity and identity, linguistic and local content are presented in the WSIS Plan of Action in paragraphs C8.23 f, I, j, k and o.

nually until 2016, when it will reach $4.2 trillion, or 5.3% of the GDP. China ranks third in the classification of the most lucrative counties; in fact, the contribution of Internet to the economy represents almost 6% of the national GDP, behind Great Britain (8.1%) and South Korea (7.2%) but ahead of the European Union (3.9%), Japan (4.9%) and the USA (4.9%). However, other scholars argue that the impact of the Internet on developing countries such as China and Malaysia is undermined by the growing commercialization and disparities among its users and that, the Internet might enlarge existing structural inequalities within the global political economy (BCG 2012).

In 2000, Network Solutions Inc. ('NSI' which later merged with VeriSign) began to provide registration services for Chinese-character domain names with extensions such as ".com", ".net" or ".org". As confirmed by Xue at that time, even though the services offered should be considered in their "testbed" stage, they had a marked impact on the Chinese market (2004, p. 564). The same year China was considered the most important market for VeriSign's International Domain Name system. Indeed, the American company confirmed that "of the registered names, 84% (of the applications to ICANN for IDN authorization) were either in Chinese, Japanese or Korean" (Lewis 2003).

The importance of the DNS remains unchanged. Indeed, according to the latest data on the domain name industry provided by VeriSign, the fourth quarter of 2012 closed with a base of more than 256 million domain name registrations across all Top-Level domains (TLDs), an increase of 6.1 million over the third quarter. Worldwide registrations have grown by 26.6 million year over year. As regards China, it is worth noting that the order of the top TLDs in terms of zone size changed slightly compared to the third quarter; in fact ".cn" moved up the ranking from the eighth to the seventh most common TLD. Of the 20 largest ccTLDs, the only countries that exceeded a 4% quarter to quarter growth are China, Tokelau, India and the Russian Federation (VeriSign 2013, p. 1–3). According to another report published in February 2013 by the Chinese Internet Information Center, at the end of 2012, China had 13.4 million registered domain names, a 73.1% year over year increase. Moreover, of these names, around 7.5 million (56%) had a ".cn" extension while 4.8 million, 36% of all domain names, end with ".com" (CNNIC 2013).

3. The Story of the DNS in China—the Most Important Steps

China's first attempt to regulate the Chinese DNS dates back to January 1996 when the State Council, guided by Premier Zhu Rongji, established the "Leading Panel for Informatization Work (LPIW)". This step was important because it brought to an end the possibility of self-governance of the Internet (CNNIC 2011). The LIPW played a fundamental role in the supervision of the setup of the Chinese Internet Information Center (CNNIC), which incorporated the Computer Network Information Center of the Chinese Academy of Social Science. The CNNIC's task was to manage registration of the ".cn" domain following the "Provisional Regulations for the Administration of Domain Name registration on China's Internet Network" (CNNIC 2011)[2]. The CNNIC realized that Chinese Internet users were looking for a Chinese-character domain name system especially because of their difficulties in remembering and properly spelling web addresses and email addresses in the Latin script. This was an economic problem also for foreign and domestic enterprises that hoped to make their domain name easy to remember. It was for this reason that the CNNIC launched an experimental registration system and held the first "Conference on the issues of Chinese-character domain names" in Beijing in October 1998.

It was clear that China's Internet authorities represented by the Ministry of Information Industry (MII) and the CNNIC wanted to simplify content regulation in order to achieve their main goal: a Chinese-character DNS governed by the Chinese administration. The clash between the two systems was evident, as confirmed by the 2000 project designed to develop domain names using Chinese character addresses on top of Latin script addresses. The project was gradually extended to "four territories and two coasts", that is, Mainland China, Hong Kong, Macao and Taiwan after the Chinese Domain Name Consortium was established. It is important to note that United States companies had introduced Internationalized Domain Name (IDN) registration a few days earlier. At that time the situation was tense especially on the Chinese side, as reported in the South China Morning Post: "China's domain name authorities dramatically oppose foreign firms registering Chinese language domain names. They sent a complaint to [ICANN] arguing that the US government had no right to authorize any company to manage domain names with Chinese characters because Chinese character domain names have unique... cultural and historical implications" (Zhou 2000).

2 In September 2002, the CNNIC was recognized by the Ministry of Information Industry as the registry both for ".cn" domain and the three top level domains (Countries, Categories and Multi-organizations) in Chinese characters.

On the other hand, it is also important to remember that it was also for these reasons that the Internet Engineering Task Force (IETF) created an ad hoc working group on IDN in order to "specify the requirements for internationalized domain names and to specify access and a standard protocol based on the requirements" (IETF n.d.). Moreover, the ICANN stated that all competing standards issued by the relevant standard body and all competing encoding schemes should conform to the standard (ICANN 2000).

In other words, a decade ago the situation was very different; in fact, the nascent Internet community was new to an international system like the ICANN and the Internet Engineering Task Force (IEFT) and at that time the DNS governance regime could be considered more "West-centric" than today (Xue 2004, p. 565). In this respect it should also be remembered that the first "official" Chinese Internet connection was postponed several times in 1992 and 1993. Indeed, the official document, "Evolution of the Internet in China" published by the China Education and Research Network, states that the "US government prohibited any socialist country from accessing the Internet that contained a wealth of science and technology information and other resources" (CERN 2001). On the other hand, the American approach was less political; a report by Cindy Zheng from the San Diego Super Computer mentioned "some concerns about which organization was going to host the NIC.cn (Network Information Center) in the PRC. Some erroneously thought that NIC was the focal point for all the network connotations. Everywhere I went, I explained how NIC works in the US in order to clear up any misunderstandings on NIC's functionalities so that hopefully the future NIC for the '.cn' domain would not be an authoritative unit" (1993). At the beginning of the 1990s the management of the ".cn" DNS registry was far from being organic due to the bureaucratic competition of that time. The biggest difficulty was to "identify who should be in charge of the assignment and management of domain names, and how the domain name server should be set up and managed" (Ermert & Hughes 2003, p. 201). This trend is clearly described also in the above-mentioned report by Cindy Zheng who wrote about different approaches to whether the ".cn" name system should be organized according to a geographical substructure or with a second level generic domain according to the existing gTLD scheme (Ermert & Hughes 2003).

At the beginning of the last decade China began to adopt a more collaborative approach towards international institutions involved in the DNS policies. However, many ccTLD registrars continued to complain about the authoritative stance of the ICANN which demanded that ccTLDs be placed under the management of their respective counties. Also in this case the ICANN confirmed its status, presenting itself as a "unique, authoritative root of DNS" (ICANN 2001). In May 2002 both the CNNIC and the non-governmental Internet Society of China

("ISC")[3] expressed their support of the ICANN in their "Suggestions on ICANN Reform" (CNNIC & ISC, Suggestions on ICANN Reform). If on one hand both institutions recognized that there were "two major types of ICANN function related entities: Internet name and address resources managers (ccTLDs, gTLDs, RIRs, technical experts) and users of such resources (individual Internet users, ISPs, major network operators and governments)", on the other hand they also pointed out that the "Asia-Pacific region is special: there are so many distinct countries with a large population and very different ethical cultures. Meanwhile, the high speed of Internet development in the Asia-Pacific region is the focus of global attention. Compared to the other four regions, we believe that Asia-Pacific should have a larger quota of representatives". Nevertheless, they confirmed the importance of the government "in guaranteeing the stable operation of the Internet" (CNNIC & ISC 2002).

At that stage the main goal of the Chinese government was to be part of the ICANN policy-making process in order to defend national security interests through the international institution. This more collaborative approach could be considered a milestone in the participation of China in Internet governance. Its involvement continued throughout the decade, reaching its climax in April 2013 during the public 46th ICANN meeting held for the first time in China, when the opening of the first new global engagement office in Beijing was announced. It is worth noting that in March 2013 numerous Chinese character gTLDs passed the ICANN's initial evaluation process, suggesting that China is a priority in terms of how ICANN rolls out new gTLDs. The symbolic importance of the event was confirmed by ICANN itself, which declared that the Beijing conference was the largest in ICANN's 15-year history with more than 2,000 attendees. In recent years ICANN has faced the largest expansion of Internet addresses since its creation in 1998; in 2012 nearly 2,000 businesses and groups submitted bids for almost 1,400 names for non-English languages and ICANN received more than 100 proposals, the majority of which was the Chinese equivalent for 'company' (gogosi 公司) and 'online' (wangluo 网络). Both of these will be reviewed after the decision of the ICANN Board.

At the same time, despite the major contribution of China to several projects, not only some issues still remain unsolved, but the role of ICANN and its US backing appears basically unchanged. The involvement of China in the international Internet policy making process is particularly remarkable in three cases, which I discuss below: the implementation of the International Name System (IDS)

3 ISC is a Chinese non-governmental organization comprising 140 members from the Chinese Internet industry including private companies, schools and research institutes. The ISC receives support from authorities such as the Ministry of Information Industry, the Ministry of Education and the State Council Information Office.

standards; the disapproval for the management of root servers and the support expressed for the multi-stakeholder model at the end of the World Conference on International Telecommunications in December 2012 (WCIT-12).

4. Three Issues from the Chinese Point of View

4.1. China and the International Domain Name System

After the ICANN conference in Beijing, the Internet Society of China (ISC) published its "Comments on the new gTLD batching process from the Internet Society", in which it expressed its hope "that ICANN would support new gTLD applicants from developing countries and regions and take the lead in the International Domain Name system (IDNs) of developing countries and regions that have a close relationship with local culture and languages" (ICANN 2013, p. 9). The adoption of the International Domain Name system is one of the most important issues for ICANN, which supports the implementation of the World Summit on the Information Society action line C8 ("Cultural diversity and identity, linguistic diversity and local content") and the UNESCO Recommendation concerning the Promotion and Use of Multilingualism and Universal Access to Cyberspace.

For historical reasons the DNS adopted naming conventions using simple Latin characters taken from the letters A–Z, digits and the hyphen ("–"). This was the result of the ARPANET project which was basically developed by English-speaking graduate students working in American universities. The main focus of the ARPANET project was not the language but the underlying networks and computers that were to be interconnected. Indeed, as Klensin pointed out, "the hostname rules chosen in the mid-70s weren't just <ASCII because English uses ASCII> […]. ASCII isn't sufficient to fully represent English—there are several words in the language that are correctly spelled only with characters or diacritical marks that do not appear in ASCII" (2003, p. 16). It is again Klensin to mention the controversies arising around the need to transform the system so as to have "fully internationalized names that are visible, comprehensible and predictable for end users" (2003, p. 18).

As the Internet became popular in other parts of the world, the absence of support for non-Latin scripts became a notable deficiency. The problem was therefore discussed by the Internet Engineering Task Force which finally proposed the "Punycode" system that would map Unicode characters representing characters from many of the world's scripts in ASCII—and vice versa. The Punycode system did not completely solve the problem because even though second and lower domain labels could be expressed in a particular script, the top level domain would still have to be expressed in ASCII (Cerf 2012, p. 6). Neither has the implementation of IDNs with new top levels domains been very successful so far; this was confirmed by the call from ICANN for proposals for new top level domains in 2012. IDNs supporters still believe that enabling users to navigate the Internet in their native language enhances the linguistic diversity of the online population; yet, the process of creating an unlimited number of gTLDs in any script—promoted by ICANN in January 2010—demonstrated that IDN implementation is still far from reaching its target as was confirmed by the mere 6% of new IDNs out of a total of 1,930 new gTLD requests.

Noteworthy, according to the statistics published by the EURid-UNESCO World Report on Internationalized Domain Names Deployment (EURid and UNESCO 2012), China represents an exception from two points of view. In the first place, the official introduction of IDN in the Chinese Internet dates back to 2002; since 2005, Chinese keyboard searches for ".cn" on domain servers were also developed and Chinese Internet companies created browser add-ons to translate a domain into another name that could be looked up on national servers and enable Internet users to enter local character strings in browsers. In the second place, China was also the most active country in applying for IDNs with 73 scripts (of which 7 were contested). In any case, the result after the first round of ICANN IDN implementation showed a further consolidation of English supremacy and of the Latin script trend, as confirmed by the ASCII requests for gTLDs such as .abudhabi, .dubai, .kyoto, .osaka, and .tokyo.

4.2. Root Servers, US Dominance

Even though China's regulatory policy has become more systematic and transparent and China's Internet authorities are now aware of the importance of international collaboration, the main problem of DNS management still remains. As stated above, "the A-Root File lies at the heart of the DNS" (Ermert & Hughes 2003, p. 197). It is possible to argue that the Root name servers still play a critical role in the Internet infrastructure because they are the first to translate human readable host names into IP addresses that are used in communication between Internet hosts. The policy statement about the management of the Internet Domain System issued by the National Telecommunications and Information Administration defines root server as "a set of thirteen files servers, which together contain an authoritative database listing all the TDCs. Currently, NSI operates the 'A' root server, which maintains the authoritative root database and replicates changes to the other root servers on a daily basis. Different organizations, including NSI, operate the other 12 root servers [...]. Universal name consistency on the Internet cannot be guaranteed without a set of authoritative and consistent roots. Without such consistency messages could not be routed with any certainty to the intended addresses" (NTIA 1998, p. 4).

The management of these host servers is naturally strategic; as mentioned above, at present there are 13 name servers. This does not mean that the number is limited to 13 physical servers; in fact every operator uses redundant computer equipment to provide a reliable service. Moreover, nine out of the thirteen servers operate in multiple geographic locations. The US presence is still the most prominent one with ten out of thirteen servers originally located on American territory, and three more located outside, in Stockholm, Amsterdam and Tokyo. It is worth highlighting that nine out of the thirteen servers operate in multiple geographic locations using the anycast system, a network addressing and routing system in which datagrams from a single sender are routed to the topologically closest node in a group of potential receivers (though it may be sent to several nodes, all identified by the same destination address).

In China the root name servers are mainly located in Beijing, the three operators are the Internet System Consortium, Netnod (formerly Autonomica and located in USA, now available from the site in Stockholm, but also at 35 other locations) and VeriSign. VeriSign is still considered the biggest player; in 2000 it took over Network Solutions Inc. (NSI), one of the biggest domain name registration companies, and is still contracted directly by ICANN to manage the A-Root servers on its behalf. Despite the attempts made by ICANN to decentralize DNS management, supervision is mainly performed by the DNS Root Server System Advisory Committee, an ICANN agency. It should also be noted that the root zone is still controlled by the United States Department of Commerce which must approve any change to the root zone file requested by ICANN. Thus, ICANN needs approval from the government for any modifications, also to change country zones such as ".cn". Last but not least, ICANN is under American jurisdiction, established as a non-profit corporation under Californian law.

4.3 China (but not only) Asks for a Change

At the end of the World Conference on International Telecommunications in December 2012 (WCIT -12) several issues were raised, partly stemming out of the reasons illustrated above. China supported the new Russian article on the Internet which included a provision aimed at the multi-stakeholder model and which states: "Members States shall have equal rights to manage the Internet, including the allotment, assignment and reclamation of Internet numbering, naming and addressing and the identification of resources and to support the operation and development of the basic Internet infrastructure" (ITU 2012).

Prominent figures like Vincent Cerf stated that the WCIT-12 decisions "have the potential to put a government handcuff on the Net. To prevent that—and keep the Internet open and free for the next generations—we need to impede a fundamental shift in how the Internet is governed" (2012). As Rezwan forecast, the next billion users would represent a major challenge because they would contribute to making the Internet more fragmented and with more visible international borders (2007). DNS and Root servers management and regulation are important issues that have to be solved; what Erment and Hughes said in 2003 sounds even more pertinent nowadays:

> "[…] indigenous Chinese attempts to define standards for a Chinese language name system are being challenged from across the Pacific. The DNS, as it has developed so far, therefore, appears to be an inherently political technology that determines the formation of a centralized power structure. Any movement away from this will depend as much on the development of new standards and architecture as it will on the ability of states to put in place a more satisfactory system of global governance" (Ermert & Hughes 2003, p. 208).

Also for the Internet, technical policies and decisions cannot be separated from politics. In the words of Lawrence Lessig,

> "in the real space we recognize how laws regulate—through constitutions, statutes and other legal codes. In cyberspace we must understand how code regulates—how the software and hardware that makes cyberspace what it is, regulate cyberspace as it is. […] We can build, or architect, or code cyberspace to protect values that we believe are fundamental, or we can build, or architect, or code cyberspace that allow these values to disappear. There is no middle ground. There is no choice that does not include some kind of building. Code is never found, it is only ever made, and only ever made by us" (1999a, p. 6).

The more active role of China in Internet governance as well as the results of the last WCIT-12 confirm that China wants to be involved in creating the code. An exclusion of the most populated country of the world from active Internet governance could imply a further *balkanization* of the cyberspace, confirming the idea of a so-caled 'digital cold war'. To a large extent, that would frustrate China's attempts to become part of an international policy-making community.

5. Way Forward—The Importance of a Constitutive Choice (and a more Collaborative Approach)

The design of the DNS structure confirms the importance and value of the constitutive choice presented by Starr. Indeed, also in this case it is possible to note how the development of a new technology represents a chance for a more extensive restructuring of rules and relationships. More in depth, "the more a society is tied to the world economy, the more likely constitutive moments will arise from changes in international communications regimes—that is, the norms and policies institutionalized in various kinds of international agreements [...]" (Starr 2005, p. 6). The near future will tell us how sound the initial constitutive choices of the DNS and IDNs will be. In this respect Starr explains that "international competition, conflict and coordination provide an imperfect 'discipline' on the range of decisions sustainable in the long run" (2005, p. 7).

What is clear is that China's Internet authority now recognizes the importance of international collaboration, playing an active role in the policy-making process and working hard on the implementation of Chinese-character domain names, as confirmed in the above-mentioned recent comments published by the Internet Society of China at the end of the 46th public meeting of ICANN in which the same institution confirms that "a large number of special studies and reviews should be carried out by ICANN to promote new gTLD. [ISC] hopes that all the work will be carried out under principles of fairness, openness and justice to protect the rights and interests of new gTLD applicants, domain name registrants and Internet users" (ICANN 2013, p. 9). If, on one hand, the worries of the West after the WCIT-12 were justified, on the other hand, it is important to recognize that the times of the "four territories and two costs" project appear distant and, more generally, that China will have a more assertive approach than before—a good reason to be optimistic about the future of Internet governance, at least from the point of view of IDNs.

ACKNOWLEDGEMENTS

I would like to acknowledge the support provided by my PhD program supervisor Prof. Giuseppe Richeri and important suggestions offered by Prof. Gabriele Balbi (Università della Svizzera Italiana) who helped me give a structure to this chapter and find the most pertinent sources. I hereby owe my thanks to Prof. Rolf H. Weber, Roxana Radu and Jean-Marie Chenou who have given me the possibility of developing some ideas I presented in May 2012 during the workshop "The Global Governance of the Internet: Intergovernmentalism, Multistakeholderism and Networks", hosted at the Graduate Institute of International and Development Studies, in cooperation with the Global Internet Governance Academic Network (GigaNet).

Andreas Kuehn

Chapter 8
Extending Cybersecurity, Securing Private Internet Infrastructure: the US Einstein Program and its Implications for Internet Governance

This chapter addresses US government efforts to "securitize" its connections to the Internet and resulting, potentially restrictive effects on multistakeholder Internet governance. National security considerations brought forward public policy and technical implementations that extend cybersecurity into the realm of privately-owned communications and other critical infrastructure. Using the US Einstein program as an example of such efforts, this chapter argues that governments will curtail the space for multistakeholderism in Internet governance when cybersecurity issues pertinent to national security are at stake. The following sections will briefly outline developments in multistakeholderism in Internet governance, cyber threat landscape and network monitoring capabilities. The reminder of this chapter will draw on these elements to discuss their relations with cybersecurity in the context of current US cybersecurity policy and technical implementations and how these technological capabilities enable the technical securitization of the Internet, a response to the developing cyber threats.

1. The Setting

1.1. Multistakeholderism in Internet Governance

Governance and control of the Internet and its underlying telecommunications infrastructure have been the subject of perennial policy debates, in addition to the controversy on adequate representation and participation in its policy-making. Before the movement towards liberalization, privatization and competition in the 1980s and 1990s, telecommunications services were considered a public utility with one (usually state-owned) monopoly operator (Brock 1994; Müller 1993; Chowdary 1998). There was no telecom regulation in the PTT era, since the government was the operator; independent regulators were created as a byproduct of the liberalization. Where transnational coordination was needed (e.g. international telephony, radio spectrum, or satellite orbits), it was considered an intergovernmental affair and subsequently dealt within the ITU (Cowhey 1990; Drake & Nicolaïdis 1992). Driven initially by private companies, data communications networks emerged and turned into a global Internet in the late 1990s that was administered by its own technical and operational community (Drake & Wilson III 2009). Those new private networks escaped the ITU's intergovernmental regulatory supremacy of voice communications at that time. Struggles about the Internet's root zone, (Mueller 2002; Simon 2006), however, led to the creation of ICANN in 1998. ICANN, a private entity overseen by the US Department of Commerce, was charged with the management of the Internet's address resources, a central technical function of Internet governance. With the World Summit on the Information Society (WSIS) in Geneva and Tunis in 2003 and 2005, respectively, the international political dimension of Internet governance emerged, resulting in an actual implementation of multistakeholder governance within the United Nations (Mathiason 2009, pp. 97–125). Mueller (2010) espoused that the inclusion of the global civil society "achieved a degree of legitimacy, acceptance, and elaboration in Internet governance that goes well beyond other sectors" and strengthened civil society's position in ICANN (p. 105). WSIS brought together various civil society activists in the Internet policy realm (Mueller 2010, pp. 88–95); its public engagement of civil society and private business in intergovernmental policy deliberations was carried over in the annual Internet Governance Forum (IGF) since 2006 (Mathiason 2009, p. 126–145). While there are several issues with multistakeholder governance (e.g. Mueller 2010, p. 264; Scholte 2011, p. 7), opening up closed intergovernmental institutions to non-state actors in the wake of globalization is a remarkable institutional change. Nonetheless, those institutional achievements in global governance should not be taken for granted and may be only a temporary phenomenon. In the ITU's 2012 World Conference on International Telecommunications (WCIT-12), for instance, some nation states attempted to add extensive cybersecurity provisions to the existing treaty on International Telecommunications Regulations (ITRs), and consequently reasserted the pre-eminence of governments, since the ITU is an intergovernmental organization. The next sections will address cyber threats and technological capabilities responding to those threats to set the stage for the discussion on the securitization of the Internet. In this discussion, particular attention is given to the relation between Internet governance and cybersecurity and how governments apply a traditional, state-centric notion of security that may adversely affect multistakeholder governance.

1.2. The Developing Cyber Threats Landscape

The US federal government defines a cyber threat as "any identified effort directed toward access to, exfiltration of, manipulation of, or impairment to the integrity, confidentiality, security, or availability of data, an application, or a federal system, without lawful authority" (DHS 2010). Cyber incidents reported by civilian federal agencies increased dramatically in the past decade along with the growth of the Internet and a general improvement in our detection capabilities. From 2006 to 2010, the number of reported incidents increased by 650 percent, to 41,776 (GAO 2011). In 2011 the number elevated to 43,889 incidents (OMB 2012). The incidents fall into one of five categories (percentage as of 2010): a) Unauthorized access (14%); b) Denial of service (1%); c) Malicious code (30%); d) Improper usage (18%); e) Scans/probes/attempted access (11%); and f) Unconfirmed incidents under investigation (26%) (GAO 2011). The last category "unconfirmed incidents under investigation" is of particular interest to this research since they include incidents detected through Einstein's intrusion detection system. For the Defense Department, on the other hand, cyber incidents have declined from a peak over 70,000 in 2009, and leveled off in 2011 and 2012 to around 50,000 (US Congress 2012).

Network-based threats have become better organized, more well-financed and professional in recent years. Today's threats landscape encompasses new, multifaceted threats, including so-called Advanced Persistent Threats (APTs), phishing, IP spoofing, large-scale botnets, distributed denial-of-service attacks (DDoS), and man-in-the-middle attacks. A 2009 US National Research Council report, warning of increased cyber attacks, stated that "the US information technology infrastructure is likely to remain vulnerable to cyberattack for the foreseeable future" (Owens et al. 2009). In addition, the likelihood of state-sponsored espionage and the potential for attacks on critical infrastructure by states or terrorists is often discussed.

A threat landscape describing only cyber attacks on the US is incomplete without also mentioning cyber threats towards other national territories stemming from the US. The US is not merely affected by cyber attacks but a significant portion of botnet attacks originates here, and the US is home for leading hacktivists who lead off the digital fight against oppressive governments (Goldsmith 2010). Possibly most relevant, the US government possesses highly classified, sophisticated offensive cyber attack capabilities; a fact that is hardly officially acknowledged but causes a severe policy headache in other nation states (McAfee 2010).

1.3. Technological Capabilities to Secure Networks

Deep packet inspection (DPI) is a technology for scanning and analyzing Internet traffic and making decisions about how to handle it in real-time. It is an enabling technology that can be used for many different purposes. For instance, it can be used to detect and block network security threats through IDS/IPS applications, to prevent "exfiltration" of private or classified information, or for censorship and surveillance. It can also be used by ISPs for copyright policing, bandwidth management, online behavioral advertising, and cybersecurity (Mueller & Asghari 2012; Mueller et al. 2012; Kuehn & Mueller 2012; Mueller & Kuehn 2013).

DPI capabilities were first developed for intrusion detection and prevention systems. Intrusion detection systems (IDS) allowed network operators to passively detect incoming or outgoing traffic associated with recognized forms of malware (viruses, Trojans, worms, and other dangerous code). Intrusion prevention systems (IPS) utilize IDS but supplement its recognition capabilities with programmed actions that stop or block the intrusion before it takes effect (Sourdis 2007). Both, IDS and IPS are based on signatures, a predefined set of values that describes a particular pattern in the network traffic. If the signature matches a particular pattern in the network traffic, predefined actions are triggered. An IDS merely recognizes and reports suspect network activities, whereas an IPS takes automated actions to stop the malicious activities. Consequently, with this approach only attacks previously known to the signature provider can be prevented.

Einstein, the program under consideration here, is an essential part in the department of homeland security's efforts to protect federal government systems and networks within the .gov top level domain and relies on these DPI-based intrusion detection and prevention capabilities.

2. Cybersecurity and the Internet's Securitization

Cybersecurity initiatives by national governments attempt to constrain the growing number of Internet threats, such as spam, phishing, malware, denial of service attacks, and network intrusion. Some national governments, however, (e.g. China and Russia) see control of message content and media as part of their cybersecurity efforts. Undoubtedly, cybersecurity has turned into a key area of Internet governance.

As a network of networks with most of its infrastructure operated and owned by private entities, effective Internet security requires coordinated, swift actions of various independent actors and institutions. This includes Internet service providers (ISPs), computer emergency readiness teams (CERTs), and enterprise network operations centers (NOCs), etc. Informal, trusted links that span organizational and jurisdictional boundaries connect these entities together. This structure enables a decentralized, collaborative effort, not coordinated by hierarchy or markets, referred to as "peer production" (Benkler 2006; Benkler & Nissenbaum 2006). Cybersecurity is a deeply operational affair that constitutes a form of peer production. Not a single actor alone, but the networked structure of those peers produce security on the Internet (Johnson et al. 2004; Schmidt 2012; Mueller et al. 2013). While governments participate on equal grounds with non-state actors in those informal networks, they encourage voluntary collaboration (e.g. sharing of cyber threat information of corporate networks with CERTs) or require notification of cyber incidents (e.g. US data breach law) through their policies and laws.

With its growing importance to Internet governance, cybersecurity has been regularly discussed in local and global IGF and ICANN meetings, where open multistakeholder arrangements assured access to participation for all entities involved in the production of Internet security[1]. In recent years, however, numerous nation states have promoted cybersecurity in their political agendas and framed it as a matter of national security. Declaring the information infrastructure as "a strategic national asset", President Obama, for instance, made the security, trustworthiness, and resilience of the US information infrastructure a policy priority (The White House 2009). Within governmental non-civilian agencies, military circles and the intelligence community, including affiliated private contractors, reframed the Internet's security towards their interests and capabilities.

Because of state sovereignty in matters of national security and international telecommunication treaties (e.g. articles 34, 35 and 37 of the ITU constitution), cybersecurity became more of a national affair. The sovereignty principle would bar non-state actors from debates on national security matters, undermining multistakeholderism in Internet governance. Cybersecurity policy shifted into the realm of politics, power and control that was to prevent the use of the Internet as a weapon against one's own critical infrastructure. This evolution is referred to as militarization or securitization of the Internet (Deibert & Rohozinski 2008). There is a danger that this will escalate into a cyber arms race, threatening freedom and openness of the Internet as we know it (Deibert 2011). These developments seem premature and problematic with regards to authority and proportionality; why call the military in when law enforcement should be able to handle it?

---

1 Governments have their own, closed institutional structures and forums for intergovernmental dialogues on cybersecurity, such as the Council of Europe's 2001 Convention on Cybercrime, the 2004 London Action Plan, or the ITU's 2007 Global Cybersecurity Agenda, for example. Within ICANN, law enforcement has held closed meetings for its community.

In security studies, securitization is a rhetorical device, a speech act that necessitates and legitimates urgent actions to an existential threat that "if [...] not handled now it will be too late, and we will not exist to remedy our failure" (Buzan et al. 1998, p. 26; see also Hansen & Nissenbaum 2009). While previous work largely focused on the securitization of cyberspace from a policy perspective, the focus here is on the institutionalized results of a securitized Internet: technical implementations, organizational adaption, practices and laws. Examples that are meant to make cyberspace more secure, representing various degrees of securitization, include the US Einstein program, as discussed in this chapter.

3. The US Einstein Program

The chapter presents empirical findings of research conducted at Syracuse University on the implications of deep packet inspection (DPI) on Internet governance[2]. The contribution of this chapter is an analytical description of US cybersecurity policy and related technology deployments that took place between 2003 and 2013. It addresses the emergent securitization of private information infrastructure under current cybersecurity policy. Methodologically, actor-centered institutionalism (Scharpf 1997) was used to conceptualize the ongoing cybersecurity policy process as negotiations between the DHS, DoD, NSA, US-CERT, and ISPs. Document analysis and interviews with technology vendors, government officials, academics and activists were used to collect data on Einstein.

The Einstein program was intended to protect US government networks against cyber-espionage, data exfiltration, and cyber threats (DHS 2010a; DHS 2012, see fig. 5 for a timeline of the program). Developing over three independently deployed instances, Einstein first tracked network flow data; then graduated to intrusion detection, and finally culminated in both intrusion detection and prevention systems (IDS/IPS) employing deep packet inspection (DPI) capabilities[3]. Table 1 provides a brief overview of the Einstein program. While at a national level private information infrastructure was subordinated to the government's cybersecu-

2 See: www.deeppacket.info.

3 The US government, in particular the NSA assisted by major US telecommunications companies, deployed DPI capabilities in its secret warrantless wiretapping efforts that came to light in 2005. These are related events that predate and occur simultaneously with the Einstein program and constitute a relevant element in the monitoring and intercepting of US communications infrastructure. The warrantless wiretapping controversy is beyond the scope of this chapter. See also Klein (2009).

rity mandate, US government policy on cybersecurity was amenable to international government cooperation from 2011 on (The White House 2011)[4].

Table 6: Overview of the Einstein program

Program Phase	Development Started	Deployment Launched	Description
Einstein 1	2003	March 2005	(Block 1.0) Network Flow Information ("NetFlow"), including centralized data storage
Einstein 2	January 2008	August 2008	(Block 2.0) Intrusion Detection System, to assess network traffic for malicious activities; (Block 2.1) Security Incident and Event Management (SIEM), to enable data aggregation, correlation, and visualization; (Block 2.2) to augment threat information visualization and to provide mechanism for information sharing and collaboration
Einstein 3	2010	2012	(Block 3.0) Intrusion Prevention System

Launched in 2003, Einstein 1 was as a key capability of the then newly formed US-CERT within DHS. Einstein 1 collected network flow information to detect anomalies, indicating potential network security threats. As a voluntary program, adoption by government agencies remained at a low, single digit number. The classified 2008 Comprehensive National Cybersecurity Initiative (CNCI) boosted cybersecurity and incorporated earlier efforts under one umbrella. CNCI extended cybersecurity beyond US government networks, addressing the protection of privately-owned critical infrastructure. Einstein 2 deployed signature-based and anomaly-based intrusion detection (IDS) capabilities, scanning temporary copies of network traffic for malicious network activities. Threat indicators and signatures were provided by the NSA and DHS to be deployed at the network monitoring devices, however, the NSA's direct participation was reduced in later stages of the program.

4 Also, the DHS has signed international agreements (MoA) with India and Israel on the sharing of critical cyber threat information (DHS 2012).

Figure 5: Protecting networks and critical infrastructure in the US[5]

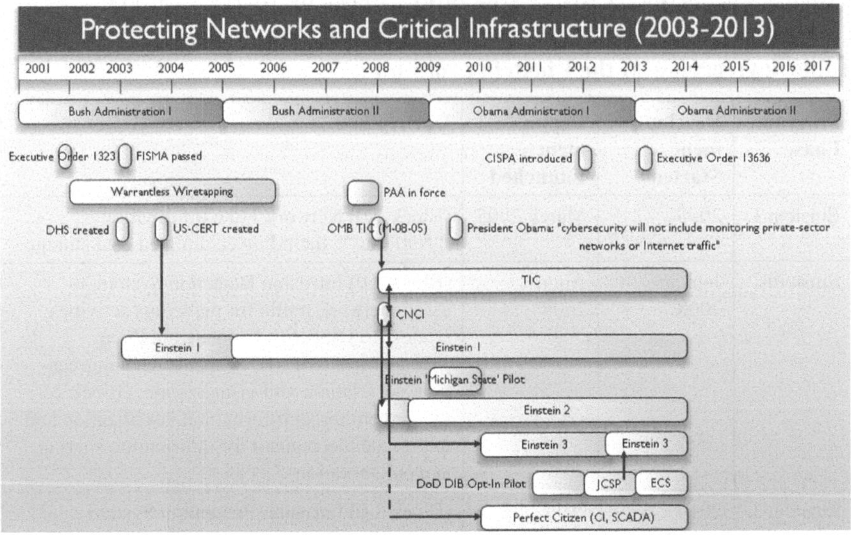

Over the course of the program, Einstein 2 was made mandatory for all federal agencies, providing US-CERT with enterprise-wide situational network security awareness. In its next iteration launched in 2010, intrusion prevention (IPS) capabilities were added to Einstein 3. This enabled Einstein 3 not only to detect intrusions but to automatically respond if attacked. At the agency's Internet service provider (ISP)—a governmental or commercial entity—redirected traffic was put through the Einstein 3 equipment. In its early phase the IPS equipment was operated and owned by DHS on the premises of the ISP. In a trial referred to as "The Exercise," IPS technology developed by the NSA was deployed. Later, the ISP's own equipment furnished with DHS threat signatures was used. As the program progressed, the DPI technology required greater coordination and some degree of organizational centralization. The ties between the private ISPs, DHS, DoD, and NSA proved to be especially sensitive. Subsequently, those relationships were progressively restructured due to privacy and surveillance concerns. This transformed the civilian DHS into a "trusted intermediary" between the private sector on the one side, and military and intelligence agencies, on the other.

In a related DoD effort, Einstein 3-like capabilities containing signature-based DNS sinkholing and e-mail filtering shielded defense contractors' networks. Sub-

5 This timeline includes elements that have not been addressed in this chapter, but are part of the larger cybersecurity picture such as the NSA's warrantless wiretapping program, DHS's Trusted Internet Connections (TIC) initiative, proposed legislation (e.g. the Cyber Intelligence Sharing and Protection Act), etc.

sequently moved to DHS, the pilot was instantiated as the "Enhanced Cybersecurity Services" (ECS) program in early 2013 (DHS 2013). By signing an executive order on "Improving Critical Infrastructure Cybersecurity", President Obama effectively extended ECS to critical infrastructure (The White House 2013). Government agencies, defense industrial base (DIB) companies and critical infrastructure operators were able to receive Einstein 3-cybersecurity through contractual arrangements with telecom providers AT&T and CenturyLink and defense companies Lockheed Martin and Raytheon.

4. Conclusion and the Way Forward

In the US Einstein program, cybersecurity was extended in terms of policy scope and technological capabilities, shifting functional authorities and organizational responsibilities between the civilian Department of Homeland Security (DHS) and the military Department of Defense (DoD). The case at hand shows that cybersecurity, and the Internet's securitization in particular, is construed and institutionalized as a co-evolution of technology and policy. Blurred boundaries and government-private sector cooperation via DHS as intermediary extended cybersecurity efforts into the private realm (see also Dunn-Cavelty 2008), but also limiting to some extent the degree to which military and intelligence agencies directly managed government-owned monitoring equipment in private ISPs networks. The conceivable consequences, this chapter argues, are critical for multistakeholder Internet governance. A fundamental substrate of Internet governance, namely cybersecurity, will be shifted under the auspices of national security to private agreements between national governments and large corporations.

For protecting the nation state, infrastructure, and individuals in cyberspace, a secure Internet is an essential cybersecurity policy objective. With the technological capabilities and the legal basis at hand, we will likely see an increase and further extension of Einstein-like programs into private networks, including major Internet exchange points. While technological progress may contribute to more effective intrusion detection and prevention, this chapter demonstrated the relevance of organizational and functional centralization in protecting US government networks (see also: Mueller & Kuehn 2013). Moving forward, two aspects will play critical roles in the extension of ECS: cooperation and standards. While early instances of Einstein deployments were at the agency level and take-up was marginal, the *cooperation* with large commercial ISPs will likely transform it into a comprehensive, large-scale deployment.

Leveraging on already provided access services, existing technical infrastructure, and customer-provider relations, commercial ISPs can offer Einstein-like capabilities as "managed security services" to their customers. Customers on their end may benefit from such services when, for example, classified knowledge on cyber threats (e.g. undisclosed information on zero-day exploits provided by the NSA) is provided through these arrangements, adding a level of protection which is not available from alternative sources. Common *standards* provide guidance and shared practices across various industry sectors. The US National Institute of Standards and Technology (NIST) is developing a cybersecurity framework that will provide minimal standards for cybersecurity (NIST 2013). While the use of the cybersecurity framework is voluntary, agencies with regulatory powers over critical infrastructure sectors may declare some minimal standards mandatory. There seems to be no obvious backlash to the further extension and the blurring of boundaries, despite widely expressed concerns on the implications of cybersecurity on society.

While not related to US government efforts to secure networks, in the 2013 NSA surveillance scandal (Greenwald & MacAskill 2013), leaked information showed that the NSA and the FBI were secretly accessing stored, comprehensive Internet communications on servers of nine global US-based Internet companies. This revelation disclosed parts of the technical capabilities that the NSA has in its arsenal to protect national security. Experts familiar with Internet surveillance and signal intelligence were not necessarily surprised to hear what the NSA was doing, but the magnitude and the comprehensiveness of the operations were startling. While it heightened public attention in the US and internationally on the dilemma between security and surveillance, its consequences for global Internet communications and Internet governance still have to play out. It is clear that long held assumptions on online privacy and security are fundamentally shattered, particularly after it became public that the NSA cracked and circumvented widely used encryption technologies (Perlroth et al. 2013).

It is safe to assume that the uncovered NSA surveillance negatively affects people's confidence in governments, one's ability to communicate securely and privately over the Internet, and US Internet companies that have collaborated in the NSA's data collection efforts. While the US government's cybersecurity efforts are a separate endeavour, critical voices see the balance between surveillance and security out of whack. They have gained evidence for their arguments since those revelations. What the long term implications thereof will be and how it will affect the further developments and deployments of the Einstein and the ECS programs and the like internationally remains to be seen.

In conclusion, securitization has the potential to remove cybersecurity from public Internet governance debates due to reservations of national security. Civil society is left only with little room for engagement in these pressing issues. Beyond impacts on multistakeholderism, securitization puts restrictions on an open and free Internet.

Andreas Schmidt

Chapter 9 Open Security. Contributions of Networked Approaches to the Challenge of Democratic Internet Security Governance

Discussions on Internet security and the appropriate institutions to contain Internet-related risks and threats are filling the conference rooms and meeting tables of academics, policy makers, and cyber intellectuals. Policy makers and national bureaucracies have reacted to rising numbers of Internet security incidents and the perception of increased vulnerabilities. Over the past years, traditional security institutions such as military, intelligence and law enforcement have increased their attention on questions of Internet security. Every other week, another country updates its cybersecurity strategy, proposes new Internet security-related legislation, or sets up yet another cybersecurity initiative.

Ideas about appropriate designs for Internet security institutions are exchanged in countless policy forums. Yet little of the institutional and organizational innovations that have been facilitated by Internet-based technologies appear to spill over to the sphere of security policy. Official Internet security polity is designed along the trodden paths of public-private partnerships and national security provisioning by traditional security institutions. Discussions about new forms of distributed collaboration among private and public organizations are scarce in the domain of Internet security (Dunn-Cavelty & Suter 2009). Furthermore, research on those actors and their collaborative endeavours that have kept the Internet up and running after numerous security incidents has literally been absent. At the same time, recent revelations about secret security and surveillance measures stress the problem of designing an Internet security polity architecture that adheres to democratic standards.

This chapter aims at addressing the aforementioned shortcomings by discussing two types of networked governance: the prevalent form of public-private cooperation, public-private partnerships and the more distributed, bottom-up model of Internet security communities. The challenge in Internet security governance is to find an institutional architecture that provides security in an efficient way. At the same time it needs to prevent mission creep, provide sufficient checks against centralisation of authority, and facilitate sufficient degrees of transparency and accountability. This chapter argues that security communities can moderate some of the normative deficiencies of partnership-based forms of public-private cooperation.

This chapter is organised as follows. The next section discusses public-private partnerships as a currently prevailing organizational approach to Internet security governance. The ensuing section then describes the so-called Internet security communities with their distributed bottom-up collaboration as an existing alternative to provide similar services as public-private partnerships (PPP). The final two sections then compare both approaches, elaborate on the normative value of peer-producing distributed networks in the domain of Internet security and ponder ways to increase their utility.

1. Public-private Collaboration

1.1. PPP as Panacea to the Cybersecurity Polity Problem

The regulatory and polity challenge for Internet security has quite a simple cause. States, whose core feature according to liberal-conservative theory is to uphold order, provide public security and protect citizens from criminals and external aggressors, neither own nor have direct control over the technical systems that make up the Internet. Private companies, which own these components, have economic interests that are not necessarily congruent with the public's need for security. Furthermore, states can have conflicting security interests, complicating attempts for transnational collaboration.

States have responded to these challenges by setting up public-private partnerships as the perceived "panacea for this problem" (Dunn-Cavelty & Suter 2009, p. 179). The underlying idea of PPP as it was defined by scholars of New Public Management is that a partnership between legal entities from the private sector and public authorities is in some cases the most efficient way to achieve certain goals or public goods (ibid., p. 180). In reality though, the term PPP is applied to such a wide range of modalities of public-private cooperation that "the majority of so-called PPP in CIP [critical infrastructure protection; A.S.] are not really PPP at all" (ibid., p. 181) and that "referring to a PPP is a euphemism which does not resolve the main challenge to identify and implement an effective governance framework" (Irion 2012, p. 13). Dunn-Cavelty and Suter aim at re-establishing a narrow concept of PPPs and posit that their defining feature is that they are project-based, rather than program-based, have measurable goals and outcomes, and are usually based on formal contracts among players with complementary intentions (2009, pp. 181–182). A desktop-research report by the European Network and Information Security Agency (ENISA 2011) chooses the opposite direction and implicitly creates a wide conceptualisation of PPP.

Irrespective of what the best conceptualisation of PPP might be, the popularity of these partnerships among policy makers has obviously spilled over to the domain of Internet security. Both in Europe and in the US it appears to be the preferred governance mechanism. In Europe for example, the EU has followed the idea of the European PPP for Resilience (EP3R), a project started in 2009[1]. With costs of cybercrime apparently still rising, the European Commission considers its EP3R by now to be ineffective as it "has...no operational powers and... cannot intervene to fix NIS [network and information security; AS] problems" and "has no formal standing and cannot require the private sector to report incidents" (2013a, p. 28). This critique on informal, non-enforceable information exchange under the EP3R regime has resulted in a European directive proposal that would mandate sharing of certain information and grant to-be established national "competent authorities" some authoritative control over attacked ICT systems (European Commission 2013b). The proposed EU-model would establish a new organizational security network, but one that differs from existing Internet security communities set up by technical experts. The NIS directive draft proposes a "cooperation network", in which the Commission and the planned national "competent authorities" share information on risks and actual attacks. A "cooperation network" will help to overcome some of the knowledge problems caused by insufficient sharing.

In the US, a number of legislative proposals have aimed at a similar direction, seeking to establish more formalised PPP models. Dating back to the Clinton administration, initial forms of private-public cooperation have been voluntary and focused on information sharing under the umbrella of *Information Sharing and Analysis Centers* (ISACs) (White House – National Security Council 1998). In the subsequent years and especially after the events in September 2001, an increasing number of private-public partnerships on all governmental levels were set up to enable a seamless flow of information to effectively respond to incidents (Nyswander Thomas 2013, pp. 9–14). Apparently under the auspices of the *Critical Infrastructure Partnership Advisory Council* (CIPAC), councils for private players in critical sectors and their governmental counterparts were established, interconnected by a number of liaising councils[2]. Since 2008, collaboration in the defence

1 For a thorough analysis of EP3R, see Irion (2012).

2 The CIPAC and its subgroup, the Cross-Sector Cyber Security Working Group (CSCSWG), facilitate cooperation mostly on policy development between *Sector Coordinating Councils* (SCC) and their governmental counterparts, *Government Coordinating Councils* (GCC). Some of the larger IT companies, which are also members of the IT sector's SCC, the *IT SCC,* have grouped together in the *Industry Consortium for Advancement of Security on the Internet* (ICASI) since 2008, establishing "a <forum of trust> in which industry leaders can work together." (Nyswander Thomas 2013, p. 22)

sector has intensified. The *DIB* [Defence Industrial Base] *Collaborative Information Sharing Environment,* the *Joint Cybersecurity Services Pilot,* the *DIB Cyber Pilot* and the *Joint Cybersecurity Services Pilot* have created venues for reporting incidents and sharing information about ongoing attacks, risks and vulnerabilities. These projects included in various combinations civil and military bureaucracies within the Defence sector, defence contractors and their Internet Service Providers (Ibid., p. 24–25). The most comprehensive for incident response is the *National Cybersecurity and Communications Integration Center* (NCCIC), which allows national authorities and the private sector to share information about ongoing or upcoming security issues and functions as the "national response center during a cyber or communications incident" (Ibid., p. 19). And finally, the National Cyber Forensics Training Alliance (NCFTA) brings together technical experts with law enforcement to facilitate national and international investigations in computer- and Internet-based crime.

Despite the breadth of cybersecurity PPPs in the US, a number of shortcomings remain: too few small and medium-sizes businesses take part in them; building trust continues to be a problem among a large number of participants; and the perspective of cybersecurity as a public good, not often shared in the private sector, appears to be a prerequisite for engaged participation (Nyswander Thomas 2013, pp. 25–30). As a means to overcome these shortcomings, legislators have proposed new or supplementing organizational approaches and mandatory cooperation by private-sector organizations. Plans for a so-called National Information Sharing Organization (NISO) or a central "cybersecurity exchange" would create a centralised, national clearinghouse or exchange point for information sharing, incident response, and mutual assistance across all sectors in private businesses and government, supplementing or replacing existing PPPs; a "civic switchboard" would examine weaknesses in existing PPPs and foster collaboration among different PPPs (Ibid., pp. 40–46).

1.2. Critique of PPPs

Quite a few scholars of organizational aspects of Internet security are critical of PPPs to ameliorate the Internet security situation. Dan Assaf, Amitai Aviram, Kristina Irion, Myriam Dunn-Cavelty and Manuel Suter have all highlighted the problems of applying the PPP model to the Internet security domain. In their view, the underlying goals of PPPs clash with those of any cybersecurity arrangement. PPPs strive for efficiency; they involve partners from the private sector, the ultimate economic interests of which do not necessarily overlap with the public's interest and can therefore impede the production of the public good cybersecurity[3]. Cybersecurity arrangements strive for security, which often implies inefficient precautions, secrecy, walled-gardens within and between participating organizations. Therefore, "the interests of the private industry and of the state in CIP are only partially convergent" (Dunn-Cavelty & Suter 2009, p. 182).

This convergence problem has raised doubts whether PPP is the best organizational approach to cybersecurity. Bauer and van Eeten (2009) argue that some of the misaligned incentives for owners of ICT infrastructure that contribute to the Internet security malaise can be reversed by appropriate regulation, e.g. by delegation to a respective regulatory agency (similarly, Irion 2012, pp. 14–15). Irion sympathises with a "safe harbour style regulation"[4], which would establish a system of enforced self-regulation at the EU level (2012, p. 22). Furthermore, she proposes "open and transparent" deliberations on Internet security governance on the European level, accessibility for "all stakeholders" including civil society, co-regulation e.g. to set technical standards and benchmarks that are relevant for the safe harbour regulation. (Ibid., pp. 21–24) Analysing the US public-private partnership governance model for critical information infrastructure protection (CIIP), Dan Assaf concludes that public interest in security is not thoroughly aligned with business interest in profit maximization. His solution: a shift from self-regulation to enforced self-regulation (Assaf 2009, p. 81). Introducing "explicit public accountability and oversight mechanisms" (Ibid., p. 76) would allow for an increased consulting of public interests in cybersecurity provisioning. Some of the elements of accountability Assaf mentions, such as a rationalised and professionalised bureaucracy, judicial review, and transparency (Ibid., p. 80), are apparently considered in Western capitals, as the description of policy debates in the previous section has shown.

---

3 Cybersecurity is often described as a public good or semi-public good. According to Assaf, cybersecurity is "not a pure public good," even though "it is non-rivalrous in consumption and it generates positive externalities." But "it is, at least to some extent, excludable." (Assaf 2007, p. 32) National security however is deemed a public good as it is "both non-excludable and non-rivalrous in consumption." (Ibid., p. 31) One could argue though that national security is a club good as it by definition excludes human beings living in other countries. Elke Krahmann reasonably differentiates between the different concepts of national security and their impact on the public-good-character of security: "If security is defined as the absence of threat, it appears to meet the criteria of a collective good. If security is defined in terms of deterrence, it seems to be a club good. Finally, if security is understood as the survival of a threat, it appears to be a private good. …Moreover, it is the understanding of security as the absence of threat that has led to the argument that peace, rather than national defence, is the archetypical collective good…." (Krahmann 2008, p. 386).

4 "'Safe harbour' style regulation is another approach to manipulate operators' incentive to contribute to and comply with private CIIP standard-setting in order to benefit from an exemption from a legislative default" (Irion 2012, p. 18).

In contrast, Dunn-Cavelty and Suter argue in favour of a more hands-off role for the state. An "expanded model," a "networked approach to governance" or "network governance" would be the more appropriate way to deal with the problem of how to secure critical infrastructures. Under the condition of high functional and technical specialisation, national bureaucracies would lack the knowledge to specify the required outcomes. The state therefore needs to acquire a different role in public-private cooperation and act as "coordinator and stimulator" of self-regulating networks (Dunn-Cavelty & Suter 2009, p. 184).

These networks could then make up for many of the deficiencies of PPPs[5]. For example, Dunn-Cavelty and Suter pick up Aviram's argument (2004, pp. 23–28) that pre-existing networks are better at enforcing norms than governmental bureaucracies that lack the technological skills to effectively monitor the performance of cutting-edge PPPs (Dunn-Cavelty & Suter 2009, pp. 184–185). However, the first argument—that governmental bureaucracies lack the capabilities required for effective monitoring of PPP performance—is rendered invalid by the recent leaks on Western intelligence agencies, the US National Security Agency (NSA) and the UK Government Communications Headquarters (GCHQ). The leaks reveal substantial technological surveillance capacities of national intelligence agencies (see also Kuehn in this volume). Apart from that, the argument in favour of networks in order to increase cybersecurity is convincing.

2. Social Production of Internet Security

The existing literature both on the theory and empirics of the "networks approach," or networked governance, in the Internet security domain by and large ignores the different manifestations networks can have. The same holds true for policy discussions in the US, Europe, and other regions (e.g. on New Zealand: Shore et al. 2011). Apparently, they fail to acknowledge both the theoretical possibility and practical existence of a different form of public-private cooperation in the Internet security domain—voluntary collaborative networks among individuals from both private and public organizations, delivering services akin to those of formal PPPs. From the perspective of traditional security governance, the idea of security provisioning by networks firms and public authorities is by itself still somewhat new (Eilstrup-Sangiovanni 2007, pp. 10–19). The idea of security being pro-

[5] To some extent, Dunn-Cavelty and Suter replace one fuzzy concept with another one. Network governance can have many forms, ranging from Anne-Marie Slaughter's state- and bureaucracy-centric "networks of government officials" (Slaughter 2004, p. 1) to Michel Bauwens' concept of the "partner state" (Bauwens 2012), the purpose of which is to incubate general welfare-oriented P2P projects.

vided by distributed global networks of technical experts is nothing but awkward and counter-intuitive for pundits of international relations. But it has both empirically happened (Mueller 2013, Schmidt 2012) and is theoretically feasible, and represents a stringent specialisation of the networked model.

When Powell introduced the idea of networks as an organizational supplement to firms and markets, trust was among their defining characteristics and represented the means which enabled transactions in networks. In ideal-type markets and hierarchies, it is money and authority that make things happen. Much of the literature deals with inter-organizational networks, i.e. networks in which firms or other types of organizations are the decisive nodes. Powell gives the example of networks of manufacturers and their external suppliers in a vertical disintegrated car industry (Powell 1990, p. 321). A network of geographically concentrated firms thus serves as an alternative to a vertically integrated firm (Carney 1998, p. 457). The concept of trust though introduces a level of analysis problem, as the building of trust between organizations involves a strong inter-human element. Powell hypothesised that common "ethnic, geographic, ideological, or professional" characteristics would create a homogeneous group with mutual trust among "participants" (1990, p. 326). Nevertheless, the focus of the literature on business networks has generally been on firms.

A different, more prominent role of the individual in production networks became feasible with the emergence of online communities and Internet-based, distributed, self-organised, autonomous collaboration (see also chapter 1 in this volume). Most prominent examples of this type of peer production are open source software (OSS) projects like Linux or content production websites such as Wikipedia. In its ideal-type variant, open source software projects use an organizational approach that by and large eschews the organizational principles of authority and monetary incentives, which are are the sources of activities in hierarchies and markets. While this mode of production is probably applicable for the production of any intangible, informational good and service, the need for secrecy requires organizational precautions that result in a different, rather closed and exclusive form of peer production. The following section elaborates on such Internet security communities that are based on individuals, their mutual deep interpersonal trust and intrinsic individual motivation.

The innovations in forms of production also affect the possibilities of public-private cooperation (PPC), of which PPPs are only a subset[6]. In practice, public-private cooperation can span phenomena as different as the Internet security community with its trust-based coordination mechanisms, co-financed PPP botnet

6 "PPP are only one of many possible forms of cooperation" (Dunn-Cavelty & Suter 2009, p. 185).

mitigation centres, and the recently exposed secret surveillance programmes with the private sector as data provider and national intelligence agencies as sponsor and central data integrator and analyst. The reality of PPC allows international, egalitarian, flat, and open structures just as they encompass secretive contracts between governments and private service providers for the alleged purpose of national security.

However, the theory of state-private cooperation and collaboration lacks inclusion of flat, non-hierarchical networks. Dan Assaf (2008, pp. 6–7) has defined the "regulatory continuum" covering the forms in which critical information infrastructure protection (CIIP) could be provided, ranging from government ownership, to (enforced) self-regulation to market based provisioning. It is the mode of self-regulation, more specifically "self-organizing networks" (Dunn-Cavelty & Suter 2009, p. 180), which Dunn-Cavelty and Suter consider as the best organizational approach to CIIP. Apparently, the regulatory "continuum" from hierarchies to markets runs via networks. However, networks can take non-hierarchical and non-market forms that hardly fit into the center of Assaf's regulatory continuum, the two ends of which are demarcated by pure markets and pure hierarchies. To consider the full range of possible forms of public-private cooperation, all possible manifestations of networks require a distinct consideration. The following section looks into one particular form of networked provisioning of Internet security.

2.1. Internet Security Community

Response activities to Internet security incidents are not only driven by incident response PPP or Computer Emergency Response Teams (CERTs), but also by distinctive communities or ad-hoc groups, whose members are part of a wider security network. The Internet security community is a loosely coupled network of security experts who are organised and collaborate in partly temporary, partly permanent sub-communities. Just like the Internet is often dubbed as the network of networks, the Internet security community is the community of security communities. This section analyses some key characteristics such as access criteria, hierarchies, structures and boundaries within the overall community, and the motivations of its members to contribute. The findings of this section, which have partly been described in earlier articles, are based on a research project that has analysed technical response activities that followed large-scale security incidents (Schmidt 2012; Mueller et al 2013; Schmidt 2013a; Schmidt 2013b)[7].

[7] One caveat though: my research project has not aimed at mapping the entire landscape of Internet security communities. The description of existing communities and their characteris-

2.2. Communities

The Internet security community is a network of individuals, organizations, groups, and communities working on different aspects of Internet security. There is no hard and clear definition for *Internet security community,* though. The term itself is commonly used by those who take part in these communities. Individual communities are organised around a variety of criteria such as technologies, Internet services, temporary security issues, professional specialisation, or the sector of an individual member's affiliation.

Most prominent among the Internet security communities is presumably the CERT communities, the ideational umbrella of all *Computer Emergency Response Teams* or *Computer Security Incident Response Teams* (CSIRTs). CSIRTs function as operational teams that support individuals and organizations to adequately respond to a security attack[8]. Such CSIRTs are set up and maintained by large corporations or political bodies willing to consolidate responses to security incidents, to establish support centres for affected organizations or, in the case of corporate CSIRTs, organizational units. Different CSIRTs cover different organizations, sectors, regions, and countries. Their communicational cultures differ widely. While academic CSIRTs are accessible and communicative, staffs of military CSIRTs are usually rather tight-lipped. Many CSIRTs are publicly funded organizations or teams therein. From an organizational perspective, the CERT complex is a mixed bag of everything. Military CERTs certainly are governmental hierarchies. Other CERTs like the Dutch govcert.nl or the Estonian CERT.EE are teams within national authorities and serve as facilitators of more or less informal public-private cooperation. The *Forum of Incident Response and Security Teams* (FIRST) serves as an umbrella for all CERT activities worldwide and provides Internet security experts from around the world with opportunities for meet-ups and trust-building to foster collaboration under or outside the FIRST umbrella. TERENA's[9] incident response task-force, TF-CSIRT, is an umbrella for European CERTs with again a focus on trust-building to foster voluntary information exchange and collaboration among the participants. It has helped to create an informal collaborative network between CERTs in Europe. While the term CERT gives the impression of similarity among these institutions, there are respectable differ-

tics are therefore probably cursory and incomplete. Future research will hopefully complete the picture.

8 CERT is a registered trademark of the *CERT Coordination Center* (CERT/CC) of Carnegie Mellon University. But generally, both terms are used synonymously. CERT/CC was established in 1988.

9 TERENA is the acronym of the *Trans-European Research And Education Networking Association,* the European umbrella organization of national academic and research networking providers.

ences with regard to accountability, secretiveness, geographical focus, political control, and their utility for national political agenda. CERTs usually have some kind of organizational structure and are either formal legal entities or teams within one. But they have also formed informal communities for collaboration and information exchange between CERTs.

The so-called operational security communities represent a fascinating new organizational phenomenon of security production and form the core of the Internet security community. CERTs, visible and popular as they may be, usually do not have the capabilities, capacities, let alone the authority to implement technical measures required to cope with an ongoing attack. Attacks are discovered and mitigated at the screens of network and system administrators, security analysts and other technical personnel. This is where operational security communities step in. These communities facilitate cooperation among operational staff to mitigate or solve ongoing attacks, incidents on the Internet. Several communities have emerged, often dedicated to distinct operational aspects of the Internet such as the resolution of domain names, traffic routing, or Internet root services. Partly, existing informal communities have taken up security related tasks when the security situation of the Internet started deteriorating in the early 2000s. Partly, entirely new communities with a focus on security issues were created. As a response to the achievements and weaknesses of the response to a series of larger and sophisticated botnets, an influential operational community was established in 2010 under the umbrella of an Internet non-profit organization that had been active in providing core Internet services for some twenty years. This operational community includes experts from a variety of fields of Internet security. They range from ISPs, content hosting providers, hardware and software vendors, financial institutions, DNS and email services, registrars, law enforcement organizations, CERT teams, and otherwise remarkable security expertise. This operational community arguably gathers Internet security expertise in a very comprehensive form.

These operational security communities by and large incorporate the same organizational principles that characterise many other technical communities. One unifying characteristic is that they have been established ad-hoc by technical experts who wanted to empower themselves to deal with ongoing security incidents. At a time when market solutions e.g. against botnets were not available and public authorities were particularly clueless, security experts had to join their forces to be able to quickly monitor, understand, and mitigate security situations. Malware has been of particular importance for adversary-launched attacks on ICT systems. Consequently, the response to almost any adversary-inflicted incident requires a thorough search and analysis of malware. Malware researchers from AV and security companies or academia exchange information, clues, intelligence, and botnet samples via a few mailing-list-based communities.

Recent developments suggest that the existing landscape of operational Internet security communities is being altered or at least supplemented by new variants of the networked approach. An example of such a newly formed network is the Cyber Security Forum Initiative (CSFI). CSFI is the result of a private initiative, and incorporated as a US non-profit organization. The Forum, which appears to have close links to US military, aims at educating the US military on cyber warfare and facilitating collaboration and information sharing inside government, military, law-enforcement and industry (CSFI 2013). While it is a "volunteer group" (Klimburg 2011) just like the Conficker Working Group, it differs from the widespread type of mailing-list-based Internet security groups in important aspects. Different from these mailings-list-based communities, thorough vetting is no prerequisite for basic membership at the CSFI, but some specific projects require US citizenship and security clearance. Active contribution is not a requirement to remain part of the group. This approach has allowed the CSFI to gather some "5000 Cyber Security and Cyber Warfare professionals" (ibid.), which are inconceivable for traditional operational-security groups, managed via the social network LinkedIn. Apparently, CSFI cooperates with US military organizations, as frequent postings for jobs that require US clearances and are related to US military indicate. CSFI also held joint recruitment sessions with the NATO Cooperative Cyber Defence Centre of Excellence (2011), and a dedicated "cyber-warfare division." This sort of community however is fundamentally different from traditional communities of technological experts with a role in operational Internet security.

2.3. Characteristics

Civil, bottom-up Internet security communities[10] have a number of characteristics that differ from other distributed forms of collaborative production of digital goods that have emerged with the rise of the Internet over the last two decades. Probably the most remarkable among them are global production endeavours that follow the principle of open source or peer production. This form of production has been defined as distributed collaboration among volunteers who contribute their time and work based on non-monetary, intrinsic motivation, resulting in goods that are freely shareable (Benkler 2006). Some of these criteria can be found in security communities, too.

[10] Here, I focus on this more narrow conceptualisation of Internet security communities and ignore this more recent phenomenon of communities which perceive themselves as vigilantes for national Internet security rather that non-national Internet security and which closely cooperate with military cyber-units.

The goods and services of the security community are, other than those of the poster children of peer production, not directly consumable or usable goods such as a Linux distribution, a Wikipedia article, or a LibreOffice suite. These security-related services are created by and targeted at operational security professionals in organizations providing services or goods that are affected by Internet security incidents. The community has served as an organizer, facilitator, and co-ordinator of global incident response endeavours, thereby helping to re-establish the functionality of the Internet after significant incidents (Schmidt 2012). Virtual response teams are formed *ad hoc* to deal with such incidents. Standing communities with various technical and organizations focuses serve as forums to relay sensitive information to affected and interested parties; they also serve as communication hubs for distributed, collaborative solving of technical and organizational problems. Those focuses span from malware analysis, backbone security, anti-phishing, anti-spam, or DNS security, to name but a few. Furthermore, information exchange within these standing communities enriches situational awareness about ongoing and arising threats, attacks, vulnerabilities, or incidents. Finally, the community ensures rapid collective assistance for those members that have become victims of an attack.

The communities are operated and organised by volunteers, just as the contributions and information shared with the communities are the result of voluntary efforts. Hence, they appear to be organised and coordinated neither by money nor by power, the two common coordinative mechanisms of markets and hierarchies. Individual motivations are akin to those that can be found in classic open source software communities, ranging from technological interest ("an itch to scratch"), the prospect of indirect appropriation, pleasure of creating solutions, to values. Hunting down the "bad guys", however, is a motivation that is presumably unique to these security communities.

Probably the most striking difference compared to popular peer production platforms is that security communities are access restricted and apply ex-ante quality assurance mechanisms. While access criteria vary among the communities, they tend to comprise one or more of the following: an operationally influential position, a proven track record on security issues, high degrees of professionalism, and being part of the personal web of trust of existing members. Furthermore, member are expected to adhere to community rules such as responsiveness towards requests of co-members (the so-called 'no lurkers'-rule), refraining from commercial appropriation of community services, and ensuring the confidentiality of shared information. Some open source communities have similar personnel selection mechanisms in place for roles that have the authority to decide which contributed code eventually goes into release builds of the software. (Dafermos 2012) The reason for such staff selection is that a "bad apple" with such roles could have a devastating effect on the products and services of the community. Quality control is not provided with "many eyes" to which "all bugs are shallow" as in open source projects, but by ensuring that only responsible, sensible, like-minded persons get delicate roles.

Once a person is proposed for membership, a vetting process is initiated, in which the aspirant is examined regarding the community's specific set of access criteria. For some groups, usually mailing lists, the responsibility lies with a single maintainer of the list. In most communities, however, candidates are vetted either by the group's board or in a joint effort by all community members. Some communities have recently introduced sophisticated tools for community-based initial peer vetting of aspirant and continuous rating of existing members.

A community member will usually only vouch for a new aspirant if a deep trust relationship between them already exists. The communities' glue is trust. A network operator cutting the Internet connection of one of his customers needs to have a great deal of trust in his community peer, who had asked for such a measure, despite working for a competing company. This deep trust is based on long-term collaboration and knowledge about the technological savviness of the peer community member. It also requires a somewhat unusual relationship between employed community members and their employers. In the words of an interviewed community member: "The level of trust within the group is higher than with any employer of the people". Communities' policy usually is that no information is shared with third parties outside the community, which includes the employer, as long as the sharer hasn't explicitly consented to sharing with others. This model of split loyalty, or from the perspective of the employer, reduced loyalty, is known in open source software communities. To give an example, in OSS communities a community member might value the community's interest in clean software design and a lean set of features higher than his employer's interest in additional features; therefore the feature might not get implemented even if the developer is paid by the employer to contribute to this OSS project (Benkler 2013, p. 224). While there are no actual figures about the percentage of community members who are incited by the employers to spend some of their working or professional time on security communities, it is probably safe to hypothesize that the majority of the employers profit from their employees' community membership in some way. The split-loyalty model however serves as a barrier against corporate and governmental aspirations to dominate a community's agenda, both in open source projects and in Internet security communities.

3. PPP vs. Internet Security Community

Reflecting on theoretical and practical differences of security provisioning networks is not purely an academic amusement. Different characteristics may yield different political consequences. This section therefore briefly compares PPPs with Internet security communities with regard to their normative value for Internet security governance. Two important characteristics from the perspective of democratic security governance are the distribution of authority and accountability.

There are some strong overlaps between PPPs and peer production communities in the Internet security domain. In a brief desktop research paper, ENISA has identified a wide range of characteristics for PPPs in the domain of network and information security. (ENISA 2011) The similarities between these organizational types are apparent, as Table 1 shows. They are unsurprising as both approaches are specialisations of networked governance. They seemingly differ in their evolution, as peer security communities are created and developed exclusively by bottom-up initiatives, membership is always voluntary, and Internet security communities hardly provide deterrence services.

Table 7: Characteristics of organizations, their manifestations in PPPs and in security communities[11]

Organizational criterion	Possible manifestations in PPPs	Manifestation in peer security communities
Organizational structure	Run by one from within; run by a coordinating entity; democratically peer led	All options
Roles and Responsibilities	Chair/secretariat/coordination by industry/gov't/mix	Chair provenance not relevant; no secretariat; peer-coordination
Duration type	Persistent community groups; working groups; rapid response groups	All options
Participation Type	Subscription; mandatory; voluntary	Voluntary
Interaction Type	Face-to-face meetings; virtual co-operation	Both
Membership rules	Accession; rights and responsibilities; exclusion	All options

[11] Except for the rows below "Links", left and centre columns are compiled from ENISA (2011).

Organizational criterion	Possible manifestations in PPPs	Manifestation in peer security communities
Formal information usage agreements	NDAs; traffic light protocol; deed of confidentiality	NDAs; TLP
Scope	Deter; protect; detect; respond; recover	Usually all but deterrence
Services	Research/analysis; information exchange; rapid response; and 16 other services	Most of them
Threat types	natural hazards; system failure; cyber-crime; terrorism/nation state	Focus on system failure and cybercrime
Community coverage	Geographic; focus (sector; cross sector; thematic);	All options, but usually sector-independent
Evolution	Top down; bottom up; top down, grown bottom up	Presumably exclusively bottom up
Incentives	Cost savings; sharing a problem; privileged, scarce information; reputation	Similar for employers. Members: Diverse intrinsic motivations.
Links	Bi/trilateral (with mirror organizations in other countries); other PPPs; CERTs; regulator	Individuals as liaisons
Members	Organizations	Individuals
External authority	Persuasion; coercion if if legally granted	Persuasion only
Geographical focus	Predominantly (sub-)national; regional	Global/none; regional; national; local
Accountability	Very limited	Very limited
Culture	Ditto. Also: focus on national assets, against adversarial countries	Geeky; technological; "one Internet"; against "bad guys"
Legal foundation	Legal entity or part of existing legal entity, usually based on formal agreement	Usually virtual organization

From the perspective of democratic governance, the key differences between both types of networked governance lie in their membership, geographical reach, culture, and in particular their authority and accountability. First, members of PPPs are organizations from either private businesses or public authorities. In security communities, members are individuals. Consequently, the incentives for participation differ between these two organizational approaches. In PPPs, private organizations follow economic incentives or legislative coercion. In security communities, it is an individual security pundit who needs to be motivated to participate voluntarily or at least find an employer willing to fund an employee's time spent on security communities with an unclear return on investment.

The second difference is a consequence of the first: The culture in security communities, which have been set up and are run by operational technical experts or technical security analysts, likely differs from the culture of those set up and chaired by corporate or public managers. The motivation of the members of PPP, public and private organizations, is to save costs, get better information, and help to protect member organizations or the cyber infrastructure of a nation. Opposed or at least supplemental to this is the community's interest in a functioning and working Internet on the global scale. The third fundamental difference is the geographical focus of the arrangements. PPPs tend to concentrate on national or at best regional affairs, e.g. the above-mentioned EP3R. But even if an organization like FIRST aims at the global level, much of the relevant operational collaboration that has been initiated and fostered by meetings in the lobby of FIRST conferences still happens in peer security communities. Security communities on the other hand do not have a national or regional focus per se. However, as they are built on deep personal trust, which best grows with similar backgrounds and frequent interactions, the membership of security communities appear to mostly come from Western countries.

Fourth, PPPs arguably have a greater potential of authority than peer communities, both internally with regard to its members and externally towards non-members. Internal authority, i.e. the ability to influence the behaviour of its members, is influenced by a number of factors like members' incentives to participate in the first place, the type of participation and members, the organizational structure, and forms of confidentiality. This is not to say that distributed networks have no coercive capabilities, on the contrary. Aviram describes that *private legal systems* can be effective means to enforce certain behaviour among their members (Aviram 2004, pp. 17–23). The calculus by members to adopt to certain rules or implement an unfavourable policy is that the overall net value of participation and community membership is deemed higher than the costs of implementation. Nevertheless, the portfolio of coercive means in a formal PPP with mandatory participation, high confidentiality, a monopoly of scarce, valuable information embedded in a national security culture is higher than in a voluntary bottom-up network of technical experts with individual motivations. External authority in both cases depends on the ability to persuade non-members. PPPs on the national or regional level can be granted direct (legal provisions) or indirect (a darker "shadow of hierarchy") coercive means by legislators, e.g. to create blacklists of unwanted Internet websites or bodies to set security standards.

Fifth, probably one of the most decisive elements of democratic governance is the capacity to hold those making generally-binding rules accountable to the public. As Assaf has rightly stressed: "The choice of actor to whom an entity is accountable has consequences for the outcome to which that entity is accountable, and hence is quite substantial" (Assaf 2009, p. 73). The substance and actual policies in a certain security governance regime, in which decision makers are accountable to the public, are different from those in a regime, in which decisions are only scrutinized by a handful of backbencher with non-disclosure agreements. Accountability, "the state of being answerable to someone" (Ibid.) with the potential to sanction unwanted behaviour, can come in various forms, usually categorized as *direct, exit, external* and *voice* modes of accountability (Mueller 2009, pp. 94–97). Functioning as mechanisms to oversee corporations or PPPs, consumer choice could punish unwanted behaviour in transparent and diverse markets and lead to *exiting* existing relations. As *external* reviewers, "rationalised and professionalised bureaucracy [and] judicial review" (Assaf 2009, p. 80) can help to oversee the activities of market players and public authorities. Finally, transparency and voting are the nominal sovereign's means to hold players in the security governance field accountable by raising their *voice* or *directly* removing them from their assignments. As to existing PPPs in the domain of CIIP, Assaf has already argued that existing "accountability mechanisms are insufficient for ensuring the public interest" and subsequently called for "additional public accountability mechanisms" such as transparency and voting (Ibid., pp. 76, 77).

At first sight, the accountability of the Internet security community is rather bleak from the public's perspective. On the one hand, given the community's non-transparency, there are no opportunities for the public to raise voice, let alone to take direct actions. Furthermore, the public cannot circumvent the activities of the communities, as the latter acts in total opaqueness. The information that is exchanged there, the actions that are taken—it all happens behind the scenes affecting unknown Internet-related services. Furthermore, the public has no direct external agent serving as the community's reviewer. I don't know of any community member coming from a traditional ICT civil society organization. On the contrary, quite a few members of influential communities come from law enforcement organizations that have been exposed to occasionally serving as proxies for US intelligence agencies.

On the other hand, the accountability of the community is not that bleak if it is viewed from the angle of its individual members. They can vote the chair of a community (though many of them likely have a meritocratic leadership); they can raise voice on the community's mailing-lists or in real-world meetings; they also can exit the community and set up different ones. The latter however might become increasingly difficult as network externalities of each community rise in an arguably consolidating community landscape. All in all, one might argue that the members indirectly serve as the public's imaginary external reviewer. This argument is supported by the diverse set of intrinsic motivations that make individual community members contribute their time and effort to Internet security issues.

4. Opening Security

The Snowden leaks have exposed an almost sinister cooperation between states and internet companies, undermining individuals' privacy, their freedom of expression, technical integrity of communication and information systems to unilaterally foster national or hegemonic interests. The more important it thus is to contemplate about future paths of Internet security governance and ignore the state of Internet *realpolitik* for a moment[12].

The Internet security community can be developed in different directions. Elsewhere (Schmidt 2013b), I argued that the community can be subtly altered by traditional powerful actors aiming to serve their monetary or power-related interests. But a different path for the community towards a non-national, global, user-serving, more accountable security provider is conceivable, too. First, the community needs to preserve its variety of mindsets. Its cultural diversity with persons coming from different backgrounds—national, professional, ideological, ideational—serves as a check-and-balance against its instrumentalization by traditional powerful actors. From the public's perspective, it is of importance that hacker-personalities remain part of the community to check those from or with close relations to traditional, overly secretive traditional security organizations.

Second, a profound goal should be its further globalisation. Currently, the community is predominantly composed of experts from the US, presumably followed by European countries. To create a true global institution that serves the global integrity of the Internet, these communities need to include a higher percentage of persons from other parts of the world. If states want to engage in some governance innovation as "partner states" (Bauwens 2012), they could sponsor communities at all geographical levels to regularly convene in a relaxed atmosphere, and create collaborative infrastructures.

[12] The sheer scale and scope of that secret surveillance and monitoring public-private partnership marginalizes any previous debate on public-private partnership for critical information infrastructure protection or against cybercrime. This monitoring regime appears not to have been established by chance, by accident or only as a consequence to 9/11. There are strong indications that it is an implementation of a long-term foreign policy strategy which has its intellectual roots in the 1990s (Schmidt 2004). From that perspective, debating the future role of the Internet security community appears to be somewhat academic, indeed.

Third, the public interest is arguably best served when collaboration is fostered by intrinsic motivations of its member rather than by political or direct economic interests of its membership. Therefore, the existing community model with individuals—not organizations—as members needs to be further strengthened.

Fourth, the community needs to avoid and combat any attempts by traditional powerful actors to hierarchize the community. Centralising the locus of authority and knowledge counter the federative, power-balancing structure of the community.

Fifth, the community should evaluate ways to become more transparent and open. A thorough analysis of levels of secrecy required for its internal informational goods might reveal opportunities to share more uncritical information and thereby build trust with the public. Granularly opening security data and creating true public spaces for non-members might also lead to security innovations. These suggestions certainly are only very rough ideas. After the Snowden leaks though, it is apparent that deep thinking needs to be invested into the design of global Internet security governance architecture.

Conclusions and Way Forward

Roxana Radu / Jean-Marie Chenou

From Nested Dilemmas to Democratic Internet Governance

In a world in which new technologies have become indispensable, the governance of technical resources allowing for the interoperability of global networks, the principles embedded in technical codes and standards, and the norms for transnational policy-making are constantly questioned. While the institutionalization of cooperation between private and public actors is a broader governance feature of which the regulation of the Internet is just an example, what is characteristic of this new issue-area is the overlap of multiple modes of governance in use, each of them bringing about stringent contestation of roles and responsibilities. Such nested dilemmas operate on different levels and actions taken to address any one of them inevitably affect others.

The Internet represents a nascent space for exploring overlying forms of authority, which might be negotiated in high political and economic fora, but may, just as well, be decided on in front of a computer, in a collaborative endeavour of peers. This book offers a substantial discussion of the many forms of interactions between different types of governors operating transnationally, and the new norms and principles stemming out of such exchanges. From collective action to institutional competition for policy-making, the governance transformations that the Internet has witnessed in the past two decades echo structural changes in regulatory approaches. Processes of governance in a globalised world constantly oscillate between the public and the private, as well as between the formal and the informal. Internet governance epitomises the *bricolage* entailed by the repeated attempts by a variety of actors to strike a balance between these elements and to create an efficient framework (Cerny 2010). As a result, institutional orders are constantly evolving and moments of crisis occur. The World Conference on International Telecommunications in 2012 (WCIT-12) was one of these outbursts of the crisis that reveal the underlying tensions in Internet governance.

This volume is seizing upon this time of change and offers a reflection on emerging norms and principles such as multistakeholderism or Internet freedom, and their role in mediating institutional contestation and reforming the current governance structures. Referring to the complexity of policy arrangements in this issue domain, Drezner asserted that the "scholarly research on the Internet encapsulates all the theoretical problems with the literature on globalization and global governance, only in a more concentrated form" (2007, p. 91). The challenge of this book has been exactly this. In examining current developments following the WCIT-12, the contributors adopted a multidisciplinary approach drawing on global governance, law, and security studies, combined with insights from their own work as practitioners. Engaging both the theory and the practice of nascent governance modes, the chapters of this volume show many examples of problems and shortcomings of the status quo. They also indicate ways forward that we might explore in order to imagine possible futures for the Internet, both for studying and for reforming it.

As noted by Sylvan in the first chapter of this volume, the Internet governance scholarship has spent a lot of time focusing on institutions and frameworks rather than on everyday interactions. This focus has contributed to reproducing abstract dichotomies like bottom-up vs. top-down, public vs. private, state vs. market etc. These dichotomies reflect the often antagonistic nature of Internet governance debates. However, as illustrated by the examples discussed in this book, the frontiers between the categories are blurry and unstable. Critics of intergovernmentalism often actively participate in the work of the OECD and rely on the WIPO to ensure the protection of intellectual property rights. Private companies advocate for a government-free Internet while cooperating with the US NSA in surveillance programmes. Autocratic regimes call for democratic representation at the global level while curtailing democratic participation at the domestic level.

With this book, we aimed to move beyond these dichotomies to analyze the existing and emerging principles and processes of cooperation in Internet governance, placing emphasis on a set of issues that need to be addressed by future processes. Internet governance necessarily involves a variety of actors, on a transnational level, and includes private and public features. Drawing on their diverse backgrounds, the contributors investigate developments in the post-WCIT environment, as well as broader trends in particular sub-domains of internet governance, such as Internet security. Their conclusions are varied, yet they all insist on some basic features of democratic Internet governance: legitimacy, cooperation, participation, and accountability. These principles echo the changes that are increasingly demanded in current Internet governance debates, notably through the design of an institutional architecture that is inclusive, transparent and effective.

Legitimacy

Underlying the issues discussed throughout the book is the question of legitimacy, which is vital not only for building, but also for maintaining and consolidating forms of authority. Hybrid forms of governance are particularly affected by this since they do not draw legitimacy from the state. As explained by Rioux *et al.* in Chapter 2, the global governance of information and communication technologies (ICTs) is no longer centred on a single intergovernmental organization. The decentralization of the sources of authority generates new challenges for legitimacy in technology-mediated global communication, ranging from the protection of critical infrastructure to control over the domain name system. Not only do such challenges alter the position of bodies such as the ITU, but they also define and defy fundamental choices for institutional trajectories, as Rioux, Company and Adam assert.

Both Weber and Jamart insist on the importance of human rights as a crucial source of legitimacy for future processes. As Jamart explains, global constitutionalism embraces the idea that a constitution should govern our globalized world, keeping in mind that the form and substance of such a global constitution may have little to do with that of domestic constitutions. There is a continuum of global constitutionalism visions ranging from support for a world government that would resemble domestic governments (Fassbender 1998) to accounts of the emergence of global civil constitutions (Teubner 2004), yet conceptualizing the global Internet governance discussion along these lines is relatively new. Upholding nascent principles such as Internet freedom might bring us a step closer to achieving a higher degree of legitimacy.

Building on Mena and Palazzo (2012), Weber also includes procedural fairness as a legitimacy element. This means that power imbalances should be neutralized in decision-making procedures. The first step in this direction might be to acknowledge the existing power differences. The field of Internet governance has long been dominated by US actors, both governmental and from the private sector. Hill argues that their practices constitute a form of "techno-imperialism", which disregards the interests of other stakeholders or places in an unequal position the largest part of developing countries. The extraterritorial effects of US domestic policies bring into question the factors shaping global legitimacy. The Prism surveillance program is the most recent instance of this, stirring calls for adherence to democratic standards. Jamart discusses the different groupings of states that proposed reforms for balancing out the US hegemony. Russia, China, Tajikistan, Uzbekistan, as well as India, Brazil and South Africa have been very vocal about creating an institutional environment in which formal equality among states is observed and power differentials offset. While this may appear more legitimate to state actors, it is nonetheless contested by civil society organizations and private sector stakeholders, which may not be able to participate fully (including voting rights) in decision-making processes convened by traditional institutions.

As Doria explains, the legitimacy debate is closely connected to the multistakeholder mode of governance sanctioned in the WSIS process. Kuehn's chapter on the Einstein program of the US also reveals legitimacy concerns related to the context of the securitization of cyberspace, considering some of the implications of the decision-making process within the Department of Defense for the regulation of the Internet more generally. Similarly, Hill questions the imposition of technical norms on developing countries—via bodies such as ICANN or IETF, which embed particular Western conceptualizations, as revealed in the design of the Domain Name System (see Chapter 7). In this context, the lack of agreement over security-related matters at WCIT-12 stems from basic contestation over locating authoritative decision-making and this debate might open the door for an incisive inquiry into restructuring rules and relationships for including all stakeholders.

Cooperation

The possibility of neutralizing the status-quo and the current power imbalances does not appear to be too distant in the future when considering the long history of cooperation in the creation and development of the Internet. The distributed architecture of the global network of networks allows for the introduction of new standards, ensuring the capacity to communicate across different platforms and to innovate at different levels. Yet, effective international cooperation for the global governance of the Internet has been much more discussed than experimented with in practice, in particular in high politics arenas.

Several challenges undermine this type of cooperation. First, as developed by Doria in her chapter, all different groups have their own limitations when it comes to cooperation. Governments are sceptical of the very idea of multistakeholder participation. Private sector organisations lack transparency and accountability, which makes cooperation difficult. Civil society organisations are sometimes inflexible, which make negotiations and consensus-building challenging. Finally, technologists hardly believe that their actions are full of economic, political and social consequences and need therefore to be discussed beyond their usual circles.

Another challenge to cooperation is the competition in the realm of security. Cybersecurity issues are often perceived as a matter of national interests by powerful states. Emerging powers often see Internet governance as a field where their sovereignty is at stake, as illustrated by the involvement of China in DNS management (see chapter 7). Beyond governments, the culture of security communities and cybersecurity programs is not one of openness.

As more stakeholders are recognizing that international cooperation is indispensable, the form to be taken by collaborative endeavours remains to be seen. The book stresses that cooperation between the US and emerging powers might lead to enhanced legitimacy, for example in China (as Negro explains). International organizations could also rely more on networked models of cooperation, in order to overcome institutional conflicts such as the one between ITU and the ICANN. Global cooperation could include formal multistakeholder forums with strict legitimacy rules (as described by Weber in this volume), but also intergovernmental cooperation (see Chapter 4 and 7), and other informal means of cooperation in networks.

Cooperation, argues Doria in Chapter 6, needs to go beyond the intergovernmental level. It could also be a form of networked governance, for example through the creation of global communities specialized in issues like Internet security (as discussed by Schmidt in chapter 9), or through an enhanced role for stakeholders organised in dynamic coalitions. These models that already exist in the Internet Governance Forum, are a way to improve communication and cooperation among stakeholder groups. They focus on particular issues, in which interests can be shared among stakeholder groups, like for example stopping spam, or protecting children online. According to several chapters in this book, cooperation can be associated with multistakeholderism.

Multistakeholderism

While all authors agree that multistakeholderism is the *modus operandi* of Internet governance, they point to the different problems that make this approach deficient. On the one hand, they ask what the political stakes are. With its implementation and application on a global scale, the multistakeholder model helps address some of the legitimacy concerns (powerful voices represented), while diffusing responsibility and making accountability more difficult to reach. Such a governance structure also offers a disguise for pursuing agendas that benefit particular actors more than others, especially if their lobbying power is greater.

On the other hand, the chapters in this volume also explore the normative dimension of multistakeholderism. When we say that all stakeholders are equally entitled to participation in decision-making, are we ready to accept all of them? The case of hackers stands out. Similarly, when techno-imperialism prevails, how do we make sure that the interests of the underprivileged are treated with the same degree of interest and attention? Doria discusses the potential of multistakeholderism to generate a true participatory democracy. One of the main challenges might be the ability of multistakeholder governance to go beyond recognition of the variety of stakeholders towards redistributive regulation as a way to empower marginalized actors (Gurumurthy and Gurumurthy, 2008).

Currently, in spite of the open participation rhetoric, the actual engagement of stakeholders depends on the ability to travel, speak English, have technical knowledge, etc. Even when equal-footing participation in shaping policy- and decision-making processes at the international level is possible, questions arise with regard to how the representation of broader communities is done and the extent to which the different Internet governance communities are riddled with corruption (Sutherland 2012).

Not only multistakeholderism suffers from several shortcomings, its emerging experimentation is also endangered by recent evolutions of Internet governance. As Kuehn shows, cybersecurity programs, especially in the US given their global scope, undermine multistakeholder participation as it exists in other domains. Cybersecurity issues are believed to be too important to be open to public participation. The lack of transparency and openness of cybersecurity communities (Schmidt), as well as the deliberate actions by governments to prevent participation, are increasingly problematic for democratic Internet governance, as illustrated by the Snowden revelations.

Multistakeholder governance is likely to be left to peripheral issues if important measures are not taken. If multistakeholder governance is the best solution for Internet governance (Weber) and the way towards participatory democracy (Doria), it needs to be reformed in order to address the most pressing challenges of Internet governance. For example, Hill suggests that the core issues of Internet governance should be put on the table and deep reforms should be considered. Some solid description of multistakeholder governance models exist (Weber, Doria), and some emerging principles are identified (Jamart), their application in the discussion of fundamental Internet governance issues still needs to be experimented. Among these issues, inequalities, in the use as well as in the governance of the Internet, must be addressed.

Accountability

As an emerging domain for global governance, the Internet poses a series of particular challenges to accountability rooted in its specific evolution over the past four decades. Such challenges stem from two diverse sources: on the one hand, they are spawn by the modus operandi of its *sui generis* institutions, as the international technical bodies exercising public governance functions to ensure the continuous functioning of the Internet (ICANN, IETF, etc.); on the other hand, they result from the gradual adaptation of intergovernmental organizations (ITU, WIPO, OECD, etc.) following involvement in global Internet policy-making.

In the late 1990s and early 2000s, Internet governance was synonymous with ICANN, the organization responsible for the technical management of the Internet. While its establishment in 1998 as a non-profit corporation 'for charitable and public purposes' under Californian law has been controversial[1], its evolution has not been less contentious with regard to accountability. Its expansive mandate as

[1] The entity was created to overtake the functions previously performed through a series of contracts between the US Department of Defence's Advanced Research Projects Agency (DARPA) and the University of Southern California and the establishment of ICANN was motivated by an appeal to formal accountability ("As Internet names increasingly have commercial value, the decision to add new top-level domains cannot be made on an ad hoc basis

the unique authority in charge of the management of the Internet domain name and unique identifiers has raised a series of concerns related to the 'virtually unconstrained power'(Weber and Gunnarson 2012, p. 13) entrusted to its Board of Directors, whose decisions cannot be reversed even in cases in which they contravene to ICANN's bylaws or other written commitments and can only limitedly be contested. As this example illustrates, the international bodies that are entrusted final decision-making power over the technical functioning of the Internet were not originally designed as externally accountable institutions, yet the rules they set in place have a global impact.

In the second case, the critique has revolved around the mismatch between the state membership and voting rights within IGOs and the need to include non-state actors (both profit-oriented and non-profit) in the process, in particular with the rise of new governance modes. A series of reforms have been undertaken in the past decade to open up to external stakeholders, yet their effectiveness remains under-researched. According to Weber, accountability in multistakeholder settings requires an active involvement towards increased expertise in stakeholder groups. One of the key issues is transparency. The opaqueness of many Internet governance processes, especially in cybersecurity matters prevents accountability, as Schmidt discusses in Chapter 9. The important role of technologists also represents a challenge for accountability, which requires a communication effort by the technologists (Doria in this volume).

The increase in the general level of expertise that is required for accountability in Internet governance also generates new policy issues. Going back to Sylvan's chapter, the interactions between particular types of governors such as daily users of Internet are able to gradually change the way in which we conceive of the Internet. As we all turn more technologically-savvy, are we willing to accept a monitoring system in which our individual behaviour is placed under surveillance in order to prevent or be able to track potential negative actions?

Summing it All Up

The chapters of this volume have shown how the evolution of the Internet has been marked by debates which—beyond the regulation of Internet—affect the international system more broadly. We have considered Internet governance in the making from three complementary angles. In part one, we looked at the institutional dynamics explaining the emergence and the evolution of Internet policy-making at the global level, as well as principles that shape its transformation. In part two, we examined multistakeholderism as the dominating mode of governance and

by entities or individual that are not formally accountable to the Internet community"), DNS White Paper, 63 Fed. Reg at 31742).

pointed to its shortcomings and potential ways to reform it. In part three, we explored the example of Internet security as a case-study of the competing logics of national interest and global cooperation. Each of the chapters of this book explores ways forward to make global Internet governance more democratic. They insist on legitimacy, participation, accountability and cooperation as basic features of future processes. These conclusions are important at a time when Internet governance is probably entering a new phase of change.

As noted in several chapters of this book, the coming years might be crucial for Internet governance. The Enhanced Cooperation process is being discussed and might lead to a reform of the governance system. Ten years after the WSIS, all Internet governance efforts will be evaluated in the light of the Millennium Development Goals. The Tunis Agenda called for a "multistakeholder effort" to build an "inclusive development-oriented information society" (WSIS 2005, § 83). What has been done so far? What remains to be done? This book offers some illustrations of the progress made in the last 15 years. It also identifies some serious limitations of the current model. The ways forward that are explored in each chapter of this book will be essential elements of the coming debates.

Publikationen aus dem Zentrum für Informations- und Kommunikationsrecht der Universität Zürich

erschienen bei Schulthess Juristische Medien AG, Zürich

Band 1 **Neues Fernmelderecht – Erste Orientierung**
WEBER ROLF H. (Hrsg.),
mit Beiträgen von Fischer Peter R., Geiser Jean-Maurice, Gunter Pierre-Yves, Haag Marcel, Hoffet Franz, Maurer François, Ramsauer Matthias, Rieder Pierre, Stampfli Katharina und Weber Rolf H., Zürich 1998

Band 2 **Symposium Schluep – Querbezüge zwischen Kommunikations- und Wettbewerbsrecht**
WEBER ROLF H. (Hrsg.),
in Zusammenarbeit mit von der Crone Hans Caspar, Forstmoser Peter, Zäch Roger und Zobl Dieter,
mit Beiträgen von von der Crone Hans Caspar/Groner Roger, Mestmäcker Ernst-Joachim, Nobel Peter, Schwarz Mathias/Klingner Norbert und Weber Rolf H., Zürich 1998

Band 3 **Informatik und Jahr 2000 – Risiken und Vorsorgemöglichkeiten aus rechtlicher Sicht**
WEBER ROLF H.
Zürich 1998

Band 4 **Daten und Datenbanken – Rechtsfragen zu Schutz und Nutzung**
WEBER ROLF H./HILTY RETO M. (Hrsg.),
mit Beiträgen von Druey Jean Nicolas, Gaster Jens-L., Hilty Reto M., Kemper Kurt, Sieber Ulrich und Weber Rolf H., Zürich 1998

Band 5 **Neustrukturierung der Rundfunkordnung**
WEBER ROLF H.
Zürich 1999

Band 6 **Rechtsschutz von Datenbanken (EU – USA – Schweiz)**
KÜBLER PHILIP
Zürich 1999

Band 7 **Informationsqualität – Ein Beitrag zur journalistischen Qualitätsdebatte aus der Sicht des Informationsrechts**
ZULAUF RENA
Zürich 2000

Band 8 **Werbung im Internet – Rechtsvergleichende, lauterkeitsrechtliche Beurteilung von Werbeformen**
JÖHRI YVONNE
Zürich 2000

Band 9 **Rechtlicher Regelungsrahmen von raumbezogenen Daten**
WEBER ROLF H.
Zürich 2000

Band 10 **Geschäftsplattform Internet – Rechtliche und praktische Aspekte**
Weber Rolf H./Hilty Reto M./Auf der Maur Rolf (Hrsg.)
Zürich 2000

Band 11 **Finanzierung der Rundfunkordnung**
Weber Rolf H.
Zürich 2000

Band 12 **Der Softwarepflegevertrag**
Widmer Michael
Zürich 2000

Band 13 **Datenschutzrecht vor neuen Herausforderungen**
Marketing – E-Commerce – Virtuelle Bank – Sachdaten
Weber Rolf H.
Zürich 2000

Band 14 **Geschäftsplattform Internet II – Rechtliche und praktische Aspekte**
Weber Rolf H./Hilty Reto M./Auf der Maur Rolf (Hrsg.)
Zürich 2001

Band 15 **Digitale Verbreitung von Rundfunkprogrammen**
und Meinungsvielfalt – Entwicklungen, Probleme, Lösungen
Weber Rolf H./Dörr Bianka S.
Zürich 2001

Band 16 **Die Übernahme von Allgemeinen Geschäftsbedingungen in elektronisch abgeschlossene Verträge**
Schwab Karin
Zürich 2001

Band 17 **Geschäftsplattform Internet III – Kapitalmarkt – Marktauftritt – Besteuerung**
Weber Rolf H./Hilty Reto M./Auf der Maur Rolf (Hrsg.)
Zürich 2002

Band 18 **Rechtliche Rahmenbedingungen für verwaltungsunabhängige Behördenkommissionen – Untersuchung am Beispiel der geplanten Fernmelde- und Medienkommission**
Weber Rolf H./Biaggini Giovanni
Mitarbeit: Dörr Bianka S./Peduzzi Roberto
Zürich 2002

Band 19 **Elektronische Signaturen**
Schlauri Simon
Zürich 2002

Band 20 **Zugang zu Kabelnetzen – Spannungsfeld zwischen Netzbetreiberfreiheit und offenem Zugang**
Weber Rolf H.
Zürich 2003

Band 21 **Elektronische Signaturen und Haftung der Anbieter von Zertifizierungsdiensten – Eine Darstellung am Beispiel der Regelungen in der EU, Deutschland, Grossbritannien und der Schweiz**
DÖRR BIANKA S.
Zürich 2003

Band 22 **Geschäftsplattform Internet IV**
WEBER ROLF H./BERGER MATHIS/AUF DER MAUR ROLF (Hrsg.)
Zürich 2003

Band 23 **IT-Outsourcing**
ICT: Rechtspraxis I
WEBER ROLF H./BERGER MATHIS/AUF DER MAUR ROLF (Hrsg.)
Zürich 2003

Band 24 **Rechtsfragen rund um Suchmaschinen**
WEBER ROLF H.
Mitarbeit: Spacek Dirk
Zürich 2003

Band 25 **Schweizerisches Filmrecht**
WEBER ROLF H./UNTERNÄHRER ROLAND/ZULAUF RENA
Zürich 2003

Band 26 **Kinofilmverwertung in der Schweiz**
UNTERNÄHRER ROLAND
Zürich 2003

Band 27 **E-Health und Datenschutz**
BERGER KURZEN BRIGITTE
Zürich 2004

Band 28 **Unternehmensinformation und Recht – Eine Übersicht**
STÜCKELBERGER BALZ
Zürich 2004

Band 29 **Schutz von TV-Formaten – Eine rechtliche und ökonomische Betrachtung**
SPACEK DIRK
Zürich 2005

Band 30 **Kulturquoten im Rundfunk**
WEBER ROLF H./ROSSNAGEL ALEXANDER/OSTERWALDER SIMON/
SCHEUER ALEXANDER/WÜST SONIA
Zürich 2006

Band 31 **Zugang zu Premium Content**
WEBER ROLF H./OSTERWALDER SIMON
Zürich 2006

Band 32 **Sorgfaltspflichten bei der Datenübertragung**
FAVRE KATIA
Zürich 2006

Band 33 **IT-Sicherheit und Recht – Grundlagen eines integrativen Gestaltungskonzepts**
WEBER ROLF H./WILLI ANNETTE
Zürich 2006

Band 34 **Privatvervielfältigung im digitalen Umfeld**
BAUMGARTNER TOBIAS
Zürich 2006

Band 35 **Das Recht der personenbezogenen Information**
WEBER ROLF H./SOMMERHALDER MARKUS
Zürich 2007

Band 36 **Staatliche Massnahmen gegen Medienkonzentration**
KELLERMÜLLER HANSPETER
Zürich 2007

Band 37 **Der Mehrwertdienst im Fernmelderecht**
HUBER KARIN
Zürich 2007

Band 38 **Telecommunications Competition and Its Driving Force**
WU JUN
Zürich 2008

Band 39 **Media Governance und Service Public**
WEBER ROLF H.
Zürich 2007

Band 40 **The Information Society and the Digital Divide Legal Strategies to Finance Global Access**
WEBER ROLF H./MENOUD VALÉRIE A.
Zürich 2008

Band 41 **Netzzugang in der Telekommunikation**
AMGWERD MATTHIAS
Zürich 2008

Band 42 **IT-Governance als Aufgabe des Verwaltungsrates – Kriterien einer sorgfältigen Pflichterfüllung unter Berücksichtigung der strategischen Rolle der IT im Unternehmen**
WILLI ANNETTE
Zürich 2008

Band 43 **Der ASP-Vertrag**
CHRISTIAN M. IMHOF
Zürich 2008

Band 44 **Zivilrechtliche Haftung von Internet-Providern bei Rechtsverletzungen durch ihre Kunden**
FRECH PHILIPP
Zürich 2009

Band 45 **Public Key Infrastructure**
MARKWALDER DANIEL
Zürich 2009

Band 46 **Shaping Internet Governance: Regulatory Challenges**
WEBER ROLF H.
Zürich 2009

Band 47 **Rundfunkübertragungsrechte an den Olympischen Spielen im europäischen Kartellrecht**
Medienmärkte, gemeinsamer Erwerb durch die European Broadcasting Union und Exklusivvergabe
HELLWIG IRENE
Zürich 2009

Band 48 **Spyware**
Rechtliche Würdigung ausgewählter Fragen sowie Empfehlungen an die Praxis unter besonderer Berücksichtigung des Eidgenössischen Datenschutzgesetzes
BUCHER MANUEL
Zürich 2010

Band 49 **Internet of Things**
Legal Perspectives
WEBER ROLF H./WEBER ROMANA
Zürich 2010

Band 50 **Datenschutz v. Öffentlichkeitsprinzip**
Erläuterungen zu den Spannungsfeldern am Beispiel des Zürcher Informations- und Datenschutzgesetzes
WEBER ROLF H.
Zürich 2010

Band 51 **Online Marketing und Wettbewerbsrecht**
WEBER ROLF H./VOLZ STEPHANIE
Zürich 2011

Band 52 **Internet-Access-Providing-Verträge mit geschäftlichen und privaten Endkunden**
Eine vertragsrechtliche Analyse nach schweizerischem Recht unter besonderer Berücksichtigung des Rechts der Europäischen Union
ORSOLYA FERCSIK SCHNYDER
Zürich 2012

Band 53 **Classification of Services in the Digital Economy**
WEBER ROLF H.
Zürich 2012

Band 54 **Neuer Regulierungsschub im Datenschutzrecht?**
WEBER ROLF H./THOUVENIN FLORENT
Zürich 2012

Band 55 **Die Erzwingung unangemessener Preise im Kartell- und Fernmelderecht – Eine rechtsvergleichende Untersuchung**
MICHAEL VLCEK
Zürich 2013

Ausserdem erschienen:

Regulatory Models for the Online World
WEBER ROLF H.
Zürich 2002

Towards a Legal Framework for the Information Society
WEBER ROLF H.
in collaboration with Roduner Xenia
Zürich 2003

The manufacturer's authorised representative in the EU is Springer Nature Customer Service Centre GmbH, Europaplatz 3, 69115 Heidelberg, Germany. If you have any concerns regarding our products, please contact ProductSafety@springernature.com

Printed and bound by CPI Group (UK) Ltd, Croydon, CR0 4YY
01/10/2026
02225967-0019